collaboration

アート / 建築 / デザインのコラボレーションの場
Collaboration: Art, Architecture, and Design

川向正人 + オカムラデザインスペースR
Masato Kawamukai + Okamura Design Space R

Collaboration: Art, Architecture, and Design

First Published in Japan on May 10, 2015
by Shokokusha Publishing Co., Ltd.
8-21 Tomihisa-cho, Shinjuku-ku, Tokyo 162-0067 Japan
Tel +81 3 3359 3231
http://www.shokokusha.co.jp

Editing: Masato Kawamukai + Okamura Design Space R
Publisher: Masanori Shimoide
Printing and Binding: Sanbi Printing Co., Ltd.

© Masato Kawamukai + Okamura Corporation 2015
ISBN 978-4-395-32038-7 C3052

Any unauthorized duplication (copying), reproduction, or recording to magnetic, optical, or other media of the content of this book, whether in whole or in part, is strictly prohibited. Please contact the publisher for authorization.

collaboration

目次

コラボレーションとは　川向正人 ——————— 6

第1章 風鈴
　　伊東豊雄 × takram design engineering ——————— 19

第2章 透明なかたち
　　妹島和世 × 荒神明香 ——————— 55

第3章 PARTY PARTY
　　小嶋一浩＋赤松佳珠子 × 諏訪綾子 ——————— 87

第4章 ぼよよん
　　青木淳 × 松山真也 ——————— 123

第5章 Flow_er
　　平田晃久 × 塚田有一 ——————— 157

第6章 白い闇
　　ヨコミゾマコト × 上田麻希 ——————— 193

第7章 波・紋
　　古谷誠章 × 珠寶 ——————— 227

オカムラデザインスペースRの記録 ——————— 258
コラボレーションという変曲点　北川原温 ——————— 266
時間に触れる異空間　内藤廣 ——————— 268
気づくことの大切さ　芦原太郎 ——————— 270
ショールームを展示空間に使うこと　中村留理 ——————— 272

CONTENTS

This is Collaboration   Masato Kawamukai ——— 7

CHAPTER 1 Furin
Toyo Ito × Takram Design Engineering ——— 19

CHAPTER 2 Transparent Form
Kazuyo Sejima × Haruka Kojin ——— 55

CHAPTER 3 Party Party
Kazuhiro Kojima + Kazuko Akamatsu × Ayako Suwa ——— 87

CHAPTER 4 Boyoyong
Jun Aoki × Shinya Matsuyama ——— 123

CHAPTER 5 Flow_er
Akihisa Hirata × Yuichi Tsukada ——— 157

CHAPTER 6 Invisible White
Makoto Yokomizo × Maki Ueda ——— 193

CHAPTER 7 Ripple
Nobuaki Furuya × Shuho ——— 227

A Record of Okamura Design Space R ——— 258

Collaboration as Inflection Point   Atsushi Kitagawara ——— 267

Another Dimension for Touching Time   Hiroshi Naito ——— 269

The Importance of Noticing   Taro Ashihara ——— 271

Using a Showroom as an Exhibition Space   Ruri Nakamura ——— 273

コラボレーションとは

建築史家・建築評論家
オカムラデザインスペースR委員長
川向正人

アート、サイエンス、インダストリーの総合化

　2003年に始まったOKAMURA Design Space R（以下、ODS-R）は、「建築家と建築以外の領域の表現者とのコラボレーション」を統一テーマとする企画展です。創設時に作成した企画書では、ODS-Rを「アート、建築、デザインの協働の場」と位置づけ、「ニューオータニ・ガーデンコートにあるスペーシャスなオカムラ（岡村製作所）のショールームの一角に、年に1度、まったく斬新な企画で創出される展示とトークのための空間です。毎年異なるジャンルの複数のアーティストが、アートの枠組みを超えてサイエンスとインダストリーの新領域にまで踏み込む意欲的なコラボレーションを展開し、その知と美の新たな形式によって多領域に向けて確かなインパルスを発信します」と創設の趣旨を説明しています。

　アートをサイエンス、インダストリーとの関係の中で捉え直して、その総合化を図ることは、1851年に開催されたロンドン万国博覧会のテーマでした。そもそも、それは18世紀に始まる産業革命とか市民社会形成の核となったテーマでありました。世界の構図が大きく変わろうとする21世紀に入って、再び、われわれの知、創造、生産、ライフスタイルが根幹から問い直される時代になってきました。こうした時代の要請を強く感じつつ、近代の時間の経過とともに次第に内的結び付きを失っていったサイエンス、インダストリー、そして建築を含むアートを、もう一度コラボレーションを通して総合化してみようというのが、ODS-Rを始めた理由です。

　ODS-Rは前半5回と後半7回、計12回開催されましたが、振り返ってみますと、前半5回は、いわば手探りする試行錯誤の段階だったように思われます。この前半5回の記録は、すでに刊行されています。本書は、第6回の伊東豊雄とtakramのコラボレーションから始まる7回を収録しています。開催順にご紹介しますと、2008年「風鈴」（伊東豊雄、takram design engineering）、2009年「透明なかたち」（妹島和世、荒神明香）、

This is Collaboration

Architectural Historian and Critic
Chairman, Okamura Design Space R Planning and Executive Committee

Masato Kawamukai

A Synthesis of Art, Science, and Industry

Launched in 2003, Okamura Design Space R (ODS-R) is a series of temporary exhibitions under the common theme of collaboration between an architect and a creator from some domain other than architecture. The initial proposal positioned the ODS-R as "a forum for collaboration between art, architecture, and design" and "a space for a completely original annual exhibition and talk event held in a corner of the spacious Okamura Corporation showroom at New Otani Garden Court," and explained the project's objective as "having artists from different genres engage each year in ambitious collaborations that step beyond the boundaries of art into new realms of science and industry, creating new forms of wisdom and beauty whose impact ripples through multiple domains."

Reexamining art in the context of its relationship to science and industry, and seeking a synthesis among them, was a theme of the Great 1851 Exposition in London. Indeed, it was a theme at the very core of the industrial revolution and the formation of civil society that began in the eighteenth century. In the twenty-first century, with dramatic changes taking place in the composition of the world, fundamental questions are again being asked about our knowledge, creativity, production, and lifestyle. Acutely sensitive to these demands of the age, we started the ODS-R project out of a desire to try once again to synthesize—through collaboration—science, industry, and the arts, including architecture.

The ODS-R exhibition extends through 12 editions, which can be divided into a first and second stage. In retrospect, the first five exhibitions might be described as a trial-and-error stage as we groped our way forward. A record of that early period has already been published. This book contains a record of the seven second-stage collaborations beginning with the 6th ODS-R exhibition. These include, in chronological order, *Furin* (Toyo Ito with Takram Design Engineering) in 2008, *Transparent Form* (Kazuyo Sejima with Haruka Kojin) in 2009, *Party Party* (Kazuhiro Kojima and Kazuko Akamatsu with Ayako Suwa) in 2010, *Boyoyong* (Jun Aoki with

2010年「PARTY PARTY」（小嶋一浩＋赤松佳珠子、諏訪綾子）、2011年「ぼよよん」（青木淳、MONGOOSE STUDIO）、2012年「Flow_er」（平田晃久、塚田有一）、2013年「白い闇」（ヨコミゾマコト、上田麻希）、2014年「波・紋」（古谷誠章、珠寶）の7つのコラボレーションです。2015年の現在、数段グレードを上げて大活躍されている方々ですが、ODS-Rにご登場の時期も、どなたも「目覚ましい」という表現がふさわしい活動ぶりでした。そのような建築家に、「今、最も興味のあるテーマに取り組んでください」とお願いするところから、コラボレーションが始まるのです。

　コラボレーションによるアート、サイエンス、インダストリーの総合化を試みるというのは簡単ですが、本当に、コラボーションによって創造の世界が切り開けるのか、目指す総合化が実現するのか。それには、どう考えて、どういうプロセスをたどればよいのか。解きたい課題は、これです。

　さて、ここで登場する伊東豊雄は、コラボレーションが異なる領域の単なる橋渡しではないこと、そもそも、二項対立的に捉える思考をとらないことを前面に押し出してきました。ややもすれば、建築家が舞台を整え、そこに建築以外の領域の表現者が登場して何かを試みるという形式のコラボレーションになりがちです。そうすると、どうしても最初から役割分担ができ、場合によっては、上下関係すら生じてしまいます。同じ目線で同じ地平に立つ、いわゆるフラットな関係になりません。伊東は本書に収録した鼎談でも強調していますが、既成の秩序・位置関係・役割分担をすべて消すところから議論を始めます。takramの言葉を借りれば、それでも「群」はある方向に確実に進んでいくのです。むしろ、無意識のうちに前提にしてしまう概念・方法・制度・関係といったものを排除して、完全に自由な状態をつくれば、状況を正確に読んで「群」はある方向に進んでいくのではないか。そして、新しい世界、新しい秩序、新しい原理原則に到達するのではないか。伊東とtakramは、いわば同じ世界観を共有しつつ、フラットな関係で、ODS-Rのコラボレーションを始めたのでした。

Mongoose Studio) in 2011, *Flow_er* (Akihisa Hirata with Yuichi Tsukada) in 2012, *Invisible White* (Makoto Yokomizo with Maki Ueda) in 2013, and *Ripple* (Nobuaki Furuya with Shuho) in 2014. Today, in 2015, all of these architects have elevated their work to even higher levels, but their accomplishments were already remarkable at the time of their ODS-R exhibitions. The collaborations began when we asked each to tackle the topic in which they were most interested at the time.

It is easy enough to talk about creating a synthesis of art, science, and industry through collaboration, but could we really attain the kind of synthesis that we sought, one that opened up new worlds of creativity? What conceptual approach, what process, did we need to follow to make this happen? *That* was the issue we wanted to solve.

It was just around then that Toyo Ito appeared, staking out a clear position that collaboration is neither a bridging of different domains nor something to be approached as a matter of dichotomy. There is a tendency for collaborations to take the form of an architect creating a stage upon which a creator from a different field is asked to appear and give something a try. This inevitably leads to a division of labor from the outset—in some cases even a hierarchy—rather than what might be called a "flat" relationship in which all see from the same perspective, standing on the same ground. As Ito emphasizes in his roundtable discussion in this volume, he began the discussion by erasing all preexisting orders, positioning, and divisions of labor. To borrow a term from Takram, even without such things the "swarm" still moves steadily forward in some direction. Indeed, it may well be only when the concepts, methods, systems, and relationships that we unconsciously take for granted are removed, and a state of complete freedom created, that the swarm is able to accurately read conditions and move forward together, arriving in new worlds with new orders and new rules and principles. Ito and Takram began their ODS-R collaboration sharing what might be called a common worldview and a flat relationship.

How wonderful it would be if we could minimize the preconditions for each edition as much as possible, creating the freest possible state to pursue collaboration within flat interpersonal relationships, and ultimately arriving at the discovery of new world

毎回、できるだけ前提条件を減らして可能な限り自由な状況をつくり、フラットな人間関係でコラボレーションを進めて、最終的に新しい世界の秩序・システム・原理を見出すところまで到達できれば、どれほど素晴らしいことか。われわれの日常行為は、実はさまざまな制約を受けています。自由どころか、がんじがらめに制約されています。ですから、可能な限り自由で、フラットな人間関係の場であること、そこで互いに力を引き出し合うようなコラボレーションが行われること、この2点が、第6回が進むにつれて次第に意識化され、ODS-Rの目標に加わったように感じています。

サイト

　コラボレーションの概念は、ODS-Rの創設趣旨文を書いた2002年の時点では、今日ほど一般的ではありませんでした。しかし、アート、サイエンス、インダストリーが、それぞれの領域で20世紀の間に生み出した成果を再び持ち寄って総合化するには、コラボレーションが有効です。実際、コラボレーションの考え方は、21世紀の進行とともに一般社会に急速に浸透していきました。同時に、コラボレーションによって真に成果を上げることの難しさも認識されつつあります。日本語で書けば「協働」ですが、真に成果を上げるためには「知恵と力を出し合って共に働く」必要があります。さらにいえば「つくってみる」、「作用・効果を出してみる」必要があります。そのときに、持ち寄る知識や方法に違いがあっても、少なくとも、広い意味での世界観や基本理念が共有されなければ、真のコラボレーションが成立しないこともわかってきました。

　ODS-Rでは第1回から、すでにできあがった作品の展示ではなく、その場で制作することに挑戦してきました。会場にはホテル・ニューオータニに隣接するニューオータニ・ガーデンコート2階、3階に広がるオカムラのショールームの一角を使います。これは通常の美術館とはまったく異なる状況で、建築家もコラボレーターも、その対応に最も強い関心を示し、また最も苦労するところでもあります。

orders, systems, or rules and principles? In our everyday activities we are subject to all sorts of constraints. Not free at all, we are actually tightly bound. This is all the more reason to prioritize a forum that is as free as possible, with flat interpersonal relationships, and to foster collaboration in which each elicits the most from the other. As the 6th edition moved forward, we became more clearly conscious of these two points, which seem now to have taken their place among the ODS-R objectives.

Site

At the time we wrote the ODS-R Aims of Establishment in 2002, the concept of collaboration was not as widespread as it is today. Nevertheless, collaboration is an effective means of reuniting and synthesizing what was achieved during the twentieth-century in the fields of art, science, and industry. Indeed, the collaborative approach has rapidly permeated general society as the twenty-first century has progressed. At the same time, the difficulty of achieving real results through collaboration is also becoming apparent. Written in Japanese, the word for collaboration (*kyodo*, 協働) literally means "working together," and truly productive collaboration demands working together in a way that pools the wisdom and strengths of each. In addition, there is also a need to make something, to produce an effect or result. We realized that even though there may be differences in the knowledge or methods that the parties bring together, for true collaboration to occur they must share, at least in broad terms, the same worldview and basic principles.

From its inception, the ODS-R has sought not to exhibit pre-existing works but to have something new created on site. The venue is a corner of the Okamura showroom, which extends across the second and third floors of the New Otani Garden Court adjacent to the Hotel New Otani. How to deal with this space—with conditions so completely unlike those at a typical museum—has been a source of great interest and great struggle for both architects and their collaborators.

The showroom is expansive, in some places directly adjacent to the urban bustle of

ショールームは広くて、ある場所ではホテル・ニューオータニの持つ都市的にぎわいにじかに接し、別の場所では緑豊かで静謐な同ホテルの庭に面しています。ODS-Rでは、ショールームのどの一角を展示に使ってもよいことにしましたので、展示場所の選び方に、これから構想を固めて制作するための基本理念のようなものが、すでに鮮明に出てきます。例えば「都市」とか「自然（庭）」といった言葉は、ショールームのある場所を具体的に指すと同時に、展示の基本理念を示すものにもなります。場所性の最初の読取り方、そして制作への生かし方が、最終的に制作された作品に強く反映されているのには、いつも驚かされます。

　今日では、建築を含む現代アートのどの領域でも「サイト・スペシフィック」は共通の前提条件です。この前提条件が共有されているからコラボレーションが成り立つともいえます。ODS-Rでは、まず企画実行委員会で企画建築家を選び、ショールームの中の場所とコラボレーターを決めるのは、その企画建築家に委ねることにしています。

　場所に関して、もう1つ、企画建築家とコラボレーターが決断しなければならないことがあります。展示期間中もショールームは開館していますので、立ち上げる展示空間をこのショールームと連続させるのか、それとも切断するのかを決めなければなりません。ODS-Rの創設趣旨からすれば、連続させてほしい。周囲に開かれた空間であってほしい。しかし、ショールームを訪れればわかるように、そこでは、オフィス家具の世界的メーカーのショールームとして、現時点で可能なアート、サイエンス、インダストリーの総合化がすでに達成されています。開かれた空間としてショールームと連続しつつ、だが埋没せずに、展示によって新しいメッセージを発し、新しい方向性を打ち出すのは、並大抵のことではありません。

　ショールームがあるのは、現代都市TOKYOの高いポテンシャルを感じさせる紀尾井町界隈。宿泊施設のほかに種々の店舗やイベント空間を内包して人・物・情報が激しく行き交い、現代都市そのもののようでもある巨大ホテルの内部。窓の外には広大な回遊

the Hotel New Otani and in others facing the verdant tranquility of the hotel's gardens. For the ODS-R, we decided that any corner of the showroom could be made available for the exhibition. Right from the beginning, from selecting the location, creators had to have some kind of basic idea in place to guide subsequent concept development and production. For example, just as some sections of the showroom might be described as "urban" or "natural" (the garden), so these words also came to suggest the basic tone of the exhibition. It was always surprising to see how powerfully the initial reading of the space, and the way the space was used, came to be reflected in the final works.

Today, in architecture and all other contemporary arts, the notion of site specificity is taken as a given. That such assumptions are shared is perhaps what makes collaboration possible. For the ODS-R, the planning and executive committee first selects an architect for each edition, and then leaves to the architect the decision of which part of the showroom to use and with whom to collaborate.

There is one other space-related matter that architects and collaborators must decide. The showroom continues to operate during the period of the exhibition, so a decision has to be made about whether to connect the exhibition space to the rest of the showroom or to sever it from it. Given the aims of the ODS-R, we hope they will choose the former and create an exhibition space open to its surroundings. And yet, as a visit to the site makes clear, as a showroom for a world-class office furniture manufacturer the space already achieves the kind of synthesis of science, industry, and art that is possible today. It is no easy task to create an exhibition in an open space that is connected to the showroom without being engulfed by it—one that says something new or proposes new directions.

The showroom is located in the Kioi-cho neighborhood, an area suggestive of contemporary Tokyo's enormous potential. Encompassing a range of shops and event spaces in addition to accommodation facilities, the interior of the massive hotel is itself like a contemporary city, bustling with the frenetic comings and goings of people, goods, and information. Beyond its windows lies a vast Japanese stroll garden. One encounters many overseas tourists and businesspeople both inside and out. Surely

式の日本庭園。内外で出会う大勢の外国人の観光客やビジネスマン。開かれた感覚を持つクリエーターならば、TOKYO の鼓動・ざわめき・においと同時に、この場所が世界につながっていることを肌身に感じられる場所です。この点が、美術館の無臭・無音のホワイトキューブとは決定的に異なるところです。

　むろん、ここでは、伊東豊雄が指摘する「グリッド（格子）構造の呪縛」のような現代都市の持つ課題や矛盾も、じかに感じられます。それを解くにも、現代のアート、サイエンス、インダストリーの総力を結集しなければならないことを、この場所が教えているように感じられます。

スケジュール

　毎回、企画展開催の前年の 12 月には、企画建築家と一緒に会場を下見して、同時に ODS-R の基本的な考え方と進め方を説明します。このときに「今、最も興味のあるテーマに取り組んでください」とお願いしています。年が明けて 1 月には第 1 回のミーティングを開催して、ショールームのどの一角を使い、誰をコラボレーター（建築以外の領域の表現者）に選び、どのようなテーマ・内容の展示を行うかなどについて、企画建築家に基本構想をプレゼンテーションしていただきます。2 月には、企画建築家が推薦するコラボレーターもミーティングに出席します。ODS-R では、企画展にかかわるすべての表現行為を企画建築家とコラボレーターに決めていただきますので、3 月には、推薦されたポスター・DM のデザイナーもミーティングに出席します。4 月には展示の基本設計をほぼ終え、ポスター・DM のデザインも決まります。さらに、オープニングパーティ、会期中に開催されるシンポジウム、ギャラリートーク、ワークショップなどの日程・タイトル・内容も決めて、5 月にプレス発表です。6 月には、企画建築家から実施設計レベルの図面が提示され、床・天井の処理、水・音・においなどの問題が出る可能性がある場合には、すべてこのミーティングの議題となります。設営の具体的な段取り、

such a space would give any open-minded creator a visceral awareness of the pulse, buzz, and scent of Tokyo and a sense of connection to the wider world. In this respect, the site is decidedly unlike a museum's sterile, silent white cubes.

Certainly one can feel here the problems and contradictions of the contemporary urban environment, something like what Ito calls the "spell of the grid." But I cannot help feeling that it also teaches us that to break this spell we must bring together the full power of contemporary science, industry, and art.

Schedule

In December of the year prior to each edition of the ODS-R, we tour the venue with the exhibiting architect and explain the project's basic idea and approach. This is when we ask the architect to tackle whatever is of greatest interest to them at the time. We hold our first monthly meeting the following January, at which time the architect gives a presentation explaining his basic concept, including which part of the showroom he intends to use, his intended collaborator from outside the field of architecture, and what theme or topic his exhibition will address. In February, the collaborator recommended by the architect also attends the meeting. The architect and collaborator are responsible for deciding all creative activities related to the exhibition, so the designers they recommend for posters and direct mailings take part in the meeting in March. By April, the basic design for the exhibition is largely set and the designs for the posters and direct mailing have been decided. A press release is issued in May to announce the date and time, title, and content of the opening party and any symposiums, gallery talks, or workshops that will take place during the period of the exhibition. At the June meeting, the architect presents working drawings and the agenda covers all potential issues related to the finishing of the floors and ceilings and any use of water, sound, or smell. Also decided at this final meeting are the concrete operational arrangements and the content and program of the opening party. The exhibition itself is held from July to August.

オープニングパーティの内容と進行なども、この最後のミーティングで決められます。毎年、この企画展が開催されるのは7〜8月です。

　このミーティングには毎回、オカムラの中村喜久男会長と岩下博樹専務のほかに、関係する部長・所長が出席して、何か問題があればすべてこのミーティングの席上で議論して対応策が決められます。構想の自由度は非常に高く、例えば、町工場に小さな試作品をつくらせることも可能ですが、すべてこのスケジュール内に収めていただきます。ですから、企画建築家とコラボレーターの時間管理が大変であることは言うまでもありませんが、難しい問題への対応策もミーティングの時間内に回答するというオカムラの基本姿勢が、準備作業を円滑に進める重要な要因となっています。

7つの鼎談へ

　どの回も建築家とコラボレーターは、アート、サイエンス、インダストリーの自由な関係を楽しみ、自由な地平の上で互いに無数の接点をつくりながら、コラボレーションを展開させていきます。決められた筋書きのない状態で、実験的に、挑戦的に、コラボレーションが展開しています。それだけに一層、毎月のミーティングが重要でした。

　最終的にできあがった作品も重要ですが、本書が伝えたいのは、コラボレーションの内実です。どんなコラボレーションだったのか。正確に再現するのは本当に難しいのですが、写真・図面・スケッチを補助的に使いながら、ご本人たちに語っていただくのが最善の策と考えました。毎回、協力企業や大勢の協力者のお世話になりましたが、その方々に深く感謝しつつ、本書では、コラボレーションの核となったテーマと解法を浮かび上がらせるために、委員長としてすべてを見てきた私も加わって建築家とコラボレーターによる、7つの「鼎談」の形をとっています。

Each of these meetings is attended by Okamura Chairman Kikuo Nakamura and Senior Managing Director Hiroki Iwashita, as well as by the heads of any related divisions or departments, so that issues can all be discussed and addressed on the spot. There is an extremely high level of conceptual freedom—it is possible, for example, to have a local workshop fabricate small test products—but everything has to be contained within this schedule. Needless to say, this means the architect and collaborator face a time management challenge, but Okamura's basic stance of addressing even difficult issues within the time of the meeting has been a critical factor in moving things forward smoothly.

7 Roundtables

At each exhibition, the architect and collaborator have delighted in a free relationship among art, science, and industry, developing collaborations that created innumerable points of contact on a free horizon. Without any predetermined outline at all, each edition has involved an unfolding of experimental, challenging collaborations. This has made the monthly meetings all the more important.

The works that have resulted from these collaborations are important, but what this volume hopes to convey is the reality of the collaboration itself. What kind of collaborations were they? Accurately recreating them is difficult, so we thought the best course would be to have the principals speak for themselves, supplemented by photographs, drawings, and sketches. Each edition was made possible through the efforts of many companies and individuals who provided their support, for which we are deeply grateful. In order to bring out the topics and methods at the core of each of the collaboration, this volume takes the form of seven roundtable discussions between each edition's architect and collaborator, which I join having observed the entire process in my role as chairman of the planning and executive committee.

CHAPTER —— 1

Furin
風鈴

ARCHITECT
Toyo Ito
建築家
伊東豊雄

DESIGN ENGINEERING FIRM
Takram Design Engineering
デザインエンジニアリングファーム
takram design engineering

CHAPTER-1　Furin　21

22　第1章　風鈴

CHAPTER-1　Furin　23

ある種のホタルの群れは、あたかも全体で統率された発光体であるかのように同じリズムで輝くことがある。しかし一匹のホタルはごく近くにいる数匹の仲間に光の周期を合わせているだけであるという。近傍のみの交信が全体に波及しているのである。

都市空間のなかでも、私達は近傍の人やものの動きだけで自分の行動を判断するケースは多々ある。現代都市はあまりにも複雑、多様で全体像を把握することなど到底不可能だからである。そのような部分的、相対的な関係のみでそれぞれが動いていると、とんでもない混乱に陥りそうに思われる。しかし意外に全体の秩序が保たれているの

は、やはり近傍の関係が全体を生み出しているからである。このような全体のあり方はきわめて現代的と言えよう。

かつての夏の風物詩を彩った風鈴、300個の風鈴によって、私達はこうした近傍のみの関係から成る秩序を再現したいと考えた。ひとつの風鈴の音が或るルールに従って周辺の風鈴と連鎖する。近傍と近傍は波紋のように重なり合って現代音楽のような世界を創り出すのである。

（展示コンセプト文より）

When certain species of fireflies swarm, they sometimes flash in a synchronous rhythm that makes it appear as if they are emitting light under some unified command, yet each individual firefly is merely coordinating its own flash cycle with that of a small number of fireflies in its immediate vicinity. Communication within the vicinity has a ripple effect on the whole.

In urban spaces, too, we often decide how to act based solely on the movements of people or things nearby because contemporary cities are so complex and diverse that it is utterly impossible to grasp them in their totality. You would think that with everyone moving based only on such incomplete, relative relationships we would be thrown into terrible confusion, and yet, surprisingly, overall order is maintained because the whole is ultimately generated by relationships between neighbors. The nature of such wholes could be called profoundly contemporary.

We decided that we wanted to recreate this sort of order generated by relationships between neighbors using 300 wind chimes, that classic symbol of the Japanese summer. When any single wind chime sounds, it causes a chain reaction in the wind chimes around it based on a predetermined set of rules. Sounds rippling from neighbor to neighbor overlap with one another and generate a world of contemporary music.

(Exhibition concept, July 2008)

CHAPTER–1 Furin   25

ローカル・ルールから生まれる呼応の空間、光と音の協奏

伊東豊雄
takram design engineering
川向正人

建築家
伊東豊雄

1941年生まれ。東京大学工学部建築学科卒業。主な作品に「せんだいメディアテーク」、「多摩美術大学図書館（八王子キャンパス）」など。ヴェネチア・ビエンナーレ金獅子賞、王立英国建築家協会（RIBA）ロイヤルゴールドメダル、プリツカー建築賞など受賞

ARCHITECT
Toyo Ito

Born in 1941, Ito is a graduate of the University of Tokyo Department of Architecture. Major works include the Sendai Mediatheque and the Tama Art University Library [Hachioji Campus]. Awards received include the Golden Lion from the Venice Biennale, the Royal Gold Medal from the Royal Institute of British Architects (RIBA), and the Pritzker Architecture Prize.

川向 ─ 最初に、このオカムラのショールームの一角を使って、今、最もやりたいことを、建築家以外の表現者とのコラボレーションを通してやってくれませんかとお願いしました。このようなオファーを受けて何をお考えになったか、そこからお話しください。

杭と渦、あるいは流れと渦

伊東 ─ ちょうどそのころ、僕らは〈ジェネレーティヴ・オーダー〉という言葉を使って、最初からルールが決まっているのではなくて、何か試行を通してルールが発生するような方法で建築をつくれないかと考えていたときでした。あれから6年たって、ようやく当時考えていた建築が

Concord Born of Local Rules,
a Concerto of Light and Sound

TOYO ITO
TAKRAM DESIGN ENGINEERING
MASATO KAWAMUKAI

田川欣哉
Kinya Tagawa

渡邉康太郎
Kotaro Watanabe

デザインエンジニアリングファーム
takram design engineering

デザインとエンジニアリングの両分野に精通す
るクリエイティブ・イノベーション・ファーム。
デザインエンジニアのほか、建築家・グラフィッ
クデザイナー・サービスデザイナーといった多
様なプロフェッショナルが集う。東京とロンド
ンを拠点に 30 名ほどのメンバーが分野を超え
たプロジェクトに取り組んでいる

DESIGN ENGINEERING FIRM
Takram Design Engineering

A creative innovation firm with expertise in the
fields of design and engineering, Takram brings
together a wide range of professionals including
design engineers, architects, graphic designers,
and service designers. Takram's roughly 30 team
members work on projects from bases in London
and Tokyo.

Kawamukai — We started by asking you to use a corner of the
Okamura showroom to do whatever you most wanted to do at the
time, in collaboration with someone from a creative field other than
architecture. Let's begin with what your thoughts were when you
heard this proposal?

Stakes and Eddies, Flows and Eddies

Ito — Right around then we were using the term "generative
order" and thinking about whether it would be possible to create
architecture using methodologies based not on pre-determined

CHAPTER-1 Furin   27

できてきたところです。

建築を、水面に立てる杭ではなく、杭の後ろにできる渦そのものとして捉えるような考え方を試そうとしていたともいえます。

川向 — 歴史的に見れば、かつての建築は、本当は渦をつくりたいのに、渦そのものには手をつけず、渦を生むために杭をつくることに力を入れていたわけですね。

伊東 — 今でも建築家は、建築は杭をつくるものだと言う人が多いと思いますが。渦は絶え間なく形が変わりますが、周りの流れといつも相対的な関係を維持している。流れそのものとも若干違います。そういう渦のような建築がつくれないかと、あのころ考えていました。

川向 — 杭をつくるのではない。だが、渦そのものといっても、渦を対象に、例えば渦巻きの形をつくろうというのでもない。あくまでも流れとの関係の中で、渦にあたる建築をつくれないかということですね。おっしゃることを正確に理解できていないかもしれませんが、少なくとも、伊東さんの意識に、まず何か大きな流れが捉えられているのは確かのように思えます。

伊東 — そうですね。その大きな流れの中に、流れそのものとは少し違うものをつくろうとしている。それは、周りの流れといつも関係を持っていて、かつ、周りとの間に壁を建てない。そんな建築のあり方を、あのときも今も考えています。

〈か〉から〈かたち〉への回路

川向 — 伊東さんがおっしゃると、〈かたち〉とか〈かた〉にすごく近いようにも感じますが、その渦のようなものは、まだ〈かたち〉でも〈かた〉でもない。菊竹清訓さんの〈か・かた・かたち〉を借りれば、まさに〈か〉の状態にとどまるものではないでしょうか。

伊東 — 菊竹さんは〈か・かた・かたち〉と言われたのですが、菊竹さんから僕が唯一教わったと、この歳になって気づくことは、「身体でものを考える」ことだと思うのです。インスタレーションでも、音とか光を置いて、来た人たちがそれをどう感じるかを考えます。見るのではなくて感じる。建築の面白さは、そこに尽きる気がしています。それは理念を超えている。そこにこそ、僕は最大の価値を見出そうとしているのです。ほかの人の建築を見に行く場合も、理念は雑誌を見ればわかるじゃないですか。実際に見たときに、それ以上のことを感じないものがけっこうあって、そういうものには僕は全然興味がないし、見るまでもないと思っています。見たときに新しい発見がある建築こそが、真の建築だと思っているのです。

rules but on rules that emerged through a series of trials. Six years later, I feel like I've finally managed to create the kind of architecture I imagined then. I think you could say I was trying to understand architecture not as stakes driven into the water but as eddies that form behind them.

Kawamukai — Seen historically, it's as if the architecture of the past really wanted to create eddies but, unable to work on eddies directly, instead targeted its energies on driving the stakes that would produce them.

Ito — Even today, I think many architects would say that architecture is about driving stakes. Eddies constantly change, always maintaining a relative relationship with the surrounding flow. At the time, I was thinking about how I might make buildings that were like eddies in that they differed just a little bit from the flow.

Kawamukai — You sought, then, not to drive stakes but also not to make eddies your subject by building, say, whirlpool spirals, instead aiming to create structures that acted like eddies in their relationship to the flow. I'm not sure I fully understand exactly what that means but it seems clear at the very least that you were acutely conscious of some greater flow.

Ito — That's right. I was trying to create something that was within, but a little different from, the greater flow—something that always maintained a relationship with the surrounding flow, that didn't put up walls against it. This approach is something I was thinking about then and still think about now.

A Path From *Ka* to *Katachi*

Kawamukai — These eddies you're talking about seem to fit into Kiyonori Kikutake's notion of *ka*, *kata*, and *katachi* (idea, type, and phenomenon). In that framework, aren't your eddies things that are not yet *katachi* or *kata* but still at the level of *ka*?

Ito — Kiyonori Kikutake talked a lot about *ka, kata,* and *katachi,* and at my age I realize that the only thing I really learned from him was to think about things with my body. Even for an installation, I place sounds and lights and then think about how they will feel to the people who come. What makes architecture interesting, really, is not how things look, but how things *feel*—that's what it all comes down to. This transcends philosophy, and it's where I try to uncover the greatest value.

When I go to see buildings that other people have designed, if I

どうやって身体性を、自分の設計プロセスに入れ込めるか。そこには1本の道筋があるわけではなくて、ひとつひとつ、毎日毎日の現場とのやりとりや事務所の中の議論などの積重ねで生じてくると思うのです。

川向 ── 例えば「風鈴」展（2008）のあとの6年間を見ても、確かに、伊東さんがつくられる建築は毎回違うものです。ですが、その差異は、大きな流れにいろいろな渦が生まれるときの、その渦の差異に似ているようにも感じます。先ほど伊東さんは、大きな流れと渦という、重要なヒントを下さいました。その差異も伊東さんの身体性とか〈ジェネレーティヴ・オーダー〉から生まれてくるのだと思いますが、それは、誰にもある日常的な身体感覚から生まれるものではなく、大きな流れのような、もっと大きくて深くもある何かに根差すもののようにも思えます。源泉として生み出す力、方向づける力のようなもので、伊東さんは否定なさいますが、それは菊竹のいう〈か〉でありプラトンのいう〈イデア〉かもしれないと私は思うのです。

伊東さんの事務所ではプロジェクトごとに徹底してディスカッションすると聞きましたが、そのディスカッションは〈イデア〉の共有のためではないかと思うのです。今回のコラボレーションでも、この〈イデア〉、理念の共有のために、takram の皆さんと対話を重ねられたのではないでしょうか。

伊東 ── 大きな流れに対する渦のように、建築は自然の中に相対的に存在しているという大前提があります。そして、流れや地形、あるいは風といった自然現象をも包含する大きな共通認識のようなものも必要です。個々の問題に当たったときに、そこから、どういう〈かたち〉で解を取り出すかが一番面白いところで、うまくいくときも、いかないときもありますが、それを僕はできるだけ対話の中でやろうとしているのです。

「風鈴」展より。さまざまな高さに吊り下げられた風鈴の数々

Wind chimes hung at various heights for the *Furin* exhibition.

30　第1章　風鈴

wanted to know their philosophies I could just read the magazine articles, right? Too many of them don't go beyond that to make me *feel* anything in person. I have no interest in such places, which really aren't worth seeing at all. True architecture, I think, has to offer some new realization when actually seen.

How do I incorporate a sense of embodiment in my design process? I don't think there's any single course. Rather, I think this is something generated through an accumulation of each and every interaction on the building site and the discussions we engage in every day at our office.

Kawamukai — Looking back, for example, on the six years since the *Furin* [Wind Chimes] exhibition (2008), each of the buildings you've designed seems different. But the differences are not unlike those among the various eddies formed within some great flow. What you said a moment ago about eddies and flows was a very important hint. I expect these differences arise from your own sense of physicality, or some generative order, but this seems to be something that, rather than rising from the kind of physical sensibility we all experience in our daily lives, is rooted in something bigger and deeper, some greater flow. You deny any particular source of creative power or guiding force, and yet I cannot help thinking that this might be Kikutake's *ka* or Plato's *idea*.

I've heard that each project at your office is discussed extensively, and I assume such discussion is aimed at sharing a common idea. For the Okamura collaboration, too, you must have had repeated dialogue with the folks from Takram to share your *idea,* your concept.

Ito — I take it for granted that architecture, like an eddy in a great flow, exists relative to nature. I also think it's critical to have an overall shared understanding that encompasses natural phenomena like flow, topology, and wind. When you run up against individual problems, then, the most interesting part is how to extract from this the *katachi* (phenomenon) that offers a solution; sometimes it works out and sometimes it doesn't, but as much as possible I try to get there through dialogue.

When I try to think about things in isolation, all I can come up with are simple topographies. When Takram, as my collaborator, came up with the idea of a wave-like configuration, though, I could see the potential for this kind of airy, floating topography. This kind of input is invaluable, and dialogue is a way to think about how to embody the thing—what to propose.

自分だけで考えようとすれば、地形といっても、シンプルなものしか思い浮かばないわけで、協働者のtakramさんが波のような地形を考えてくれると、ああこんなに軽くてフワフワした地形もあるのだと、どんどんインプットされていきます。それをどういうふうに身体化して、ものとして提案できるか。対話は、その回路みたいなものです。

コラボレーションの力

川向 ── 18世紀のカントの時代には、感性が大切だとする一方で、感性の捉えたものを悟性によって統合して概念を構成しなければならないと考えました。さらに、感性と悟性だけでは、感覚が捉える具体的な世界を出て、抽象と普遍の世界に入っていくことができない。そこで、もう1つの、理性が必要だということになりました。感性・悟性・理性の三者の中で考え、実践しなければいけないと言い始めます。私は近現代建築史の研究者として、経験・具体性と抽象性・普遍性との関係をいつも考えていますが、21世紀初頭の現在は、再び両者の関係が問われる時代だと思うのです。

伊東 ── 最終的には普遍性、理念に行き着かないと、その建築は残っていかないと思っていますが、設計するときにそれを考えている余裕はない。菊竹さんだって、〈か・かた・かたち〉と言っていたけれども、これだという提案が出たときのすさまじさ。しかも、一瞬にして、とんでもない形で出てくる。え！ 今までこれだけやったのに、なんで突然これなの。事務所内は、この連続でした。だけど、そこに、この人は天才的だなと惚れ込んでしまうのですよ。
僕は菊竹さんのような天才ではなく凡庸な人間だから、どうやって飛び越えていけるか、他人の力をできるだけ借りて、そのワーッと越えていくチャンスをいつも探しているのです。

川向 ── それは、私のやっている〈住民主体のまちづくり〉と同じです。みんなの力でワーッと越えていくチャンスをいつも探っていますから（笑）。
そこで興味深いのは、その菊竹さんも、〈か・かた・かたち〉の解釈を何度か変えていることです。やはり、初期の考えに彼の独自性があって、その後は、時代に合わせるように解釈を変えています。大きな理念があって、それにふさわしい技術を工夫し、斬新な現象を生み出した点では、菊竹さんの場合、初期がとにかく素晴らしかった。それに対して伊東さんは、ずっと変わらず、この理念と技術と現象のバランスが維持されていると思うのです。

伊東 ── 菊竹さんは天才型、僕は凡才型。菊竹さんと僕の違いをもう1つ

The Power of Collaboration

Kawamukai — In Kant's time—the eighteenth century—sensibility was held as something important but it was also believed that concepts needed to be organized by integrating, through understanding, that which had been captured by the senses. Furthermore, sensibility and understanding alone were not enough to leave the concrete world of the senses and enter the world of abstraction and universality. The additional necessary element was reason. People began talking of the need to act within this tripartite of sensibility, understanding, and reason. As a scholar of the history of modern architecture, I'm always thinking about the relationship between experience/concreteness and abstractness/universality but now, at the start of the twenty-first century, I think questions are once again being raised about the relationship between the two.

Ito — If you don't ultimately arrive at some universality, some philosophy, then I think the building is unlikely to last, but there's no time to think of such things when you're in the midst of a design. Kikutake talked of *ka, kata,* and *katachi,* yes, but you can't imagine the intensity when he came up with a compelling proposal. In an instant the most outrageous shapes would emerge, suddenly and completely overturning all the work we had done up to that point. This happened all the time in his office, but you still couldn't help admiring the man's genius.

I'm not a genius like Kikutake, just an ordinary person, so it isn't easy to take the kind of great leaps that he did. I try to rely on the talents of others as much as possible, therefore, and watch closely for my chance to jump.

Kawamukai — It's exactly the same with the community-based town-building projects that I work on. I'm always looking for opportunities to use everyone else's energy to leap forward all at once. (*Laughs*)

What's really interesting, though, is that Kikutake modified his interpretation of *ka, kata,* and *katachi* several times. I suppose the earliest conception was a matter of his own originality, which he then modified to suit changing times. In terms of having an overarching philosophy, and devising appropriate techniques, and creating innovative constructions, the early Kikutake was simply amazing. By comparison, Ito, you seem to have always maintained a kind of stable balance between philosophy and technique and construction.

Ito — Kikutake was a genius; I'm ordinary. Kikutake was also like a

言えば、菊竹さんは凸型、僕は凹型です。菊竹さんは自分をバーンと出して、相手に反応させる。僕は逆で、「どうだろうか？」みたいに言いながら、相手からいろいろと引き出す。これが、僕のコラボレーションの方法でもある。「風鈴」展でも、takram さんがいろいろなイメージを出してくれました。

川向 ― 伊東さんは、普段の仕事でも、スタッフとコラボレーションしているようなところがありますね。スタッフが意見を言いやすく、だからスタッフも成長します。菊竹さんの時代と比べると、技術も素材も豊富になっていて、しかもそれを使いこなせる人々が次から次へと出てくるので、異分野の若い世代とのコラボレーションは刺激的で面白いですよね。

伊東 ― そうです。例えば takram さんがやっていることは、僕らには得体の知れないところがありますが、この人たちと一緒にやってみたいと思ったのは、彼らのセンスです。美的センスがすごく発達していて、「風鈴」展をやったときも、音の出し方、光の伝わり方、それは素晴らしいセンスでした。

蛍と風鈴～ローカル・ルール

川向 ― さて、伊東さんからコラボレーションのお誘いがあったとき、takram は、どんなことを考えられたのですか。

田川 ― お話があったのは、事務所ができて 2～3 年目の、まだ、takram がよちよち歩きをし始めたころでした。21_21 DESIGN SIGHT で展示した「furumai」という水滴で遊ぶ作品を、伊東さんの事務所のスタッフがご覧になったことがきっかけで、声をかけていただきました。

渡邊 ― 21_21 DESIGN SIGHT で行われた「water」展に出した作品は 2 つありまして、「furumai」（2007）という、超撥水技術を使ったアナログなお皿と、「shiguré」（2007）という、人が歩くと、その振動をきっかけにしてあたかも水たまりの中を歩いているかのような音を再現するデジタルなインスタレーションでした。アナログで美的な部分と、技術的な力と、

左・中：「furumai」（takram design engeenering, 2007）。皿を支える支柱を手で揺らして、水の粒で遊ぶことができる
右：「shiguré」（takram design engeenering, 2007）

Left and Center: *Furumai* (Takram Design Engineering, 2007) enabled people to play with beads of water by jiggling the pillars that supported the plates.
Right: *Shiguré* (Takram Design Engineering, 2007).

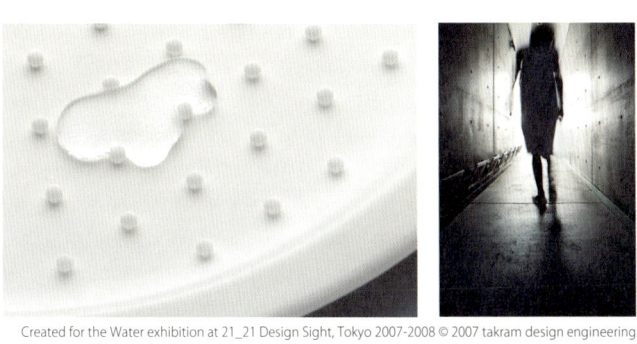

Created for the Water exhibition at 21_21 Design Sight, Tokyo 2007-2008 © 2007 takram design engineering

ridge, while I'm like a trough, in that Kikutake pushed himself out with a bang and forced the other party to react while I ask, "What do you think?" and try to pull in all sorts of information from the other party. This is the way I collaborate. For the *Furin* exhibition, Takram came up with all sorts of ideas.

Kawamukai — Even in your everyday work you seem to engage in a kind of collaboration with your staff. They feel comfortable offering up their own opinions, and are given room to grow. Compared to Kikutake's time, there is such an abundance of technology and materials now, and there are so many people coming up who are capable of using these to great effect, that you must find it fascinating—stimulating—to collaborate with young people from different fields.

Ito — Absolutely. What Takram does, for example, is in some ways unfathomable to people like me, but what made me want to work with them was their sensibility. They have a highly developed aesthetic sense and the way they applied it to *Furin*—the attack of the sound, the way the light was conveyed—was absolutely wonderful.

Fireflies and Wind Chimes: Local Rules

Kawamukai — Well, what did you think at Takram when you received Ito's invitation to collaborate?

Tagawa — The invitation came only two or three years after we started up our office, so Takram was really still just toddling about. We were contacted because Ito's staff had seen a piece that we did called *Furumai*—it involved playing with drops of water—for an exhibit at 21_21 Design Sight.

Watanabe — Actually we did two pieces for the *Water* exhibition at 21_21 Design Sight. One was *Furumai* (2007), an analog work that involved water-repellent technology, and the other was *Shiguré* (2007), a digital installation that reproduced the sound of walking in puddles when triggered by the vibrations people made as they walked around. I suppose they figured we were a team that could mix analog aesthetics and technical skills.

Ito — I thought your work was really amazing.

Kawamukai — How did Ito explain the collaboration to you?

Tagawa — He told us about "stakes and eddies" and then after that we all got very excited talking about "swarms."

Watanabe — Ito's "stakes and eddies" triggered a discussion among

どちらの側面も感じてもらえたのではないでしょうか。

伊東 ── あれはすごいなと思いました。

川向 ── 伊東さんは、このコラボレーションの企画をどういうふうに説明なさったのですか。

田川 ── 伊東さんが〈杭と渦〉の話をされて、そのあと僕らも、〈群〉の話ですごく盛り上がりました。

渡邉 ── 伊東さんの〈杭と渦〉の話に触発されて全員で話していたのは、自然界に見られる群の振舞いです。絵本『スイミー』（1963）に出てくるような、統率者がいない魚の群れや、蛍の光のようなものです。

伊東 ── 渡邉さんから、数匹の蛍が隣にリズムを合わせて光り始めると、それが伝わって全部が同じリズムになるというお話を聞いて、すごいなと思いました。

渡邉 ── 東南アジアのとあるジャングルでは、1本の木に数百匹の蛍が集まってバラバラに光り出すのですが、隣同士で少しずつリズムを同期させていきます。すると、徐々に光のグループができていく。グループが大きくなり、より数の多いほうが強い光を発して他方をのみ込む。最終的にはグループが3つになり、2つになり、最後には木全体が1匹の蛍のように輝き始める。遠くにいるメスをその光で誘うためです。

田川 ── アンコールの拍手と一緒ですね。引込み現象というか。

渡邉 ── こういった群には、実は全体を指揮するような「統率者」は存在しません。個々が守るローカルなルールしかなく、個々は隣しか見ていないのに、全体に影響が及ぶ。このローカル・ルールとグローバル・エフェクトが、チームの中での共通言語になりました。

田川 ──〈杭と後ろの渦〉は、自然界にいろいろとあるという話もしました。例えば、地下鉄の満員電車のドアがバッと開いたときに人が出ていく様子が、砂時計で砂粒が落ちていく様子と同じように見えるとか、ダイレクトに形を捉えるのではなく、個々の構成要素の関係性に着眼することで、非常に豊かな変容性に富むものが出てくるとか。それが、ローカル・ルールの一番の面白さですね。

ローカル・ルールは、個体がどう振る舞うかだけではなく、個体同士が情報をどうやって交換し、お互いに影響を与え合うかということに着目するアプローチです。このアプローチを採用すると、2匹の場合、300匹の場合、5万匹の場合に出てくる模様は、それぞれまったく違ってくる。力点と作用点の不一致が面白いという話をしました。

展示では、300個の風鈴がお互いにどういう関係を結ぶのか、入ってきた人と1個のオブジェクトがどういう関係を結ぶのかという、関係性の定義だけで止めて、そこから先に出力されてくるものについては、僕らも

us all about swarm behavior in the natural world, like the leaderless schools of fish depicted in Leo Lionni's picture book *Swimmy* (1963), or the blinking of fireflies.

Ito — Watanabe described how, if a few fireflies near each other start flashing to the same rhythm, pretty soon they'll all be all flashing in synch. I thought that was incredible.

Watanabe — In a certain Southeast Asian jungle, hundreds of fireflies gather in a single tree, all flashing out of synch, but as neighbors begin to fall into the same rhythm, they gradually form groups of light. As the groups grow, those with more members produce a stronger light and absorb the other groups. Soon there are only three groups, then two, and finally the entire tree begins flashing as if it were a single firefly. This stronger light is capable of attracting females from further away.

Tagawa — It's like the applause for an encore after a show, or the pull-in effect.

Watanabe — There is no overall leader directing things in swarms like this. Each individual follows its own local rules, and is only looking at its neighbor, and yet has an effect on the whole. Soon everyone on the team was talking about "local rules with global effect."

Tagawa — We also talked about how this idea of stakes and eddies forming behind them can be seen in all sorts of ways in the natural world. The way people pour from a crowded subway car when the doors open, for example, looks a lot like the way grains of sand fall in an hourglass. Instead of capturing a form directly, looking at the relationship among its individual constituent elements reveals an extraordinarily rich variability. This is what's so interesting about local rules.

The local rules approach looks not only at how individuals behave but also at how individuals exchange information with and influence each other. Where this approach is adopted, the patterns produced when there are two fireflies, or 300, or 50,000, are completely different. We talked about the interesting disharmony between stress points and application points. Right at the start we decided that for the exhibition we'd only define the relationships—what ties together the 300 wind chimes, and what ties any person who enters to individual objects—and as for what happens after that, we'd just enjoy seeing where things led.

Ito — At what point did we come up with the idea of wind chimes?

Tagawa — At our very first meeting. We talked about having wind

結果を見て楽しもうという話を最初にさせていただきました。

伊東 — 〈風鈴〉というテーマは、どの辺で出てきたのだっけ？

田川 — 最初の打合せです。風が吹いて音が鳴るというよりも、人が歩くとチリンと鳴るイメージを話しましたね。風鈴になった理由は、開催時期は夏で暑いし、涼しいものがいいのでは、ということでした。

伊東 — 僕が感心したのは、普通、風鈴で音を出すにはガラスを鳴らすじゃないですか。それを、上部の金属で音を鳴らすようにしたのが、すごい人たちだなと思いましたね。

田川 — 実際にガラスを叩いて鳴らすと、カーンと少し滑稽な音が鳴るんです。それをエレガントな響きにしようとすると駆動部分が大きくなってしまい、設計的には非常にハードルが高く、なかなか期待した音が出ないことがわかりました。考えてみれば、江戸風鈴もチリンチリンと鳴るものは金属でできています。ガラスの持つ透明感を生かし、光の伝播する様子を見せたかったので、音質と透明感の整合性にかなり悩みました。最終的には、ガラスが光る瞬間に、その発光の位置から離れた、天井近くに配置された金属棒を鳴らすことにしました。それを考える過程では、これはフェイクだという意見も出ました（笑）。

渡邉 — 当初、伊東さんの事務所のスタッフからは猛反対されました。音はいいけれど、これは風鈴ではないと。

田川 — 人間の視覚は横方向と上下方向の空間分解能が発達しています。人間は左右方向の音の定位には非常に鋭敏ですが、上下方向の分解能は粗いのです。これは、人間が危険を察知するときに、音で何となく方向を知り、目で最終的に位置を特定するという、視覚と聴覚の役割分担があるからです。

「風鈴」駆動部の変遷。風鈴のガラスをディンガーで叩くものから、天井付近に格納された鉄琴をハンマーで鳴らすものへ変更した

Transformation of the wind chime actuators from dingers that struck the glass to hammers that struck metal bars concealed near the ceiling.

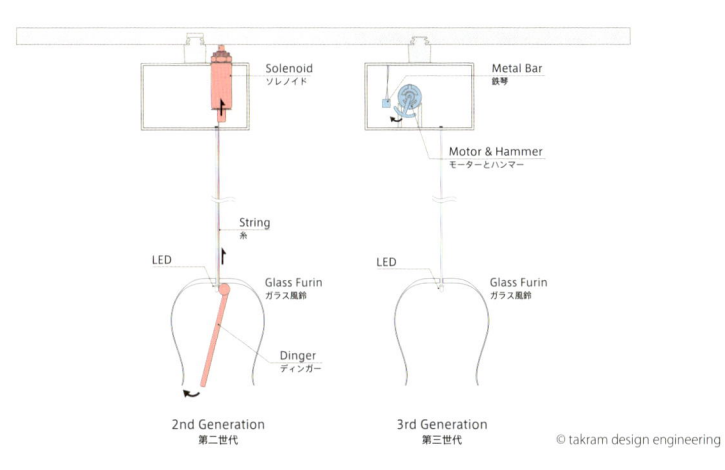

© takram design engineering

chimes that rang not when blown by the wind but when people walked. The reason for using wind chimes was that the exhibition was being held in the hot summer so we wanted to do something that felt cool.

Ito — What intrigued me was that wind chimes normally generate sound when a clapper strikes the glass globe, right? So when the team made sound using metal bars placed above the globes, I knew they were really thinking outside the box.

Tagawa — When the glass is struck, it dings in a way that's actually kind of silly, and trying to turn that sound into something with an elegant resonance meant using an actuator that was really big. The substantial design hurdles this presented made us realize that we weren't going to be able to get the sound we wanted. Then we realized that the Edo wind chimes that ring so beautifully are actually the ones made of metal. Since we wanted to take advantage of the transparency of glass in showing how the light spread, we really struggled with how to achieve consistency between the sound's tone and the sense of transparency.

Ultimately, we decided that at the moment the glass lit up, a metal bar fixed some distance away near the ceiling would be struck to produce the sound. As we were discussing this, there were some who said it would be a sham. (*Laughs*)

Watanabe — At first, the staff members from Ito's office were dead set against it. They liked the sound, but said that what we were making weren't wind chimes.

Tagawa — Human vision has well-developed horizontal and vertical

「風鈴」が並ぶ打合せスペース

Rows of wind chimes in the meeting space.

CHAPTER-1 Furin 39

目の前でピカーッと光らせながら、音の発生源が天井にあっても、ほとんどの人が光ったところから鳴っていると感じる。これは、人間が別々の感覚器から情報を同時にインプットされたときに、人間の脳がつじつま合わせのために光ったところから聞こえていると思ってしまうからです。物理的にカチンと鳴らすタイプと、違うところからきれいな音が鳴るタイプを、伊東さんがご覧になったときに「実際にものが当たって音が鳴るのは普通で、ありもしないところから聞こえてくるのは魔法みたいだ」という話をされて、そこから設計がグッと進みました。

川向 ── 風鈴だが音だけではなく光るという、どこか生命体、特に蛍のイメージが残っています。

田川 ── 確かに、風鈴自体は発光体ではないのですが、もともとの〈群〉の発想を定着させるメタファーとしての風鈴を持ってきました。風鈴は基本的には 300 個並べて聞くようなものではないが、アイデアの基点になったものを、そのまま使いました。

川向 ── 結果的には、非常に美しい風景ができました。最初は、ショールームの風景をそのまま見せようという話でしたが、最終的には、黒い布で 3 方向を囲みましたね。

渡邉 ── もちろん、音だけでも成立するかもしれませんが、この展示空間では周囲を暗くして黒い幕を張り、視覚的なノイズを下げました。光も使うことにしたのは、蛍のエピソードが背景にあります。

田川 ── このローカル・ルールの同じ仕組みを、無限に展開していけば地球を覆う展開が可能です。スペースの制限から実際の風鈴は 300 個でしたが、無限に広がる一部分を切り取ったというふうに感じられるのがベストだと思って、黒い幕の囲いを使うことにしました。

伊東 ── そうです。スパッと切り取る感じにしようと。

川向 ── 全体の構成、空間のデザインの仕方としては、音、光、そして吊り下げられた 300 個の風鈴が生み出す波形という 3 つの要素が重なっています。ですから、ただ音や光が伝播するだけでなく、それを伴って波、あるいは波紋が空間に広がっているように錯覚します。

渡邉 ── ウェーブですが、X と Y の両軸でサインカーブを直交させてつくった「風鈴配置の波」のほかに、「光が伝播していく」波の 2 つがあります。風鈴の発光をトリガーするために 2 つのルールを定めました。「風鈴の下を人が通ると光る」というものと、「隣の風鈴が光ったら、それよりも少し弱く光る」というもの。結果的にどこかで人が動くと、音と光が減衰しながら波打つかのように広がります。人の振舞いが結果的に波紋をつくる。でも波紋を描く、というプログラムを書いたわけではないのです。そこが面白い。プログラムの変数を変えることで、いろいろなパターン

spatial resolution. When it comes to hearing, though, people are acutely sensitive to positions in the horizontal direction, but vertical resolution is rough. This is because humans have evolved to sense the general direction of a threat through sound and then to determine its final location through sight, in a kind of division of labor between the senses.

Even if the source of a sound is up near the ceiling, if the sound is emitted simultaneously with a light flashing at eye level, most people will perceive the sound as being produced at the light source. This is because when people receive simultaneous inputs from multiple sensory organs, their brains seek consistency and interpret the sound as coming from the same place as the light.

When we had Ito listen to both types—the wind chimes that clinked when physically struck and the ones that produced a clean sound from somewhere else—he said, "It's perfectly ordinary for a sound to be made when something is struck, but to hear sound when there's no clapper feels like magic." The design moved ahead quickly after that.

Kawamukai — They wind chimes produce not only sound but light, too, which leaves an impression somehow reminiscent of a living organism, particularly a firefly.

Tagawa — A wind chime is not normally a source of light, of course. We initially brought in wind chimes as a metaphor to establish the idea of swarms. At its core, the exhibit is more than just 300 wind chimes set up to be listened to, but this core idea did carry all the way through.

Kawamukai — The result was a really beautiful landscape. Originally there was talk of leaving the showroom just as it was, but ultimately you enclosed the space with black cloth on three sides, didn't you?

Watanabe — The piece might have held up even with just sound alone, but we decided to make the space darker by hanging a black curtain around the perimeter to reduce visual noise. Deciding to incorporate light, of course, was based on the firefly discussion.

Tagawa — If you applied the same mechanism of local rules infinitely, you could cover the whole world. Because of space restrictions we actually only used 300 wind chimes, so we added the black enclosure in the hope of creating the sense that they'd been cut from some infinite expanse.

Ito — That's right. Cut clean away.

Kawamukai — As a matter of spatial design, the overall composition was made up of three elements: sound, light, and the wavy shapes

を用意して、時間帯によって、場のルールを変える工夫も施しました。

川向 ——〈杭と渦〉、そして〈群〉のイメージが、見事にインタラクティブなインスタレーションに具現化されて、その鮮やかさに驚きましたが、あれは、takram の通常のデザイン手法ですか。

田川 —— 僕たちは〈振り子〉と呼んでいますが、抽象と具体などの相反するものの間にこそ、豊潤なアイデアが埋まっていると考えています。僕らはプロトタイピングという手法で、常につくっては壊すという行為を繰り返します。自分と作品との対話、抽象と具体の対話、対極にあるものの間で振り子運動をしつつ、ものをつくることが、takram のメンバーの共通認識になっています。ものをただブラッシュアップするだけでは、よくも悪くも技術的改良に終わって、文化的にならない。〈振り子〉が両極の間を行ったり来たりする移動の瞬間に、アイデアの発火が起こるのです。

川向 —— この「風鈴」展は会期を延長して、インスタレーションの空間を実際のショールームの打合せコーナーとして使うことのできた、貴重な回でしたね。

田川 —— はい。新たな〈渦〉が生まれた感じでした。打合せをするテーブルの上で風鈴がチーンと鳴るシュールな状景でしたね。

未曾有の建築へ

川向 ——「風鈴」展のあとのお仕事の展開についてお話しくださいませんか。

伊東 —— 僕が田川さんたちと若干違うのは、僕ももちろん理念があって、それを具体化し、ものから理念に戻るというフィードバックは繰り返すのだけれど、僕は、理念を壊したいと思っているのです。〈ものの力〉で破壊する。理念を超えたときに、建築って面白いのかなと思っています。それは、なかなか思うようにいかないし、建築は相手があるので、また

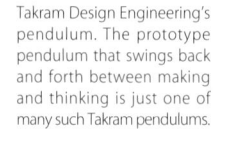

takram design engineering の〈振り子〉のイメージ。つくることと考えることの間を行き来するプロトタイピングの振り子など、いくつもの振り子がある

Takram Design Engineering's pendulum. The prototype pendulum that swings back and forth between making and thinking is just one of many such Takram pendulums.

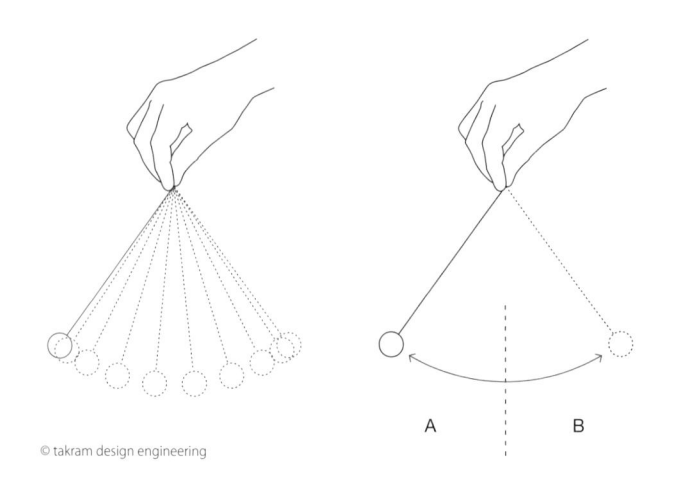

© takram design engineering

created by 300 hanging wind chimes. So it wasn't just sound and light being propagated but also the illusion that these were accompanied by waves or ripples that spread out across the space.

Watanabe — There were two kinds of waves: the "wind chime position waves" formed by arranging the wind chimes on intersecting sine curves along the X and Y axes, and the waves of transmitted light. We set two rules for triggering light emission. The first was that a wind chime's light would shine when someone walked beneath it. The second was that a wind chime would shine whenever a neighbor shone, but a little less brightly. The result was that whenever somebody moved it generated waves of attenuating sound and light. People's behavior created ripples, but what was interesting is that we hadn't created a program for creating ripples. We did, however, prepare a variety of different patterns by altering the program's variables, allowing us to change the rules governing the space for different times of day.

Kawamukai — I was really amazed at the brilliant way you embodied the notions of "stakes and eddies" and "swarms" into such an interactive installation. Was this typical of Takram's usual methodology?

Tagawa — We take what we call a "pendulum approach," believing that the richest ideas are embedded in the space between contrasting concepts like abstract and concrete. We're constantly prototyping: building things and taking them apart. Everyone at Takram shares this approach: we swing back and forth between opposites in a dialogue between ourselves and what we make—in a dialogue between the abstract and the concrete. For better or worse, just brushing things up leads only to technological improvements; it doesn't lead to anything cultural. It's in the moments when the pendulum swings back and forth between extremes that ideas are sparked.

Kawamukai — *Furin* was a special exhibition, one we were able to extend by leaving the installation in place even as the venue returned to its normal function as a meeting space.

Tagawa — That's right. It felt like new eddies were being created. It was a bit surreal hearing the wind chimes ring above the tables as people had meetings.

Toward Unprecedented Architecture

Kawamukai — Could you talk a little bit about the work you've done since the *Furin* exhibition?

天井に「風鈴」が配置された
まま、打合せスペースとして
利用された

The meeting space continued to be used for meetings with the wind chimes hanging from the ceiling.

失敗したとか、そんなことばかりですけれども。

今やっている「台中国立歌劇院」は、2015年にようやく完成予定ですが、まあ、これはいろいろなことが重なり合って、僕らも理性では判断できないことだらけです。でも、とめるわけにはいかない。その日その日を乗り越えていくことの積上げの結果、今まで感じたことのない建築になりつつあります。予想できないものというか、それは二度とあり得ないほどのものだと思っているのです。

川向 ── それは、素晴らしい建築の誕生を期待させますが、予想不可能というのは「せんだいメディアテーク」(2000) でおっしゃっていた以上のことですか。

伊東 ── はるかに。「せんだいメディアテーク」は、確かに難しかったけれど、ある時点から、こういうスケジュールで、こういう方法で仕上がっていくというのが予想できていたのですが、「台中国立歌劇院」は、いまだに何ができるのかわからないことだらけで進んでいます。こんな建築は、今の世の中にはあり得ないです。ここまで来てしまった、というのが現実です。それは、自分でも味わったことのない感動ですね。外は全貌を現し、内側もほぼ仕上がりつつあります。

渡邉 ── 予想できなかった部分は、どういうところですか。

伊東 ── まず、できるかどうかの確信が持てなかったのですよ。施工しているのは、台湾でもそこまで大きくないゼネコンなので、僕らが手取り足取り、足場の建て方まで教えているような状態でした。

川向 ── それは、ものとしてつくることが難しいということですか。

Ito — What's a bit different from Tagawa and his team—although I do experience the feedback loop of having an ideal, trying to embody it, and then returning from the thing to the ideal—is that I want to destroy the ideal. I want to destroy it with "the power of the thing." Architecture is at its most interesting when it transcends the ideal. That doesn't happen easily, and of course there are always other people involved, and I always seem to be bemoaning the latest failure. The project I'm working on now—the Taichung National Theater— should finally be completed in 2015, but you know, so many things have piled up, and so many of them are things we just can't decide rationally. Still, it isn't as if we can stop now. As a result of just trying to get through each day, though, it's turning into a kind of architecture unlike any I've ever felt before. I think it's something unpredictable— something that can never be repeated.

Kawamukai — Well, that certainly raises expectations for the birth of a wonderful work of architecture, but do you mean it's been even more unpredictable than the Sendai Mediatheque (2000)?

Ito — Far more. The Sendai Mediatheque was certainly a challenge, but at a certain point we were able to predict how it would come together using given methods and on a given schedule. With the

「せんだいメディアテーク」
（伊東豊雄建築設計事務所、
2000)

Sendai Mediatheque (Toyo Ito & Associates, Architects, 2000).

「台中国立歌劇院」（伊東豊雄建築設計事務所、2015 年竣工予定）の建設中の様子。周囲には高層ビルが建ち並ぶ

Taichung National Theater (Toyo Ito & Associates, Architects, expected completion 2015) under construction and surrounded by high-rises.

伊東 — 普通、ホールの場合は、2,000 席、800 席、200 席といった、だいたいの枠を取って、それに合わせて全体像を組み上げていきますよね。「台中国立歌劇院」は、最初に示した大きな柱状のグリッドができていて、その中に強引に 2,000 席と 800 席を組み込んでいるのです。ねじ上げていく形で。

僕は、今の世界はグリッドでつくられていて、世界の都市は全部グリッドに覆われていって、人々は均質なグリッドの中でエントロピーの極限状態のように、結局、平和な死を迎えるに違いないと思っています。そういう中にあって、全然違うグリッドで、人間の手作りというか、力の限りを尽くして、人間に力を与えてくれるような建築があってもいいかなと思っているのです。

3 〜 4 年遅れているので、役所からギャーギャー言われているし、終わったら裁判にもなりかねません。現場の設計事務所に山のようにある、役所との打合せ記録の書類も、裁判のためにとってあります。それでも、役所も施工会社も喜んでいるし、そういう中で進行していくのは、ものすごく不思議な感覚です。日本では考えられないですよね。

川向 — グリッドの軸の部分がヴォイドですよね。ある意味、「せんだいメディアテーク」の柱がヴォイドになっていて、それが縦横に並んでいる感じです。なぜ、こんなことを、という建築ですね。

伊東 — こんな面倒くさいものをどうやってつくるのかという、立場を変えれば、本当にばかばかしいことだと思うでしょう。普通は考えないと思いますよ。

「台中国立歌劇院」の中から外の風景を見ると、すごく不思議なのです。設計が始まったころには、周りに何もなかったのですが、今では周囲が

Taichung National Theater, though, there are still all sorts of areas in which we're moving ahead without any idea how things will end up. In this day and age a project like this is just unthinkable. The fact is, it's incredible we've made it this far. I've never been so impressed by anything in the same way. The exterior is beginning to fully reveal itself while the interior is nearing completion.

Watanabe — What sort of things weren't you able to anticipate?

Ito — First, I've never been certain it could be done. The general contractor that's building it isn't even one of the biggest in Taiwan, so we've spent a lot of time showing them step by step how to do things, even teaching them how to set up scaffolding.

Kawamukai — Do you mean that the building is just really difficult to actually build?

Ito — Normally, when you build a theater complex you start by blocking out spaces for, say, a 2,000-seat hall, an 800-seat hall, and a 200-seat hall, and then use these as the building blocks around which to compose the structure as a whole. For the Taichung National Theater, though, there was the grid of massive columns that we presented at the beginning and then we had to find a way to forcibly integrate—to wrench in—2,000 seats here and 800 seats there.

Today's world is built of grids; all the cities of the world are covered in grids, and it seems inevitable that people will ultimately meet their peaceful end, at the limits of entropy, in homogenous grids. Amid all this, why not have a building that's based on a completely different geometry, that tests the limits of the handmade, the limits of man's ability, and gives people strength?

We're three or four years behind schedule, the city office is constantly making noise, and we might even end up in court when it's all over. The mountain of documents recording our discussions with the city that's piling up at our on-site office is being kept in case of a lawsuit. Despite this, the city office and the contractor are both happy so we're moving forward anyway. It's a very strange feeling, and something that would be unthinkable in Japan.

Kawamukai — The grid is built around voids, isn't it? In a sense, it seems as if the tubular columns of the Sendai Mediatheque have become voids laid crosswise and lengthwise. It's the kind of building that makes you ask, "Why do such a thing?"

Ito — Frankly, if I were in a different position I might very well look upon efforts to build something so maddening as utter folly. It's certainly not the kind of thing you normally think of.

「台中国立歌劇院」大ホール
の検討模型

Study model of the Taichung
National Theater grand theater.

　高級マンションで埋め尽くされて、洞窟の中から古代人が現代社会を眺めているような、それはまさしく、グリッドで固められた洞窟の中にいるような気がします。
　「風鈴」から一貫しているのは、今の世界は視覚が圧倒的に強くて、視覚ですべてが決まっていくような状況ですが、僕はそうではなくて、音とか光といった聴覚や視覚にアプローチするような空間をつくりたいと思っています。

川向 ── これまでの建築と比べて、一気にすべてを飛び越えているという感じですか。

伊東 ── 結果的に飛び越えてしまったという感じですね。自分でも予想していなかったところに行ってしまったという。

自然界に学ぶ動的デザイン

川向 ── takram の「その後」をお話しください。

渡邊 ──「風鈴」展がきっかけになって、ミラノサローネで東芝の空間展示「OVERTURE」（2009）をつくることになりました。当時は、家庭向けの光源が白熱球から LED に移行し始める時期で、LED 光源を使ったインスタレーションを一緒につくりませんか、というお話でした。いろいろな高さに電球形のオブジェを 100 個ほど吊り下げ、来場者が空間を歩き回る中、オブジェに触れるとそれが一定のリズムで瞬き始める、というインスタレーションです。水が入っているオブジェに触れると、瞬きのリズムと同期して手の中でトクットクッと振動する感触は、あたかも小動物の鼓動のようです。

川向 ── 建築空間は、どなたの設計ですか。

Looking out from the interior of the Taichung National Theater is the strangest experience. When we started designing the building there was nothing in the surroundings, but now the area is packed with luxury apartments. It feels like being an ancient staring out at the modern world from a cave hemmed in by the grid.

What remains consistent with *Furin* is the idea that the world today is overwhelmingly weighted toward sight—that everything gets decided based on visuals—but I really want to create spaces that use light and sound and take a multi-sensory approach instead.

Kawamukai — Does it feel as though, compared to architecture that has come before, you're vaulting over everything all at once?

Ito — Ultimately if does feel as if I've made a great leap, and landed somewhere that I myself could never have predicted.

Dynamic Design that Learns From the Natural World

Kawamukai — And what has Takram been up to since *Furin*?

Watanabe — The *Furin* project led to an opportunity to create an installation called *Overture* (2009) for the Toshiba space at the Salone del Mobile in Milan. It was around the time when the transition from incandescent bulbs to LEDs for home use was just beginning and we were asked to collaborate on an installation using LED illumination. The installation involved suspending about a hundred light bulb shaped objects at various heights. When touched by visitors moving around the space, they would begin to emit light that pulsated with a regular rhythm. When the water-filled objects were held in the hand, they vibrated in sync with the pulsing light, feeling much like the heartbeat of a small animal.

Kawamukai — Who designed the architectural environment for that piece?

Watanabe — Ryo Matsui took the lead, designing the space together with us and with the Toshiba Design Center.

Tagawa — The space wasn't very large, and it was a bit convoluted, so we put up arched walls with mirrors behind them to create a sense of something more expansive.

Kawamukai — Around the same time, Ito, you were building the Tama Art University Library (Hachioji Campus, 2007), a building known for its impressive arches.

Ito — That's right. I'm surprised to learn that we were thinking about similar things.

「OVERTURE」（東芝＋takram design engineering＋松井亮、2009）

Overture (Toshiba, Takram Design Engineering, and Ryo Matsui, 2009).

Toshiba Corporation, Takram Design Engineering, Ryo Matsui Architects Inc. © 2012 Toshiba Corporation

渡邉 ― 松井亮さんが中心となり、東芝のデザインセンターとわれわれとの三者でつくりました。

田川 ― あまり広くない入り組んだ空間でしたので、アーチの壁を立てて、背後に鏡を配置して、空間が広がっているかのように見せました。

川向 ― 伊東さんも同じころに、アーチが印象的な「多摩美術大学図書館（八王子キャンパス）」（2007）をつくっておられましたね。

伊東 ― そうですね。驚きました。同じようなことを考えているものですね。

渡邉 ― もう1つ、2013年からNHK Eテレの子ども向け科学教育番組「ミミクリーズ」でアートディレクションとキャラクターデザインを担当しています。番組の監修は生物学者の福岡伸一先生です。実は福岡先生はたまたま「風鈴」展を見に来てくださって、『週刊文春』のエッセイで「風鈴」について書いてくださっていた。以前から見えないご縁があったんです。番組では「風鈴」で考えた個と群の関係を含め、自然界のいろいろな造形や構造をテーマとして据え、〈螺旋〉、〈枝分かれ〉、〈層〉などを取り上げています。

例えば、世の中に偏在する図形で、ボロノイ図というものがあります。点と点の間に垂直二等分線を引き領域を分けていくと現れる模様です。細胞の集まりのように見えますが、例えばトンボの羽根の模様はこのルールで造形されています。ヒョウやキリンのような動物の「柄」も、同じボロノイ図の造形です。

直接的な言葉や数式で説明するのではなく、わかりやすい印象的なアニメーションの中で捉えてもらう。子どもたちが科学的な目線で世の中を

「多摩美術大学図書館（八王子キャンパス）」（伊東豊雄建築設計事務所、2007）

Tama Art University Library [Hachioji Campus] (Toyo Ito & Associates, Architects, 2007).

Watanabe — Starting in 2013, we've also been responsible for art direction and character design for an educational science program for kids on NHK called *Mimicries*. The program is supervised by biologist Shin'ichi Fukuoka, who had actually visited the *Furin* exhibition and written an essay about it for the *Shukan Bunshun* weekly. Some invisible connection must have been drawing us together. For the program we address a variety of universal forms and structures found in the natural world, including the relationship between individuals and swarms that we considered in *Furin,* as well as spirals, branches, and layers.

For example, one kind of pattern that can be found all over the world is the Voronoi pattern, which is formed by dividing a territory using perpendicular bisectors drawn between given points. The patterns look like gatherings of cells, but dragonfly wings, for example, are actually formed according to this rule. The spots on animals such as leopards and giraffes are also Voronoi patterns.

Instead of explaining things directly using words or mathematical formulas, we try to encourage comprehension through easy-to-understand animations that leave an impression. We hope that the work we do encourages kids to enjoy looking at the world with a scientific point of view.

Ito — You were talking about Voronoi patterns just now, but for the library in the National Taiwan University College of Social Sciences (2013), which has finally been completed, I created a space in which

Images from NHK

子ども向けテレビ番組の「ミミクリーズ」で、ボロノイ図について扱った回から

From the episode of *Mimicries*, a television program for children, that looked at Voronoi patterns.

見ることに親しんでくれるのではと期待してつくっています。

伊東 ── ボロノイ図の話ですが、ようやくできあがった「国立台湾大学社会科学部棟」（2013）の図書館では、柱の位置と屋根の位置を全部同じにして生成していくということをやっています。グリッドとは違う秩序で、幾何学ではありますが、こうして物事が決まっていくと、かなり違った空間ができて、人間にとっては親しみやすく、自然の中にいるような親密感を味わうことができるのです。

今、岐阜でやっている図書館の「みんなの森 ぎふメディアコスモス」は、木造のうねった屋根が架かっています。地元のヒノキを使って 90 m× 80 mの大きな平面を大きな波で生成しています。それは曲げるのも大変ですが、3 方向に互い違いに厚さ 2cm ぐらいの飛騨材の板を積層して、一番厚いところでは 20 枚の板で厚さ 40cm のシェルをつくりました。それは、まさしく「風鈴」の波を下から見たものとまったく同じだと思いますよ。いろいろな形につながっていますね。

川向 ──「その後」を語ることで、あの「風鈴」にもう一度多面的に光を当てていただきました。どうも、ありがとうございました。

「国立台湾大学社会科学部棟」の図書館 (伊東豊雄建築設計事務所、2013)

National Taiwan University College of Social Sciences Library (Toyo Ito & Associates, Architects, 2013).

the positions of the columns and the positions of the roof sections all line up. Deciding things like this by following a system that's geometric but not a standard grid results in a really different sort of space, one that feels approachable for people and offers a taste of the affinity we feel for being in nature.

The library we're doing now in Gifu prefecture—the Minna no Mori Gifu Media Cosmos—is covered with an undulating roof made of wood. We're using local hinoki cypress to create a massive, wavy surface that measures 90m x 80m. Difficult to bend to begin with, we've layered 2cm-thick lumber from Hida, alternated in three directions, to create a lattice shell that's 40cm at its thickest point— that's 20 boards. Looking up at the ceiling is almost exactly like looking up at the waves in *Furin*. It's amazing, really, how things tie together.

Kawamukai— Asking you to talk about what you've done since *Furin* has really shed new light on that exhibition, and from a number of angles. Thank you very much.

CHAPTER-1 Furin 53

CHAPTER —— 2

Transparent Form
透明なかたち

ARCHITECT
Kazuyo Sejima
建築家
妹島和世

ARTIST
Haruka Kojin
アーティスト
荒神明香

56　第 2 章　透明なかたち

CHAPTER-2　Transparent Form　57

58　第2章　透明なかたち

CHAPTER-2 Transparent Form 59

厚さ 3mm のアクリルを使ったインスタレーション。高さ 2,520mm のパネルを曲げ加工ができる厚みで、極限まで薄くしたアクリルを集合させ、形をつくっていく。幅 1,660mm のアクリルピース 1 枚では自立するのがやっとであるが、それらが集合し、平面的に閉じた形となることではじめてより安定した全体として成立する。

3mm の透明なアクリルはものとしての存在感が希薄になるため、アクリルの表面における反射と視線の透過が強調される。そのため、この薄いアクリルの集合が反射と透過を繰り返し、刻々と変わる光の状態や周辺の環境と体験する人々の動きによってつくられる現象のようなものだけが現れ、実際にあるものと反射してアクリルの表面に映し出される像が混じり合いながらあいまいな全体をつくりだす。

周辺の環境を受け入れながらできあがる空間とも彫刻とも見える、透明なかたちのようなものをつくりだせればと思っています。

（妹島和世＋佐々木睦朗　展示コンセプト文より）

アクリルでできた立体物は、はっきりと目に見えたり全く存在を消したりする。そこにあるのに、ないような、でも、確かにそこにはある。パントマイムのように、見えない壁の続きを手でそっとなぞりたくなった。私は、アクリルでできた壁を境に、モチーフを対称に並べていった。人々の動きによって、壁がまるで鏡面になったかのように見えたり、または反射によってくっきりと映り込み、壁の向こう側にあるモチーフに像を重ね始める。このインスタレーションは、遠くで見ると単にモチーフが目に入り壁の存在感が消えてみえるが、近よって見ると、逆にそのモチーフの配列によって透明の壁の存在を浮かび上がらせることができればと思っている。

目に見えないあいまいな境界線が、実はたしかに空間を横切っているということを、目に映る物体を追っていくことで確認することができる。このことは、私達の身のまわりの環境の中、風景の中でも起きていることかもしれない。限りなく曖昧な推測だが、私はそう確信している。

（荒神明香　展示コンセプト文より）

This is an installation that uses 3mm acrylic. We bent 2,520m-tall panels into shape, assembling the ultra-thin material to create the forms. A 1,660mm-wide sheet of acrylic can barely stand on its own, but when multiple sheets are assembled to make a shape that is fully closed in plan view, they finally come together as a stable whole. Because transparent 3mm acrylic panels have a material insubstantiality, surface reflections and the transmission of the gaze are prioritized. Through repeated reflection and transmission, therefore, the thin acrylic assemblage is revealed as a kind of phenomenon generated by light conditions that change moment-to-moment, the surrounding environment, and the movements of the people who experience it, creating an amorphous whole that blends what is actually there with the reflected images appearing in the surfaces of the acrylic. We hoped to create a space that was sculptural but also receptive of its surrounding environment, something approaching a transparent form. *(Kazuyo Sejima and Mutsuro Sasaki, Exhibition concept, July 2009)*

The three-dimensional object made of acrylic is sometimes plainly visible and sometimes disappears completely. It exists there, seems not to, but then unmistakably reappears. As if pantomiming, I wanted to run my hands gently over the invisible extensions of the walls. I arranged motifs symmetrically on either side of the acrylic walls. Depending on how people move, the surfaces of the wall may function exactly like a mirror, or reflect in such a way that the reflections begin to overlap with the motifs on the other side of the wall. I hope that when this installation is seen from a distance the motifs will be visible while the presence of the walls fades away, but when approached the arrangement of motifs will instead reveal the presence of the transparent walls. Following the objects that are visible to the eye reveals the invisible, amorphous boundary lines that actually cross the space. This may be something that occurs in the landscapes of our own surroundings, too. Although an exceedingly vague conjecture, this is something of which I am certain. *(Haruka Kojin, Exhibition concept, July 2009)*

CHAPTER-2   Transparent Form   61

場所に潜在する
〈透明なかたち〉を顕わにする

妹島和世
荒神明香
川向正人

建築家
妹島和世

1956 年 茨城県生まれ。日本女子大学大学院
修士課程修了後、伊東豊雄建築設計事務所を
経て、1987 年 妹島和世建築設計事務所設立。
1995 年 西沢立衛と SANAA 設立。主な作品に、
金沢 21 世紀美術館 (2004) ほか

ARCHITECT
Kazuyo Sejima

Born in Ibaraki prefecture in 1956, Sejima
received her master's degree from Japan
Women's University before working at Toyo Ito
& Associates, Architects and then establishing
Kazuyo Sejima & Associates in 1987. In 1995 she
established SANAA with Ryue Nishizawa. Major
works include the 21st Century Museum of
Contemporary Art, Kanazawa (2004).

川向 — このオカムラのショールームの一角を使った、建築以外の領域の
表現者とのコラボレーションという企画を受けるにあたって、妹島さん
がお考えになったことあたりからお話しいただけますか。

3mm のアクリル壁への挑戦

妹島 — 建築家の展覧会は模型を展示することが多いです。実際の設計の
ときもたくさん模型をつくりますが、普通、模型はあくまでも建築が何
分の一かに縮小されたものとして見ています。この企画展のご説明を受
けて、はじめから模型を 1/1 のものとして考えられないか、そんなとこ
ろからもう一度、建築について何か考えられるのではないかと川向先生

Making Manifest
the "Transparent Form" Latent in a Place

KAZUYO SEJIMA
HARUKA KOJIN
MASATO KAWAMUKAI

アーティスト
荒神明香

1983 年 広島県生まれ。2009 年 東京藝術大学
大学院先端芸術表現科修了。空間を異化させ
る現象的なインスタレーション作品を展開し、
国内外で作品を発表。現在、wah document
らとともに、クリエイティブチーム「目」として
活動する

ARTIST
Haruka Kojin

Born in Hiroshima in 1983, Kojin received her
master's degree from the Tokyo University of
the Arts Department of Inter Media Arts in 2009.
She creates phenomenological installations that
transform spaces both in Japan and overseas.
She currently operates, together with Wah
Document, as part of the creative team Mé.

Kawamukai — Sejima, could you start by describing what you first
thought when you heard our plans to ask you to collaborate with
someone from outside the field of architecture in creating something
to be shown in a corner of the Okamura showroom?

The Challenge of 3mm Acrylic Walls

Sejima — Architects' exhibitions often involve displaying models. I
make a lot of models when designing actual buildings, and normally
see them as nothing more than the buildings at a smaller scale.
When you first described your plans for the exhibition, I wondered if

とオカムラさん側にお伝えしました。

通常の建築で構造家の佐々木睦朗さんと協働することが多いのですが、今回は、はじめから模型そのものを実物大と考えて成り立つような構造の考え方ができないかという話から始まりました。

テーマの〈透明なかたち〉は、透明だけれど形があるとすれば、どういう形かなと考えました。透明だと見えないけれど、それを表したいなと思いました。

川向 ── ここは美術館ではなくショールームで、しかも個展ではなく誰かとのコラボレーションという、少々難しい条件です。最近はショールームと美術館との境界が曖昧になってきていますが、ショールームは商品を展示する空間であって、美術館とは違って、作品が鑑賞者にメッセージを送ったり感動を生み出したりする場所ではありません。美も重要だが、やはり機能性が優先される空間です。

妹島 ── はじめ、ちょっと天井が低いと思いました。グルグル歩き回って、どうせショールームでやるならもっと商品の中に入り込んだほうが面白いかなとも思いましたが、実際に使われている場所なので、結局、打合せスペースに戻って、ここでやれることをやろうと考えました。

川向 ── ミーティングの最初に「3mm のアクリルを試してみたい」とおっしゃったのが衝撃的でした。どのような形態で使うのかもわからない、スケッチも何もない段階で、いかにも妹島さんらしいアンサーに、正直、衝撃を受けました（笑）。

妹島 ── 5mm の厚みは建築に出てくるけれど、展覧会だからこそ、もう少し薄いものを試してみたかったのです。天井に届くほどの 3mm 厚のアクリル板をどうたてていくか、佐々木さんにまずご相談しました。

川向 ── 妹島さんは打合せの場を有効に使われていましたね。最初に結論ありきではなく、打合せの場で、いろいろなことを探っていました。この点に関しては全然スタッフ任せにしない。ODS-R は、建築をつくるというよりは空間をつくる、形をつくる試みです。

3mm のアクリルがつくる空間は構造と仕上がりが一体的にできて、構造と空間の分節が同時にできる。ご自身が最も関心のあるテーマに、迷うことなく、まっすぐに進んでいく感じでした。しかも、どうせやるならば、ひとつ大きな問題を解いてみようと、佐々木さんとも議論されていましたね。

妹島 ── 佐々木さんには、いろいろな仕事をご一緒していただいています。とても面白い方ですけれど、すごくクリアな方だから、建築をつくるときにあまり変なことを言っても「それはあり得ないですよ」と言われてしまいます。「3mm のアクリルを現実のところでたてたい」と問えば、「た

I might think about making a model that started out at 1/1 scale, and described to you and the folks at Okamura how I thought this might be a path for thinking interesting thoughts about architecture.

In my ordinary design work I often collaborate with structural engineer Mutsuro Sasaki, and I talked with him about how this time I'd have to think from the outset about the model being life-size, with enough structural integrity to stand on its own.

The theme for *Transparent Form* arose from a sense of curiosity about what form transparency would take if it had a form. Although the transparent cannot be seen, this was something I wanted to try to express.

Kawamukai — The conditions for the exhibition were a bit complicated, given that it took place in a showroom rather than an art museum and was a collaborative effort rather than a solo show. The lines between showrooms and museums have blurred lately, but showrooms are spaces for displaying products. Unlike museums, they aren't places whose works send a message or inspire deep emotion. Certainly they're spaces where aesthetics are important, but functionality takes priority.

Sejima — Well, the ceiling did seem a bit low at first. As I walked around I was thinking that as long as I was going to do something in a showroom I should go all the way and get out among the products, but since the space was actually in use I ultimately decided to go back to the meeting area and do what I could there.

Kawamukai — When you started the meeting by saying you wanted to tackle 3mm acrylic it had a real impact. At the time there were no sketches—no idea what form you intended to produce—so this seemed both very much in character for you and, frankly, rather shocking. (*Laughs*)

Sejima — We sometimes use 5mm acrylic in buildings, but since this was an exhibition I wanted to try something a bit thinner. This first thing I did was consult with Sasaki about how to make 3mm-thick acrylic sheets stand in such a way that they would reach the ceiling.

Kawamukai — You used our meetings very effectively, too. Instead of starting with a preconceived answer, you explored all sorts of possibilities yourself, not leaving everything to staff. The ODS-R is not so much an effort to build a structure as to create a space or a form. A space made from 3mm acrylic enabled you to integrate structure and finished surface while articulating structure and space. It was as if you charged straight ahead without hesitation to address the

ちますけれど、このようなことになりますよ」と言われる。

川向 ─ しかも、妹島さんは、これが建築ではなく模型だということを真剣に考えておられました。建築の条件のどれを外せるかと。

妹島 ─「透明なかたち」展は屋外ではないのですが、ある意味で建築的な、現実のものをつくりたいと思いました。材料には材料そのものの特性があると思います。例えば、建築で 100mm の厚さを 1/100 の模型にすると 1mm ですよね。しかし、1mm の紙が持っている硬さと 100mm の木造や RC 造の壁の硬さは違うわけです。模型は現実とは根本的に違うところがある。

「透明なかたち」展は、模型のようでありながら、1/1 の原寸です。通常 3mm の厚みのアクリルは建築の素材としては出てこない。3mm というのは、もっと厚い 200 〜 300mm のものを、1/100 の模型でつくるときにたまたま出てくる厚みですよね。それを 1/1 の原寸ではじめから考えるという仕事が、果たして今後もあるだろうかと考えました。

佐々木さんとも以前から、カーボンなどを使おうとすると、計算よりも実際の素材の持っている力みたいなものがあって、計算で構造的に成り立つ、成り立たないという話はあるけれども、実際にやってみないと、どのようにシナルかといったこともわからないと話していました。だから、計算と、触ってわかる世界、この両方を合わせたものをやろうとしました。

川向 ─ 先ほどからお話を伺っていて少し意外なのは、「透明なかたち」展のミーティングでは、妹島さんが模型という概念をほとんど使われな

「透明なかたち」展の平面図

Plan drawing of the *Transparent Form* exhibition.

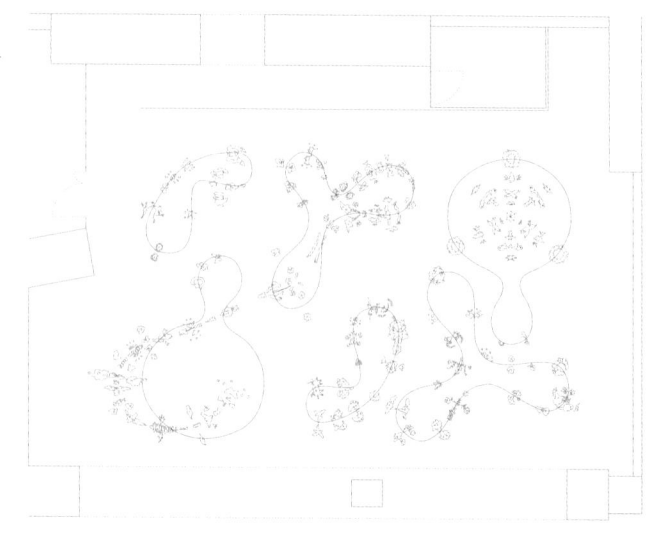

66　第 2 章　透明なかたち

topic you were most interested in. And you decided that as long as you were going to do it you'd tackle one big problem, so you talked things over with Sasaki.

Sejima — I've worked with Sasaki before on all sorts of projects. He's a lot of fun, but also very direct, so if we're working on a building and I say something strange he'll just tell me, "That's not going to happen." When I asked about putting up 3mm acrylic, he said, "It'll stand, but here's what'll happen."

Kawamukai — And you were also very serious about approaching the project not as a work of architecture but as a model—examining which architectural criteria you could do without.

Sejima — The *Transparent Form* exhibition wasn't held outdoors, but I did want to make something that felt, in some way, architectural and real. Different materials, I think, each have their own characteristics. For example, in a 1/100-scale model, something that would be 100mm in the actual building will be 1mm, right? But the stiffness of a 1mm-thick piece of paper is different than that of a 100mm wall made of wood or reinforced concrete. A model is fundamentally unlike reality.

The *Transparent Form* exhibition was like a model, but at full 1/1 scale. You just don't find 3mm-thick acrylic used as a building material; it's the kind of thing you run across occasionally in 1/100 models to represent thicker 200–300mm sheets. I figured there was probably little chance I'd ever have the opportunity to think about putting it to use at 1/1 scale again.

Sasaki had talked with me before about how when you go to use materials like carbon fiber, sometimes it may actually be stronger in use than you'd expect from your calculations, that you can talk all you want about whether or not something will be structurally sound based on the numbers but until you actually build it you can't really know how much it will give. I wanted to do something, therefore, that combined the world of calculations and the world of what can only be known through touch.

Kawamukai — One of the things that surprises me a bit as I listen to you now is that during our meetings about the *Transparent Form* exhibition you didn't employ this notion of architectural models very much. Back then you mostly spoke of the very simple and to-the-point matter of whether it was possible to build something architectural using 3mm acrylic sheets. I can remember the electric atmosphere in the room and the sense that there was a clear

かったことです。あのときは「3mmのアクリルに建築は可能か」といった実にシンプルだが、まさに正鵠を射る問題提起に、私も含めて同席者全員が気持ちの奮い立つのを感じ、同時に展覧会の進むべき方向がはっきりと見えたことを記憶しています。むしろ、模型を介さずに、3mmのアクリルを広げたり、たわめたり、視覚的に透過性を確かめたりすること自体を、これから妹島さんが試すのだろうと期待を込めて想像したのです。

妹島 ── そうですね。おっしゃる通りです。建築設計の現場で私たちは模型に不自由さを感じている、そこが大事です。厚みなどは合っても、柔らかさといった質感がずれていきます。軽やかに伸びていくはずのものが、現実には、重たくそこに存在している。模型でスケールや形態を正しく捉えていても、できあがってくるものは違うわけです。模型を介さない、パーティションとか家具ではない、だが、これは建築であるといえるようなものを試してみようと考えたときに、今までの建築とは違うものが何となく想像できて、私自身も展示構成に向かっての進み方がつかめたように思います。

川向 ── 妹島さんの作品は、勝浦の住宅「Y-HOUSE」(1994) から拝見していますが、あのころから、建築における〈自由〉というテーマは変わっていないですね。住宅であればプライバシーなどの条件から、必要に応じて不透明なパーティションも建てますが、最も大切なのは、その場所を自由に動き回れることで、少し極論すれば、平面図にシングルラインで描かれる〈透明なかたち〉が、その広がりの輪郭だともいえます。

妹島 ── その〈透明なかたち〉には穴や窓があって、違う世界とも自由に行き来できることも同じです。

川向 ── そして、そのシングルラインの実態が 3mm のアクリル板だということがすでに決まっています。これから具体的な設計作業に入っていくわけですが、妹島さんの設計は、最初に 3mm のアクリルの〈選択〉があるという点で、20世紀を越えて、どこか〈19世紀的〉ですね。それは素材の決定だともいえますが、妹島さんのつくる空間はいくつかのレイヤーの重なりによって構成されていて、その最初の、最も基本となるレイヤーの決定に当たります。

19世紀の場合も、必ず最初に〈様式〉つまり〈かた〉の選択が来ます。これが、最も基本的なレイヤーでもありました。そのほかのレイヤーには、画家や彫刻家が担当するものがありました。ですから19世紀建築は、諸芸術のコラボレーションだったのです。

さて、コラボレーションのお相手として、佐々木さんだけではなく荒神さんのお名前が挙がってきました。あれは、どのような理由からですか。

direction forward for the exhibition. Indeed, at the time I imagined you might not work from a model at all but rather engage in a visual exploration of transparency by bending and spreading out the 3mm acrylic sheets.

Sejima — Yes, that's right. It's as you remember. The important thing is that we often struggle with the limitations of models when designing works of architecture. Even if the thickness is right, the softness or texture is frequently off—something we expect to stretch with a sense of lightness may just stand there feeling heavy. Models are good for properly conveying scale and shape, but they're not at all like the thing that will result. When I decided I wanted to try building something without the intervention of a model, something that was not a partition or a piece of furniture but could be called a work of architecture, I was able to imagine something unlike architecture to date and grasp a direction for moving forward in putting together the exhibition.

Kawamukai — I've watched your architectural work since Y-House (1994), the residence you designed in Katsuura, and your interest in exploring the notion of freedom in architecture has been a constant ever since, hasn't it? When designing homes, privacy considerations require erecting some opaque partitions, but your highest priority seems to be to facilitate freedom of movement within a space that, at risk of overstating the point, might be described as a kind of "transparent form" whose breadth is outlined by a single line on the floor plan.

Sejima — That "transparent form," too, has apertures and windows that make it possible to go back and forth freely between different worlds.

Kawamukai — And for this exhibit, that single line turned out to be 3mm acrylic sheeting. At that point, you were able to move on to the concrete work of designing the exhibition, but in the sense that you began with the choice of 3mm acrylic your approach seems almost to transcend the twentieth century, to be somehow very nineteenth century. This decision to use a certain material determines the first and most fundamental of the multiple layers in the spaces you create. In the nineteenth century, architects always began by choosing a style, a *kata*. This became the building's most fundamental layer, with painters and sculptors often responsible for adding subsequent layers. Nineteenth-century architecture, therefore, involved collaboration among the fine arts.

手作業でつくる透明な現象

妹島 ― 今の諸芸術のコラボレーションというお話と関連していると思いますが、佐々木さんだけだと、このODS-Rでのコラボレーションとしては、少しわかりにくいかな、と。つまり、佐々木さんとのコラボレーションは本当に一体的ですから。それで空間表現のもう1つのレイヤーを担ってくれるコラボレーターが必要かなと感じ始めたのです。ちょうど同じころ、ブラジルのサンパウロ近代美術館で行われた「ライフがフォームになるとき－未来への対話／ブラジル、日本」（2008）という展覧会で、私もSANAAとして「Flower House」の1/2の縮尺の模型を出していました。事務所のスタッフが、その展覧会場で荒神さんの「reflectwo」を見ていて、その水平か垂直かわからないような作品の話を聞いて、それは〈透明なかたち〉に近いと感じ、連絡をとり荒神さんにお会いして、コラボレーションをお願いしてみました。

川向 ― 荒神さんは、そのころ、どのような創作活動をしておられたのですか。

荒神 ― 当時、私は学生で大学院の1年生でした。妹島さんから突然電話がかかってきたので、すごく驚きました。妹島さんは「透明な壁をウニャウニャつくるので、その中で何かやってくれませんか」とお話しされました。

妹島さんのことは知っていましたし、妹島さんの建築に共感していました。普通の建築物は見たときに重たい感じがするじゃないですか。建築物はもっと自由に、軽やかになれると思っています。私が抱くような、そういった感情を、妹島さんはそのまま造形化されています。自由ですね。でも外に出て町を歩くと同じような建物が並んでいて、それに私はすごく違和感を抱くのです。

サンパウロ近代美術館で展示した、縮尺1/2の「Flower House」（SANAA、2008）

A 1/2-scale model of *Flower House* (SANAA, 2008) as exhibited at the São Paulo Museum of Modern Art.

Well, in thinking about partners for collaboration, Kojin's name came up in addition to Sasaki's. Why was that?

Transparent Phenomena Created by Hand

Sejima — This may be related a bit to what you were saying about collaboration among the fine arts, but working with Sasaki alone wouldn't really have been the sort of collaboration the ODS-R seemed to be looking for. What I mean is, when I work with Sasaki, we really become one. I began to feel we might need another collaborator who could add a different layer of spatial expression. Right around that time, as part of my work with SANAA, I had submitted a 1/2-scale model called *Flower House* to the *When Lives Become Form: Dialogue with the Future: Brazil/Japan* exhibition (2008) at the São Paulo Museum of Modern Art in Brazil. My staff saw Kojin's piece *Relectwo* at that exhibition and when I heard them describe it as something whose horizontality or verticality was indeterminate I felt it might be close to what we were trying to do with *Transparent Form*. I contacted Kojin, we met, and I asked her to collaborate on the project.

Kawamukai — Kojin, what kind of creative work were you doing back then?

Kojin — I was in my first year of graduate school at the time, so I was very surprised to get an unannounced telephone call from Sejima. She said she was going to make a space out of wavy transparent walls and asked if I could do something in it.

I knew who she was, of course, and her architectural work really resonated with me. Most architecture seems really heavy, right? I always thought there must be some way to make buildings that were freer and lighter. Sejima's work seemed to take those feelings and give them form. It's very free. Go out and walk around the city, though, and all the buildings look pretty much the same, which makes me feel really uneasy.

Ever since I was a child I've always thought that an accumulation of handwork, taken to its extreme, might lead to some kind of understanding about things like space, architecture, or the structure of cities. Some parts may be just an accumulation of handwork, but they somehow extend out into the space, or out into the city, as a whole.

Kawamukai — That certainly seems like the sort of thing you could

左：サンパウロ近代美術館で
展示した「reflectwo」(2008、
荒神明香)。右：東京藝術大
学で展示した「R.G.BB.G.R」
(2008、荒神明香)

Left: *Reflectwo* (Haruka
Kojin, 2008) as exhibited at
the São Paulo Museum of
Modern Art.
Right: *R.G.BB.G.R* (Haruka
Kojin, 2008) as exhibited at the
Tokyo University of the Arts.

子どものころから、手の中の作業をどこまでも蓄積していったら、その
延長線上に空間、建築、都市現象みたいなものが捉えられるのではない
かと考えてきました。ある部分手作業の積重ねになりますが、それが空
間全体、都市全体に広がっていくような。

川向 ── それは、建築とのコラボレーションによって実現しそうに感じま
すね。まさにグッドタイミングで、妹島さんが建築の側から手を差し伸
べたような感じもいたしますが。

荒神 ── 例えば、「R.G.BB.G.R」という作品では、夜眠れずに天井をずーっ
と見ていたときに現れた赤や緑の光の粒々を、もしこの手でつくり出せ
たら新しい光の像をつくり出せるかもしれないと思い制作した作品です。
5 mm 幅に切ったトレーシングペーパーに顔料を塗って、人さし指くら
いの小さな輪をたくさんつくり、それを並べていって 5 ㎡ くらいの大き
な膜をつくりました。それを空間のまん中に吊して見ると、時間帯や周
りの環境が変化していくにつれて見え方が刻々と変わっていきます。同
一平面上に並べてあるはずのパーツが色の錯覚で手前、奥の距離感がわ
からなくなったりもします。小さい手作業の積重ねがいずれ広い現象に
変わっていくようなことを試みたものです。

「reflectwo」は、川を見ていたときに思いついた作品です。深夜 2 時ごろ
に川沿いを歩いていると、川の水面がピタッと止まる時間があるのです。
水面に向こう岸の風景が鏡のように映り、月とか星までも映っていて、
空の中に向こう岸の風景が浮かんでいるように見えたのです。その風景
を、大量生産されている造花の花びらを上下対称に貼り合わせ、それを
空中に浮かべていくことによって、まるで水平線がピーッと通っている
ような作品を制作しました。

妹島 ── 荒神さんは造花の花びらをアイロンでつぶすのですよ。大量生産
された造花の花びらを集めてアイロンでよりフラットにする。そうやっ
てある抽象性を得る。造花の花びらをアイロンで平らにすることで、具
体性と抽象性のバランスみたいなものが出てくるのだと知りました。

achieve through collaboration with an architect. It was incredibly good timing, then, that Sejima reached out to you from the architecture side when she did.

Kojin — *R.G.BB.G.R.,* for example, was a work I was prompted to make by the idea that I might be able to create a new way of seeing light if I could create through handwork the red and green grains of light that appear when I'm unable to sleep at night and stare at the ceiling for a long time. I painted 5mm strips of tracing paper, used them to make many tiny paper rings about the size of my index finger, then arranged them to make a huge membrane measuring about 5m^2. When this was hung in the middle of a space, the way it looked changed constantly with the time of day and changes to its surroundings. Although the rings had all been arranged on the same plane, differences in color led to the illusion that parts were at different depths, some nearer and some further away. In that piece I tried to see how an accumulation of small handwork might transform eventually into some broader phenomenon.

Reflectwo is a piece that came to me while I was looking at a river. I was walking along the river at about two in the morning and there was a moment when the surface of the river suddenly seemed to come to a complete stop. The scenery on the far bank was reflected in the mirror-like surface of the water, as were the moon and the stars, and it all seemed to be floating in midair. By recreating that scenery using mass-produced artificial flower petals pasted together in horizontal symmetry and hung in midair, I made something that seemed to be bisected by a perfectly straight horizon line.

Sejima — Kojin flattens the artificial flower petals with an iron, you know. She gathers mass-produced flower petals and then presses them with an iron to make them even flatter. This invests them with a sense of abstraction. I could see how pressing the petals with an iron produced a balance between the concrete and the abstract.

Kawamukai — People tend to think of things that are mass-produced as perfectly uniform, but there are actually many subtle variations that I imagine may sometimes feel like a nuisance from an artist's perspective. And artificial flowers are just cheap, mass-produced imitations. But even from the midst of such material, it's possible to select examples of a certain type and, though simple tasks, transform them into art—and in massive quantities. Your choice of materials and your means of manipulating them demonstrate this clearly, and I can see why Sejima was so taken with your work.

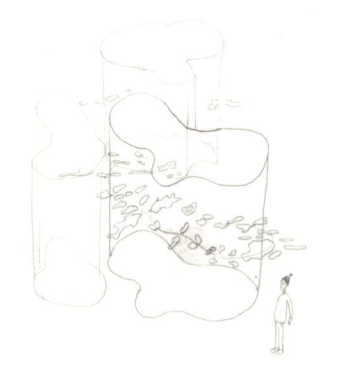

2点とも：荒神氏による「透明
なかたち」展のコンセプトス
ケッチ

Conceptual sketches by
Haruka Kojin for the *Transparent From* exhibition.

川向 ── 機械によって大量生産されたものは、すべて均質だと思われが
ちですが、実は微妙にムラがあって、アーティストの目から見ると、そ
れが〈わずらわしい差異〉に感じられる場合があるはずです。ましてや
造花は、チープな大量生産の模造品。だが、その中からでも、ある種の
ものを選択して、ある単純な作業で、それをアートに生まれ変わらせる
ことができる。しかも大量に、です。荒神さんの素材の選択と利用法は、
このことを示しており、そこを妹島さんが、高く評価なさったのも、わ
かるような気がします。

さて、荒神さんは、アクリル曲板の空間をご覧になって、どのようにお
感じになりましたか。

荒神 ── まず、「透明」だから実際には私たちには見えていない壁も存在
するかもしれない。もしかしたら、この空間に私たちの身体があること
や目の前に机があるという物理的な現実を、透明な壁が自由に、軽やか
に突っ切っていける可能性があるのではないかと感じました。そんなこ
とを考えながら、夜、車に乗っていて、薄いフィルムみたいなものを見
つけました。これが〈透明なかたち〉なのかなと思いながら手と手が合
わさるようにフィルムを挟んで見ていたら、透明だけれどもまるで鏡の
ようにも見えることに気づきました。薄い透明なフィルムが鏡に見えた
途端、すごく物質的に見えました。そこから、造花の花びらを使って、
水面に映った反転した現象を、さらに鏡のような効果を持つ透明なアク
リル曲面の間につくっていくことによって、どこかで見たような、でも、
どこにもない、幻想的でもある水辺の風景を生み出そうとしました。

図面でアクリルの壁が緩やかにクネクネと曲がっているのを見て、空間
の中にアクリルが描いた曲線の延長線上に〈透明なかたち〉を想像して
作品を配置していくことにしました。「reflectwo」で表していた水平線を、
空間を区切るアクリルの境界線に見立て、反転した風景をつくりました。

Well, what did you think when you saw the space Sejima made of curved acrylic sheets?

Kojin — First, I wondered if there might be walls that we can't actually see because they're transparent. What if there was a possibility that our physical reality—our bodily presence in this space, the table in front of use—could be cut through freely and lightly with transparent walls? As I was mulling over such things, I discovered a kind of thin film one night when I was out driving. Thinking that it might be an example of a "transparent form," I brought my hands together on either side of it and realized that even though it was transparent it looked just like a mirror. In that instant, the thin, transparent film suddenly seemed very *material*. After that I decided that using the artificial flower petals to create the phenomenon of a reflection in the water by suspending them on either side of the transparent acrylic curves, which had a mirror-like effect, might create a fantasy-like waterside landscape that was vaguely familiar yet existed nowhere. When I saw Sejima's sketches of acrylic walls curving gently back and forth, I decided to position my works where I imagined there were "transparent forms" extending out into the space from the curves described by the acrylic. I created reflected scenery in which the acrylic boundaries that divided the space acted like the horizon line in *Reflectwo*. This meant that where there was no acrylic, there was no reflected scenery. But I also wanted to betray expectations, so I tried things like not placing reflected scenery where it would be expected, creating scenery that extended beyond and swept around the actual position of the walls, and making ambiguous "transparent

「透明なかたち」展より

Transparent From exhibition.

アクリルのないところでは、反転した風景がないことになります。ただ、ここで、〈裏切り〉のようなことをしてみたくなり、あるべき反転した風景がないとか、壁の実在の位置からはみ出し回り込んだ風景をつくるとか、曖昧な〈透明なかたち〉を、もっと透明にしようと試みたところもあります。

川向 ── 妹島さんから、自立するアクリル曲面の空間をどう使うかという問いかけを受けて、荒神さんの手法で、反転あるいは鏡像関係、裏切り、透明性の増幅のようなものが示されたわけですね。

妹島 ── そうですね。アクリル素材の持つ透明性を、まったく違う次元にまで引き上げてくれています。3mm のアクリルとはいえ、決して 100% 透明ではないわけで、それを荒神さんが、どう透明に見せたかということですね。

荒神 ── 鏡じゃないの？と思われているお客さんもいらして、それが、自分の中ではうれしかったですね。

川向 ── いま話されていることは、おふたりのコラボレーションの核心にふれるものですね。現実の建築は必ず〈かたち〉を持ちます。妹島さんは、ガラスやアクリルを積極的に導入して、その〈かたち〉を消す試みを続けてこられました。今回も、アクリル面への光の当たり方の調整が、最後の最後まで続きました。

妹島 ── もう少し自由な建築はないだろうか、どうやったら〈透明なかたち〉といえるのか、そんなことをいつも考えています。

むろん、荒神さんには「リフレクトゥ」のような別の興味もあって、それぞれが、やれること、やるべきことをやってみようという〈コラボレーション〉でした。「このために、これをやってください」というのではなくて、荒神さんが考えたことを自由に試みてください、と。

川向 ── その結果、高い次元での〈コラボレーション〉になりました。

素材・現象・知覚のその先へ

川向 ── さて、その後の展開ですが、妹島さんは東京都現代美術館で「ラグジュアリー：ファッションの欲望」展（2009）の特別展示の会場構成をアクリルでされていましたね。

妹島 ── はい。「透明なかたち」展よりもっと薄くいけるなと、「ラグジュアリー：ファッションの欲望」展では、アクリルの厚みを 2mm にしました。その 1mm の差で、ますます〈透明なかたち〉に近寄るだろうということで。

川向 ── 犬島の「家プロジェクト」でも、アクリル壁を使い、こちらでは再び、荒神さんとコラボレーションしていますね。

forms" even more transparent.

Kawamukai — So Kojin answered Sejima's question of how to use a space made from freestanding acrylic curves in her own way, with reflections and mirror images, by betraying expectations, and by further amplifying its transparency.

Sejima — That's right. She took the transparency of acrylic to a whole new level. Even 3mm acrylic isn't 100% transparent, of course, but Kojin found a way to make it seem truly invisible.

Kojin — There were some visitors who thought the surface was mirrored, which pleased me very much.

Kawamukai — What you've both said really seems to touch on the heart of your collaboration together. Architecture in the real world always has a *katachi*, a specific shape. By actively using glass and acrylic, Sejima, you've constantly sought to erase this *katachi*. For this exhibition, for example, you worked right up until the very end making adjustments to the illumination on the surface of the acrylic.

Sejima — I'm always thinking about ways architecture might be made freer, and how to create things that could be called "transparent forms."

Kojin, of course, has her own separate interests along the line of *Refletwo*, and this was definitely a collaboration in which we each sought to do what we could— to do our part. I didn't tell her to do a given thing for a given reason, but rather asked her to freely try what she thought was best.

Kawamukai — And the result was a high-level collaboration, indeed.

Beyond Material, Phenomenon, and Perception

Kawamukai — Turning to your more recent work, Sejima, you used acrylic again in the spatial design of the special exhibit venue for the *Luxury in Fashion Reconsidered* exhibition (2009) at the Museum of Contemporary Art, Tokyo, didn't you?

Sejima — Yes. Based on the *Transparent Form* exhibition I figured I could go even thinner, so for *Luxury in Fashion Reconsidered* I used 2mm acrylic. I thought the 1mm difference would bring it even closer to a "transparent form."

Kawamukai — And in another collaboration with Kojin, you also used acrylic walls at the Inujima Art House Project.

Sejima — That's right. I worked with her on *A-Art House/Reflectwo* (2010) and *S-Art House/Contact Lens* (2010).

「ラグジュアリー：ファッションの欲望」展（東京都現代美術館、2009）の会場風景
© 京都服飾文化研究財団

Venue for the *Luxury in Fashion Reconsidered* exhibition.
© The Kyoto Costume Institute

妹島 ─ はい。荒神さんとの「A 邸 / リフレクトゥ」（2010）、「S 邸 / コンタクトレンズ」（2010）ですね。

「家プロジェクト」は企画展なので少しずつゆっくり変わります。現在はほかに小牟田悠介さん、ジュン・グエン＝ハツシバさん、そして、名和晃平さんの作品が展示されています。

川向 ─ 妹島さんと荒神さんによる 2 作品は、すごく冴えているなあと思いました。過疎化が進み、空き家が増え続けるところで、現代アートとして、どこか集落の過去のにぎわいとか自然の豊かさを想起させる〈現象〉をじかに提起しています。その〈現象〉がすっと訪問者の心に入り、ぐっと鷲づかみするのです。その印象はオカムラの「透明なかたち」展に似ています。

妹島 ─「S 邸 / コンタクトレンズ」は、レンズ越しに見ると向こうの家のディテールがパッとひっくり返って見えたり、人の顔が見えたり、ただの素通しもある。全部がレンズではなく、見えたり見えなかったりするのが面白い。それと、私が勝手に「花畑」と呼んでいる「A 邸 / リフレクトゥ」もあります。

川向 ─ おふたりは〈現象〉そのものをつくっていると思うのですが、建築の持っている手法は、まさに〈物自体〉をつくるものばかりで、一気に〈現象〉の提示には行かない。そこがアートとの違いです。おふたりの作品をじっと静かに眺めていると、不思議に、子どもたちの声が聞こえ、老若男女が集い、楽しく、にぎやかに暮らしていた過去の様子などが脳裏に浮かんできました。

アクリルが町並みに合っていましたね。アクリル曲面のスパンが民家の間口幅に近く、高さが民家前面の庇のそれに近いとか、周辺環境との呼

The Art House Project involves temporary exhibitions so it changes slowly, bit by bit over time. Currently there are works on exhibit by Yusuke Komuta, Jun Nguyen-Hatsushiba, and Kohei Nawa.

Kawamukai — I thought the two works you collaborated on both had tremendous clarity. In a place where depopulation is underway and the number of vacant houses is growing, they directly presented, in the form of contemporary art, phenomena that recalled the former bustle and natural bounty of the village. Such phenomena reach right in and tightly grab the hearts of visitors. The impression left was very much like that at the Okamura *Transparent Form* exhibition.

Sejima — When you look through the lenses in *S-Art House/Contact Lens* (2010), you may see the details of the houses flipped upside down, or people's faces, or maybe just clear glass. They aren't all actual lenses, so it's interesting how sometimes you see things and sometimes you don't. And there's also *A-Art House/Reflectwo*, which I like to call the "flower garden."

Kawamukai — It seems to me that you both create phenomena. The architectural method is mostly about creating things; it doesn't jump directly to presenting phenomena. That's the difference between architecture and art. As I contemplated the works that you collaborated on, for some reason I couldn't help hearing the voices of children and seeing fleeting images of a past in which men and women, young and old, all lived happy, flourishing lives together.

The acrylic was a terrific match for the townscape, too. The span of the acrylic arcs nearly matched the frontage of the local residences, and their height was about the same as the eaves on the fronts of such homes. You were really attentive to, and responsive to, the surrounding environment.

Sejima — As you said, we coordinated the height to match the neighborhood. At first I thought having the piece run parallel to the curve of the road would be the best fit, but when we tested the idea on site using models and full-size cardboard mockups we found this was much too strong—and surprisingly so.

The gentle curves of roads, you see, have been designed to handle fast-moving cars. But the roads on the island are narrow and not traveled by cars. There's a *katachi* that can continue to be made in such an environment, right? There's a weight and thickness that can be carried, and assembled, by human hands. I realized that even transparent acrylic had a *katachi*—and a weight and thickness—that could be sufficiently felt with the human body.

応にずいぶん配慮されていました。

妹島 — ご指摘の通り、高さは隣近所の高さと調整しています。最初は、道に平行なカーブのかたちが一番なじむと思ったのですが、模型や実物大のダンボールを現地に持っていって検討してみると、それだと、すごく強く表れてしまう。それは驚くほどでした。

つまり、緩いカーブはある意味で車のスピードに対応するようなカーブなわけです。島の道は細くて車は通らない。そういう環境でつくられ続けるかたちってあるわけですね。運んだり、組み上げたり、人の手でできる大きさだったり厚みだったり。透明なアクリルでもかたちやそのかたちが持つ厚み、重さなんかを人間の身体は充分に感じるということに気づかされました。

今、あのプロジェクトで考えていることは、どうやって使い続けるかということです。だから今度は、ギャラリーではなくコミュニティキッチンを用意したらと思っています。そして、気持ちのいいトイレとお風呂。コミュニティキッチンがあると、島の人の間でも、それからビジターとでも、物々交換が生まれると思います。

川向 — 昔ですと共同体が生きていて、同じ集落内では、さまざまなものが共有され交換されていました。その〈共有〉、〈交換〉から始めたわけですね。

妹島 — ええ。それから、みんなが参加できるプログラムをつくろうとしています。小さい島ですから効果が見えます。豊島や直島は大きくて車が走っているけれど、犬島は歩くしかない。少し歩くと海が見えなくなり、また少し歩くと海が見える。自分たちの世界の境界が認識できる大きさです。自分たちで何かつくると、違いが認識できる。そうなるとみんな自分の島という気持ちが生まれてくる。定住の考え方も変わってくると思うのです。

犬島は岡山市に近いから、おじいさん、おばあさんも週末になると岡山市に住む息子さんのところに行ったり、逆にビジターが島に来る。若い人が経営するカレー屋さんとかパスタ屋さんは、週の半分は岡山市内で店をやって、週末だけ島で店を開く。アーティストがどこかに作品を制作するために10人くらいが1カ月滞在したり、劇団員の30人くらいが1～2カ月滞在したり。私の場合は、2～3カ月に2～3日だけ来る。

こうやって、いろいろなリズムで人が島を使い続ける。とにかく続けていく。今の犬島の風景をリスペクトしながら、知恵を足していくようなことをやれたらいいのではないかなと、興味を持って取り組んでいます。

川向 — やはり地域づくり・まちづくりの根本は、現状の生活に寄り添うことですね。リスペクトしながら、そこに少しずつ知恵を足していく、

犬島の「家プロジェクト」。
「S邸／コンタクトレンズ」(左)
から「A邸／リフレクトゥ」(右)
が見える

Inujima Art House Project,
where *A-Art House/Re-
flectwo* (at right) was visible
from *S-Art House/Contact
Lens* (at left).

What we're thinking about now with the project is how to ensure continual use. For the next step, instead of a gallery we're thinking of preparing a community kitchen, as well as pleasant bathrooms and baths. A community kitchen, I think, might lead to bartering among the people of the island and even with visitors as well.

Kawamukai — In the old days, such communities were alive and all sorts of things were shared and traded within the same neighborhood. You've decided to start encouraging such sharing and trading, then?

Sejima — Yes. We're also developing programs that everyone can take part in. It's a small island so you can really see the impact. Teshima and Naoshima are bigger islands with automobile traffic, but on Inujima you just have to walk. You walk a little bit and you can see the ocean. You walk a little bit more and you see the ocean again. It's a place where you can perceive the boundaries of your own world. When we make things for ourselves, we can perceive a difference. There's a feeling among us that it's our own island. I think this changes the approach to residency, too.

Inujima is not far from the city of Okayama, so it's often the grandmothers and grandfathers who head into the city on weekends to visit their children while visitors from the mainland come out to the island. Young people who run curry or pasta restaurants spend half the week at their shops in Okayama and then open shops on the island during the weekends. When artists create works somewhere on the island it might entail ten people staying for a month, and there are theatrical companies that bring 30 or so people for a month or two. As for me, I spend two or three days on the island every two or three months.

In this way there are a lot of different people using the island, each

という。建築でも集落でも、妹島さんの設計姿勢は、人々の生活を克明に分析するところから始まりますね。

妹島 ── こうやったら使いやすいだろうなとか、楽しいだろうなとか、自由になれるだろうな、ということを必死にやった結果です。

川向 ── 荒神さんは、その後、いかがですか。

荒神 ── 〈コラボレーション〉の話に戻りますが、こういうことをしようというゴールが明確で、みんなの目的が一緒になれば、うまく回っていきます。2012年から、「目」という3人のチームで活動をしています。1人はディレクターでコンセプトや企画戦略を練る人。もう1人は制作の統括をしていて、現場の士気をあげるのが得意な、まさに僧侶みたいな人。そして私は〈原点〉をつくります。大学を卒業して5年ほど1人でやりましたが、それぞれの役割で力を発揮したら絶対いいものができると、ディレクターに説得されて「目」を組み始めたのです。

妹島 ──「目」が小豆島でつくった「迷路のまち〜変幻自在の路地空間〜」（2013）は、面白いと思うな。

荒神 ── あれは、たばこ屋だったところを改装して、たばこ売り場から入ると廊下がくねくねあって、洋服だんすを覗くと、文脈が違う工場みたいなものが見えたりします。その洋服だんすから出られるようになって

「迷路のまち〜変幻自在の路地空間〜」（目【め】、2013）
上：イメージスケッチ。下：たばこ屋から入り（左）、最後は冷蔵庫から外に出る（右）
© 目【め】2013、瀬戸内国際芸術祭／小豆島

Maze Town—Phantasmagoric Alleys (Mé, 2013)
Above: Image sketch. Below: Enter through the tobacco shop (left) and finally exit to the outside through the refrigerator (right).
© Mé, 2013, Setouchi International Art Festival / Shodoshima

according to their own rhythm. The key is that it keeps being used. I'm really enjoying my involvement with the project, and hope we can respect the island's scenery as it is today while adding some wisdom of our own.

Kawamukai — Yes, the key to regional or community development is to draw close to local conditions. Respecting the way of life that's there while adding wisdom bit by bit—this design approach of yours, toward both individual structures and communities, begins from a detailed analysis of how people live, doesn't it?

Sejima — It's the result of thinking really hard about what people might find easier to use, or find more enjoyable, or might give them greater freedom.

Kawamukai — And Kojin, what have you been working on?

Kojin — Turning back to collaborations, when there are clear goals and everyone shares the same objectives, they can go really smoothly. Since 2012 I've been working as part of a three-person collective called Mé. One person is the director and handles concept development and strategic planning. Another oversees production and is skilled at boosting motivation on the ground—really rather like a Buddhist priest. And I'm in charge of starting points. I worked by myself for about five years after university but formed Mé after the director convinced me it would be a way for each of us to focus our energies on different roles.

Sejima — I really liked the project you did as part of Mé at Shodoshima, *Maze Town—Phantasmagoric Alleys* (2013).

Kojin — That project involved remodeling a former tobacco shop. Entering through the shop, you passed through a series of winding hallways. Peering into a wardrobe revealed a factory-like space taken from an entirely different context. You could pass through the wardrobe, which led abruptly to a Japanese-style tatami mat room that looked as if it had been in use up until just moments before. In the end, you exited to the outside though the refrigerator in the kitchen.

Sejima — Did you connect it to the neighboring house?

Kojin — This was an area packed with pairs of houses built so close together they were practically stuck together. Apparently this was a means of blocking the wind, but the result was private spaces that were very close to each other. *Maze Town—Phantasmagoric Alleys* is a ten-year plan and I hope to connect even more buildings together eventually.

For the Utsunomiya Museum of Art's outreach program, *The Day an*

鼎談後に行われた「おじさんの顔が空に浮かぶ日」（目【め】、2014）
©目【め】2014 宇都宮美術館／宇都宮市上空

The Day an Ojisan's Face Floated in the Sky (Mé, 2014), conducted after the roundtable.
©Mé, 2014, Utsunomiya Museum of Art / The sky above Utsunomiya City

いて、出てみると急に和室があって、先ほどまでまるでここに人がいたのではないかというような部屋があったりする。最後は、キッチンの冷蔵庫から外に出ていけるようになっています。

妹島 ― それは隣の家とつないだの？

荒神 ― もともと 2 軒つながっているような家が密集したところで、風を遮るためにそういうつくりになったそうですが、プライベートの空間同士が近くにあります。「迷路のまち～変幻自在の路地空間～」は 10 年計画で、どんどんつないでいきたいと思っています。

宇都宮美術館の館外プロジェクト「おじさんの顔が空に浮かぶ日」（2014）は、この町に住んでいるおじさんの「顔」を、実際に、空に浮かべます。

川向 ― おふたりが、かなり長い時間をかけて、建築・アートの力で、個々の建築を超えた集落・町を捉え直し、それを徐々に変えていこうとしているところが、共通していて面白いですね。常識の束縛から自由になった目で見れば、疲弊して打ち捨てられた地方の町や村にも、再生に向けての素材が、いっぱい転がっている。それをうまく活用すれば、われわれは、過去・現在よりもはるかに生きやすく楽しい未来を開拓できる。おふたりと話をしていると、そんな感じがしてきます。今日は、どうもありがとうございました。

Ojisan's Face Floated in the Sky (2104), we actually sent up a giant balloon in the shape of the face of a man who lives in the town.

Kawamukai — It's interesting that you've both spent such a long time applying the power of art and architecture to go beyond individual structures and reexamine townscapes and neighborhoods, gradually working to transform them. When seen with free eyes unconstrained by "common sense," even the sort of provincial towns and villages that have grown impoverished and been all but discarded offer a wealth of material for possible revitalization. Hearing what you've both had to say makes me feel that by making good use of these materials we can surely forge a future that's more pleasant and livable than either the past or the present. Thank you very much for your time today.

CHAPTER —— 3

Party Party

ARCHITECTS
Kazuhiro Kojima + Kazuko Akamatsu
建築家
小嶋一浩 + 赤松佳珠子

FOOD ARTIST
Ayako Suwa
フードアーティスト
諏訪綾子

88　第 3 章　PARTY PARTY

CHAPTER-3　Party Party　89

90　第3章　PARTY PARTY

CHAPTER-3　Party Party　91

毎日建築をつくっている私たちですが、〈建築は「もの」ではなく「出来事」である〉と考えています。今回、2週間の展覧会の中で私たちは、「出来事」そのものを設計したい、と考えました。

記憶に残るフードで「コンセプトを胃まで届ける」諏訪綾子さんとコラボレーションすることで、食べたり飲んだり話したりという様々なアクティビティや人の気配を、光の流れとともに空間化・記憶化しようと試みました。

OFFパーティでの主役は「グラス」と光です。空間に浮かぶ112個のワイングラスのうち46個は光のアクションを引き起こすトリガーとなっています。それらは合計29種類の光の動きのパターンを生み出します。グラスの光によるざわめきを引き起こすのは、この舞台の登場人物としてのあなたです。テーブルの天板に落とされたプロジェクターによる光は人の動きと一体となって、新たな「流れ」と感じさせます。

一方、諏訪さんのフードパフォーマンスが行われるONパーティでは「大勢の人たち」とフードという新たなレイヤが舞台に加わります。

（展示コンセプト文より）

We are involved in making buildings every day, but think of them not as "things" but as "happenings." For this two-week exhibition, we decided that we wanted to create a real happening. By collaborating with Ayako Suwa, who presents memorable foods that deliver the concept right to your stomach, we tried to create in space and in memory, together with the flow of light, various activities such as eating, drinking, and conversing as well as intimations of people's presence. The star of the party during "off" times is the glasses and the lights. Forty-six of the 112 wine glasses floating in the space trigger lights that generate 29 different patterns of movement. As a character on this stage, you yourself trigger the shimmering and glittering through your interactions with the wine glasses. The light projected onto the tabletops from above unites with human movement to create the sense of a new flow. During the "on" times when Suwa performs, meanwhile, new layers of crowds and foods are added to the stage.

(Exhibition concept, July 2010)

オンとオフ、
出来事とその余韻を〈あじわう〉

小嶋一浩 + 赤松佳珠子
諏訪綾子
川向正人

建築家
小嶋一浩

1958 年 大阪府生まれ。東京大学大学院博士
課程在籍中にシーラカンスを共同設立。2005
年 CAt ／シーラカンスアンドアソシエイツ トウ
キョウに改組。現在、横浜国立大 Y-GSA 教授
（2011 年 -）。主な作品に、宇土市立宇土小学校
（2011）ほか

ARCHITECT
Kazuhiro Kojima

Born in Osaka in 1958, Kojima co-founded
Coelacanth while in the doctoral program at
the University of Tokyo. The company was
reorganized as Coelacanth and Associates Tokyo
(CAt) in 2005. Kojima has been a professor at
the Yokohama Graduate School of Architecture
(Y-GSA) since 2011. Major works include Uto
Elementary School (2011).

建築家
赤松佳珠子

1968 年 東京都生まれ。日本女子大学家政学
部住居学科卒業後、シーラカンスに加わる。
2002 年よりパートナー。2005 年 CAt ／シーラ
カンスアンドアソシエイツ トウキョウに改組。
現在、法政大学准教授（2013 年 -）

ARCHITECT
Kazuko Akamatsu

Born in Tokyo in 1968, Akamatsu joined
Coelacanth after graduating from the Department
of Housing and Architecture in the Faculty of
Home Economics at Japan Women's University.
She became partner in 2002, and the company
was reorganised as Coelacanth and Associates
Tokyo (CAt) in 2005. Akamatsu has been an
associate professor at Hosei University since 2013.

Savoring the On and the Off,
the Happening and its Reverberations

KAZUHIRO KOJIMA + KAZUKO AKAMATSU
AYAKO SUWA
MASATO KAWAMUKAI

フードアーティスト
諏訪綾子

1976年 石川県生まれ。2006年よりfood creation
の活動を開始。国内外で「ゲリラレストラン」
を開催し、人間の本能的な欲望、好奇心、進
化をテーマにした食の表現を行う。美食ではな
く、栄養源でもエネルギー源でもない新たな
食の価値を提案している

FOOD ARTIST
Ayako Suwa

Born in Ishikawa prefecture in 1976, Suwa
launched her food creation activities in 2006.
Hosting "Guerrilla Restaurants" in Japan and
overseas, she pursues expression with food
on the theme of people's instinctive desires,
curiosity, and evolution. She proposes a new
value in food other than the epicurean or as a
source of nutrition and energy.

川向 ── 私が ODS-R 第 8 回の企画建築家を依頼したとき、どのようなことをお考えになりましたか。

パーティという〈出来事〉

小嶋 ── 面白いことができるといいなと、まず、思いました。一般的に建築家の展覧会は自分がやっているプロジェクトのプレゼンテーションです。ところがこの展覧会はそれとは違って、この場所で新しいものをつくり出していくという。それは楽しそうだけれども、最初は、どちらを向いて走り出したらいいのか見当がつきませんでした。

赤松 ── とにかくテーマは何でもいい、コラボレーターと一緒になってつくってくださいということで、まず、何をすればいいのかと面食らいました。ワクワクして始まりましたが、どちらに向いてワクワクすればいいが見えなかった。

川向 ── コラボレーションという言葉は、この企画が始まった 2003 年にはまだ珍しい言葉でした。建築家にご自身の展覧会をお願いすると、事務所の内部でほとんどが準備されます。できれば、結果よりも、コンセプト・メイキングからのプロセスを拝見したい。しかも、この場所、この企画でしかできない、何か創造的なことをやろうと最初に企画実行委員会で決め、「建築家と建築以外の表現者とのコラボレーション」という、あまり例のないフレームワークを考えました。〈コラボレーション〉に関しては、最初に何をお考えになりましたか。

小嶋 ── そもそも、われわれはパートナーシップで仕事をしていますから、自分ひとりの頭の中で何かを組み立てて、いきなりポンと出すのではなく、まず十分に議論します。そういうコラボレーションは日常的に行っているし、ほかのプロフェッショナルな人たちとも一緒にやらないと複雑なプロジェクトには対応できません。

私たちの設計対象は学校が多くて、最後は特に教育委員会の人たちに「な

「宇土市立宇土小学校」（小嶋一浩＋赤松佳珠子／CAt、2011）

Uto Elementary School (Kazuhiro Kojima and Kazuko Akamatsu / CAt, 2011).

Kawamukai — What did you think when I asked you to be the architects for the eighth ODS-R exhibition?

The Party as "Happening"

Kojima — My first thought was that I hoped we could pull off something interesting. Architects' exhibitions often present whatever projects they're currently working on. This exhibition was different, though, in that we were asked to create something new to fit the space. That sounded like fun, but it was difficult at first to know in which direction we should start running.

Akamatsu — There was no set theme other than to collaborate with someone else, so the first thing we wrestled with was what to do. We began to get really excited, but weren't quite sure where to direct our excitement.

Kawamukai — Back when we started this exhibition series in 2003, the word "collaboration" was still relatively uncommon in Japanese. When architects are asked to do exhibitions of their own work, they generally prepare nearly everything in their own offices. Our planning and executive committee decided at the outset, though, that what we really wanted to see—even more than the results—was the process starting right from concept development, and the creation of something unique to our space and our exhibition. That's why we came up with the all but unprecedented idea of having architects collaborate with creators from outside the field of architecture. What were your first thoughts on this idea of collaboration?

Kojima — Well, we already work as a partnership so it isn't as if either of us puts things together all alone in our head and produces it fully formed; there's always a tremendous amount of discussion between us. We engage in such collaboration every day and it would be impossible, of course, to handle any complex project without working with other professionals.

A lot of our design work is with schools, and we have to make particularly sure that the folks from the Board of Education are satisfied when we're done. That doesn't leave much room for radical conceptual leaps. This exhibition, though, seemed to invite us to take a huge jump by engaging in collaboration, so that was really different. When giving speeches we often say, "Architecture is not just a thing, but a happening," and the exhibition seemed to offer an opportunity to create the happening without building the thing, a great chance

るほど」と納得してもらわないといけないので、発想の急激なジャンプは許されません。ところが、この展覧会は、むしろ「協働することによってジャンプしろ」と言われているようなイベントですから、そこが違います。

われわれは講演会でよく「建築はモノではなく出来事である」と言っていますが、今回の展覧会で「〈出来事〉だけつくり、建築というモノをつくらない」というのは、やりたいことをやるいいチャンスだと思いました。そこで、何かオブジェをつくるアーティストではないコラボレーターを探しました。

赤松 ── われわれとしては、ものをつくって見せることよりも、出来事そのもの、人が来て初めて始まり、人が介在することで変わっていく場をつくってみたいと考えました。〈PARTY〉のようなものです。人が集まり、みんなでワイワイやって、そこで起こること自体をデザインしようと。

ほぼ同時に、諏訪さんのお名前が出てきました。諏訪さんは、いわゆるケータリングのパーティとはまったく違う新しいことにチャレンジしておられましたので、進むべき方向がおぼろげながら見えてきました。

川向 ── 最初に、4,000㎡あるオカムラのショールーム全体を見ていただいて、どこを使ってもいいという話をしましたよね。〈PARTY〉の場所として、打合せスペース以外のところはお考えになりませんでしたか。

赤松 ── ショールームらしい場所に〈PARTY〉が入り込むのも面白いかもしれないと話をしていましたが、さすがにそこまでやると収拾がつかなくなるので、会場には打合せスペースを選びました。

川向 ── シーラカンスは、ずっと、人間のアクティビティに焦点を合わせた空間づくりをしてきましたが、今回も、その基本姿勢は変わっていませんね。

小嶋 ── 設計をする上でも「家具の次元で、こういうことが起きたら」と普段から考えていますので、いわゆる家具のショールームで同じ発想にとどまれば、僕たちにとっての日常と変わらないことになります。僕らの仕事は、昼間は日の当たる明るい、子ども目線での小学校の設計が多いですから、今回は基本姿勢は同じでも、普段やっていない〈夜〉の艶っぽいセクシーな空間をつくるチャンスだと思いました。このジャンプのために、いつもとちょっと違うスイッチを入れました。

〈気配〉と〈状況〉

川向 ── さて諏訪さんは、今回のコラボレーションのオファーを、どう受け止めたのでしょう。

諏訪 ── ずいぶん回を重ねた展覧会ですので、お声がけいただいて光栄に

to do whatever we wanted. So we set out looking for a collaborator who wasn't an artist who made objects.

Akamatsu — For our part, rather than making something to be seen, we wanted to try to create a happening, a forum that begins when people arrive and changes through their intervention—something like a party. We thought we could design what happens when people get together and make a little noise.

Right around that time we also learned about Suwa. She was trying to tackle something new—something completely different from the typical catered party—so even though things were still pretty vague, we began to get a feel for what direction we might pursue.

Kawamukai — Initially, we showed you the entire 4,000m^2 Okamura showroom and said you could use as much as you wanted. Did you consider using anything other than the meeting space as the venue for your party?

Akamatsu — We did talk about how it might be interesting to take the party out into the showroom space, but we thought things could get out of hand and decided to use the meeting space.

Kawamukai — Coelacanth has always created spaces that focus on human activities, and that basic stance remained unchanged for this exhibition, didn't it?

Kojima — When we design buildings, we're always thinking about what might happen at the level of furniture, so if we didn't go beyond that when working with a furniture showroom it really wouldn't be much different than what we do every day. In our work, we're often designing elementary schools, taking the perspective of the children who'll use them under bright, sunlit, daytime conditions. This time, even though we maintained the same basic stance, we decided it was a good chance to create the kind of sleek, sexy, nighttime space we don't normally get to work on. To make that leap, we flipped some switches that we normally wouldn't.

Intimations and Situations

Kawamukai — Suwa, what did you think when you got the offer to collaborate?

Suwa — The exhibition series already had a long history then so I felt very honored to be invited to take part, but I also had no idea what I might be able to do when working with architects. The theme was still undecided and I couldn't see what would come next—although

思いましたが、建築家の方たちと一体何ができるかが全然わかりませんでした。テーマがまだ定まっていない状態でしたから、これから何が起きるのか見えない状態で、逆に、それがすごく面白いと思いました。普段は、ある程度テーマが決まったところからスタートすることが多いので、これからテーマが決められるということにもワクワクしました。

川向 ── 毎回、私は「今、一番関心のあることを試みてください」とお願いします。これが、最大のヒントでもあります。その実現に向かって、時には共感し合い、時には衝突しながらも、何度もジャンプしつつ協働作業が進むことを期待しているわけですが、実際、どう進んでいったのでしょうか。

赤松 ── そこに人がやってくることで、いろいろな関係が生まれます。まず、そのときの〈気配〉について話し合いました。それから、どうアプローチして、どういうルートで動いてもらうか。家具を配置することで、どう人が動き、〈出来事〉が発生するか。これを延々と試しましたね。会場平面にどこかの都市の地図を落とし込んで輪郭をとってみるとか、会場周辺の地図を切り出して使うとか、何度も試行錯誤を繰り返しました。

川向 ── 確かに、最終的な平面と空間の構成がアドルフ・ロースの「アメリカン・バー」に似た高密の都市空間のようでした。

小嶋 ── それは、うれしいご指摘です。

赤松 ── 何によってルールを決めていくのかに悩んだのです。建築設計の場合、敷地や方位があり、こちらから風が吹くとか、いろいろな前提条件があります。あの会場には、前提条件となる外的な要因がありませんでしたから。

小嶋 ── ひとつ大切なのは、諏訪さんひとりで〈出来事〉をつくるとい

金沢 21 世紀美術館で行われた「ゲリラレストラン」(food creation、2008)

Guerrilla Restaurant at the 21st Century Museum of Contemporary Art in Kanazawa (Food Creation, 2008)

that very uncertainty was really interesting. Usually, by the time I get involved the theme has already been pretty much set so I was excited to be in on things from the very beginning.

Kawamukai — For each edition of the exhibition, I ask that people attempt whatever they're most interested in at the time. This is as much of a hint as they get. We always look forward to seeing how the collaborative effort to make that happen progresses, leaping ahead sometimes in harmony and sometimes in conflict. How did things move forward for you?

Akamatsu — People were going to come to the venue, so that would create all sorts of relationships. We first talked a lot about what kind of intimations we wanted to establish, how people would approach the space, and what routes they would take. How would positioning the furniture influence people's movements and generate "happenings"? We tried all sorts of things, lots of trial and error, doing things like incorporating the outlines of city maps into the floor plan or using parts of the map of the actual area around the venue.

Kawamukai — Indeed, the end result—both the floor plan and the spatial composition—became a kind of high-density urban space reminiscent of Adolf Loos's American Bar in Vienna.

Kojima — What a wonderful thing to say.

Akamatsu — We really struggled with how to define the rules. When designing a work of architecture, there are all sorts of preconditions like the dimensions of the site, its orientation, and the prevailing winds. But at our exhibition venue there really weren't any external factors to serve as preconditions in this way.

Kojima — The one important thing was that Suwa be able to create the happening alone, so that as soon as she appeared we'd be relieved of duty. (*Laughs*)

Akamatsu — That's right. We wanted to just fade into the background. (*Laughs*)

Kojima — But that wouldn't be collaboration. The boomerang came right back to us and we had to think about what architects could do when collaborating with an event professional like Suwa. By that point, though, we had a pretty good understanding of what Suwa's "food creation" actually meant, and that gave us some hints for how to move forward.

I like to create moments when little arrows seem to pop up all at once, and I think a lot about how to trigger little happenings within the gentle, everyday flow of time. We had to create a place that would be

うことでした。だから、諏訪さんにご登場いただいた途端に、僕らはお役御免になってしまう（笑）。

赤松 ── そう、われわれが背景になってしまう（笑）。

小嶋 ── それではコラボレーションではない。イベントのプロフェッショナルの諏訪さんとのコラボレーションで、建築家は何をやるのかと、自分たちにブーメランが返ってきた。ただ、この段階になると、諏訪さんの〈food creation〉が何をなさるものかという具体的イメージが共有できていて、次に進む手がかりがあった。

〈小さな矢印〉みたいなものがパッと沸き立つ瞬間をやりたくて、日常の穏やかに流れている時間に小さな事件をどう起こすのかと考えるのですが、2週間弱の期間、幻のような〈出来事〉の場所を生成しなければならない。

川向 ── 21世紀になって、「空間を生き生きさせたい」という声をよく耳にするようになりました。生命体とか有機体のイメージが、建築だけでなく都市あるいは集落にも求められるようになっています。20世紀末からその声が強まり、本当に形になってきたのは、21世紀に入ってからだと思うのですが、企画実行委員会の中で〈コラボレーション〉について議論していたときに、命を宿すとか火をともすといったことが何か魂のふれ合いのようなものから生じるのではないかと考えたことを、ふっと思い出しました。建築と非建築、建築家と建築以外の表現者との〈コラボレーション〉が、生命を、命の炎を、この場所で生み出すかもしれないという期待です。今の小嶋さんのご発言を聞いて、そんなことを思い出しました。

さて、それでは、諏訪さんの〈コラボレーション〉に対する期待をお話しいただけますか。

諏訪 ── 私は普段から〈状況をつくる〉ことを心がけています。そこに食べ物、飲み物が入ってきて、それをあじわうことで、何かを感じ取ってもらいます。その〈シチュエーション〉には、まずどういう空間なのか、例えば、光がどうあって、風がどう吹いているのかといった空間的な〈シチュエーション〉と、身を置く人がどんな時間帯に、どれぐらいの長さ、どのような経緯で滞在し、そこで何を体験するかという時間的な〈シチュエーション〉があります。

今回、コラボレーションするにあたって、建築家の仕事には空間が絶対的だと考え、時間の部分に私がどうコミットできるかを考えました。

〈ON と OFF〉

川向 ── 今のお話は、小嶋さんと赤松さんの建築思考の本質を捉え、かつ、

home to vision-like happenings for a period of just under two weeks.

Kawamukai — We hear a lot of talk these days about wanting to make spaces "come alive." People now seek a sense of the organic, of the living, both in their architecture and in their cities or neighborhoods. Such voices gained strength toward the end of the twentieth century but only really took shape, I think, after the start of the twenty-first. I can remember back when we were discussing collaboration within the planning and executive committee and talking about how, when something comes alive or a fire is lit, it always seems to be the result of some kind of interaction among spirits. In this same way, we hoped that collaboration between architecture and non-architecture, between architects and creators from other fields, would breathe life—the fire of life—into this space. What Kojima said just now brought that whole conversation back to me.

Suwa, could you talk a little bit about what you expected from the collaboration?

Suwa — I make it a practice to create "situations" in my work. The food and drink are brought in, people consume them, and they feel something. The situations define the type of space; for example, there are spatial situations, like the quality of the light or the direction of the wind, and temporal situations, like when people arrive, how long they stay, what course they follow, and what they experience.

For this collaboration, I decided to leave the spatial aspects to the architects so it was then a matter of how much I would be able to commit to the temporal parts.

On and Off

Kawamukai — That seems to capture the essence of Kojima and Akamatsu's architectural thinking, while also touching upon the key issue of how to collaborate.

Kojima — Indeed. You can see not only how well she understood our architecture but also how she arrived on the scene as an event specialist. In fact, when we started discussing things with her it was if a ray of light had appeared to show us a path out of the wilderness. We don't use the term "situation," but our aim is the same. In architecture, though, what we're careful about in our everyday work is that the way spaces work on people has to be really subtle or it quickly becomes too much. Suwa imagines a given start time and end time and then makes things happen at a given cross-section of

どう協働すべきかという核心に触れるものでしたね。

小嶋 ── そうですね。われわれの建築をよく理解し、その上で、イベントのスペシャリストとして登場してくださったことが、あらためてわかります。実際、打合せを始めたときも、迷走していたところに、進むべき方向から光が差してきた感じでした。

僕らは「状況」という言葉は使いませんが、目指しているところは同じです。ただし、僕らが日常の仕事で注意深く行うのは、建築の場合、空間の人に対する働きかけは、本当にささやかでないとうっとうしくなるからです。諏訪さんの場合は、開始時間と終了時間を想定して、ある時間の切断面の中で事を起こしていますね。建築はエンドレスなので強度を上げると嫌な感じになりますが、諏訪さんは、いい意味で強度をパッと上げています。とはいえ、今回は2時間ではなく2週間ほどのイベントですから、諏訪さんにその会場にずっといていただくわけにもいきませんでした。

赤松 ── 展覧会の期間中、ずっとパーティというわけにはいかないですから、〈ON と OFF〉を考えました。〈ON〉は、諏訪さんに登場していただく、すごく記憶に残る〈出来事〉が起こるパーティです。〈OFF〉は、〈ON〉の〈気配〉、美しいパーティのざわめいている雰囲気がかすかに感じられる、余韻のひとときです。ずっと華やかな〈ON〉の状態が続くより、〈ONと OFF〉の両方の波があるからこそ、〈OFF〉の状態で静かに佇む居心地のよさも感じられ、真の意味で体験が豊かになるのかなと。パーティの始まる前なのか、終わった後なのかとフッと考えるような〈シチュエーション〉がつくれれば、われわれの目指すものが、ひとまず達成されるかなと話していました。

川向 ── 〈ON と OFF〉は、すごく重要な考え方ですね。〈ON〉のワーッ

「PARTY PARTY」展の会期中のモードを示すダイアグラム（CAt）

Timeline indicating modes during the period of the *Party Party* exhibition (CAt).

A mode : パーティタイム

会期中 3 回、パーティを開催します。Food creation をとおして、空間と料理の融合を表現します。それは、一瞬のデキゴトであるけれど、永遠に記憶に残り続ける。テンポラリーであることを最大限に活かした、ここでしかできない体験をつくりだします。

B mode : 呼吸

3 週間の会期中、パーティがない時も、会場は呼吸し続けます。そして、次におこるデキゴトを待ちうけます。その流れはテーブルに映像や状態としてうかび上がります。

time. Architecture is forever, so raising the intensity too much can be unpleasant, but Suwa can quickly turn up the intensity in a good way. Still, this wasn't a two-hour event but one that would last around two weeks, so we couldn't tie her to the venue for the duration.

Akamatsu — Since we couldn't have a party that ran for the entire period of the exhibition, we had to think about switching between "on" and "off." During "on" times, Suwa would appear and a really memorable party would happen. The "off" times, though, would present intimations of the "on" times, as a kind of lingering sensation conveying the faint hum of a beautiful party. Rather than trying to maintain a showy "on" time all the time, creating waves between "on" and "off" seemed like it would be a richer, truer experience that incorporated the pleasant silence of the "off" times. We talked about how we would pretty much have achieved what we set out to do if we managed to create situations that caused people to wonder whether the party had just ended or was about to begin.

Kawamukai — This notion of "on" and "off" is really important, isn't it? It's no easy task to create the kind of roiling excitement of "on" times, but when you think about public facilities, what really needs to be addressed is the "off" times when the spaces become like dreary, empty warehouses. It would be really wonderful if we could enjoy the "off" times on their own terms by creating situations for savoring pleasant silences.

Kojima — The party venue was swarming with what I might call ghosts. We wanted people who went there during the "off" times, even if they were the only ones there, to feel as if some other presence filled the place, too. By going during the "off" times, you

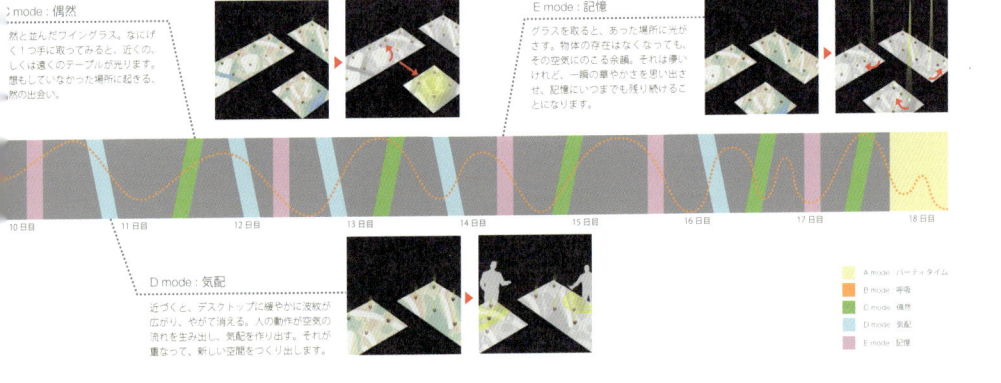

と盛り上がる状態を生み出すことも決してやさしいことではありませんが、公共施設などを考えても、〈OFF〉の状態の寒々しい空き倉庫のような空間こそ、何とかすべきです。〈OFF〉の場合も、むしろ静けさをあじわえる居心地のよい状態が生み出され、〈OFF〉としての使い方ができるとすれば、それは、素晴らしいことです。

小嶋 ── このパーティ会場では、〈ゴースト〉みたいなものがうごめいているのです。〈OFF〉に来たら、自分ひとりしかいないのだけれども、何かがいっぱいいるような感じを狙いました。〈OFF〉の場合にも、もう１つのパーティ体験ができるのです。

川向 ── そうでした。〈ON〉でも〈OFF〉でも、互いに異なるパーティが体験できる。だから、タイトルが「PARTY　PARTY」となったのでした。

赤松 ── 〈OFF〉の空間でも、〈ON〉の人がいる雰囲気を生み出せないかと考えたのです。光がフワフワと動いたり、会場のグラスを取ることが引き金になって光がパパパパッと瞬き「あれ？ 人がいるのかな？」と思ってもらえるように設計しています。この照明については、照明デザイナーの岡安泉さんにご協力いただきました。

すごく華やかなパーティの場に紛れ込んで、異次元の中に浮かんでいるような、不思議な空間体験を考えました。

食べないで〈あじわう〉

川向 ── あらためて伺いますが、諏訪さんの〈food creation〉は何を目指して、どんな活動をなさっているのですか。

諏訪 ── 表現としての食を追求し直し、普段の３食の習慣、栄養源やエネルギー源、あるいは美食やグルメなどとは異なる食の価値を確立したいと、活動を始めたものです。食べ物そのものや、食べるとかあじわうといった行為を通していろいろな表現を試みているのですが、それによって、体験した人たちの〈記憶〉、〈感覚〉、〈感情〉などの内面に働きかけることができれば、と願っています。

川向 ── より人間的な、記憶、精神、文化などにかかわる行為としての〈食〉ですね。こうした内面的なものに、どう具体的に働きかけていくのかを説明していただけますか。

諏訪 ── まずコンセプトとかテーマを最初に設けます。そして、自分自身を表現することに意識をフォーカスしていきます。重要なのは、コンセプトやテーマを単に言葉で伝えるのではなくて、〈あじわう〉もしくは〈食べる〉ことを通じて感覚的に理解してもらうことです。

川向 ── タイトルに「怒りのテイスト」や「喜びのテイスト」などもあると聞きましたが、一体どんな食べ物かと想像が膨らみます。

could experience an entirely different kind of party.

Kawamukai — And so it was. You could experience different parties during the "on" and "off" times. And that's why you titled the exhibition *Party Party*.

Akamatsu — We wondered if we could create a people-filled, "on" atmosphere even in an "off" space. We designed things with softly moving lights and made it so picking up a glass in the venue would trigger flashing lights that might make people wonder if someone was there. We had lighting designer Izumi Okayasu help us with the lighting.

We tried to create a marvelous spatial experience that was like floating in another dimension, and then slipped that into a really flashy party venue.

To Taste Without Eating

Kawamukai — Suwa, tell me again about your "food creation" activities and what you're aiming for.

Suwa — I reexamined food as an expressive medium and began my activities in the hope of establishing a kind of value in food unlike the habitual consumption of three meals a day, or nutrition and energy, or the epicurean and gourmet. I try all manner of expression through either food itself or through the act of eating and tasting, and hope that what I do has some effect on the inner memories, sensations, and emotions of those who experience it.

左:「驚きの効いた楽しさと隠しきれない嬉しさのテイスト」（food creation、2008）右:「後をひく悔しさとさらに怒りさえもこみ上げるテイスト」（food creation、2008）
© Numéro TOKYO 2008 年 8 月号（扶桑社）

Left: *The Taste of Surprising Happiness and Uncontainable Joy* (Food Creation, 2008)
Right: *The Taste of Lingering Frustration and the Anger that Wells Up Within* (Food Creation, 2008)
© *Numéro Tokyo,* August, 2008 issue (Fusosha Publishing)

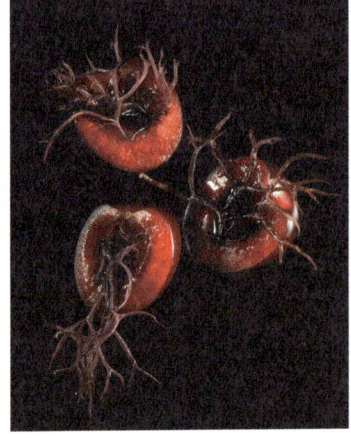

〈食べなくてもあじわえる〉プロジェクトのひとつ、「味身」(宮原夢画×諏訪綾子、2008)。身体をあじわうというコンセプト

Mimi (Muga Miyahara and Ayako Suwa, 2008), one of the *Savor Without Eating* projects. The concept was "tasting the body."

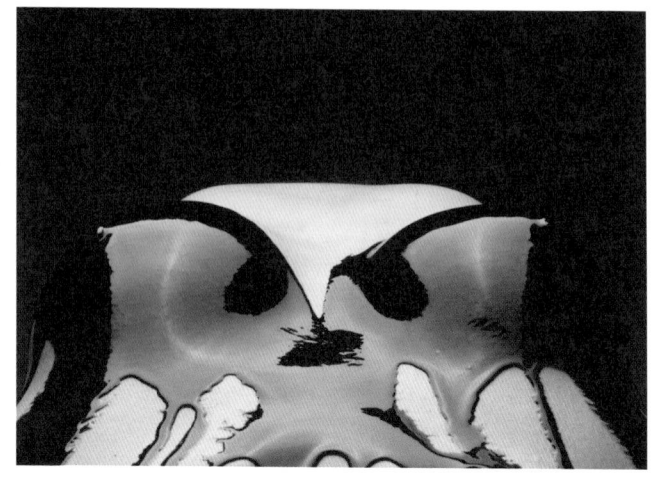

諏訪——タイトルはとても大事です。体験される方にタイトルを伝えない場合もありますし、言葉以外で伝えることもあります。タイトルはコンセプトでもあるので、すごく重要ですね。レシピを考えるときも、タイトルありきで考えますし、光の当たり方や置く場所、見る角度や見せ方も、同じ食べ物でも、コンセプトによって変わります。

川向——食として、ここだけは注意したいという点はありますか。例えば、現地にある食材を使うとか、少なくとも味がいいものをつくるとか、のどごしがいいとか、必ず守る条件はあるのでしょうか。

諏訪——究極的には、〈食べなくてもあじわえる〉と考えています。例えば、食べられないものを見て、食べたらどうだろうと想像するだけで〈あじわえる〉と思うのですね。

川向——食べられないものを前にして「これをあじわってみてください」と言うこともあるのですか。

諏訪——あります。物理的には食べていない人も、誰かが食べたり飲んだりしているのを見ることで、想像上でもあじわえますね。人間は、視覚と情報であじわう部分が多いので、50%くらいは想像上であじわえるのではないかと思っています。

パーティの〈気配・余韻・記憶〉

川向——さて、諏訪さんとのコラボレーションで、どういう場所、空間をつくったのか、もう少し、先に進んだ話をしていただけますでしょうか。

小嶋——僕らも最初は〈food creation〉が何なのかよくわかっていなかったけれど、フードを視覚や想像力で表現したり、期待と口にしたときの

Kawamukai — So you're dealing with food as behavior related to human memory, spirit, and culture, then? Could you explain in concrete terms how you address such internal aspects?

Suwa — I start by determining a concept and a theme. Then I focus my consciousness on expressing myself. The important thing is not to simply convey the concept and theme verbally but to get people to understand these things intuitively through tasting or eating.

Kawamukai — I've heard that your titles include "The Taste of Anger" and "The Taste of Joy," which certainly stir the imagination to think about what kinds of food might be involved.

Suwa — Titles are very important. There are times when I don't tell the people who are experiencing the event what the title is, and times when I tell them without using words. The title is also the concept, so it really is important. When I think about recipes, I do so with a title in mind, and even with the same food the lighting, placement, viewing angle, and presentation all change depending on the concept.

Kawamukai — Are there things you're especially careful about when it comes to food? For example, using local ingredients, or making things taste good, or go down easily? Are there conditions you always try to satisfy?

Suwa — Ultimately, I strive for food that can be tasted even without eating. For example, even when looking at something that you cannot eat, I think you can still taste it by imagining what it would be like to eat it.

Kawamukai — Do you ever present people with something they cannot eat and tell them to try tasting it?

Suwa — Sure. Even someone who is not actually eating the food can watch someone else eat and drink and taste it in his imagination. People rely a lot on sight and information when they taste; I'll bet you can probably taste about 50% through the imagination.

A Party's Intimation, Reverberation, and Remembrance

Kawamukai — Could you talk in a little more detail about the kind of place—the kind of space—that you built in collaboration with Suwa?

Kojima — We didn't know what "food creation" entailed at first, but Suwa described how it was a matter of expressing food visually and imaginatively, and addressing the gap between expectation and reality when consumed. We also experienced what she does

ズレに着目したりする話を聞き、体験もしました。諏訪さんの活動の場合、五感の中でも僕ら建築家が使っていない感覚が相当に重要だと思います。もちろん建築家も五感で空間を体験しているのですが、味覚とか嗅覚は建築の表現としては封印していますよね。建築を「なめてみなさい」とは言わないし、嗅覚も積極的に使うのは木のいい香りを楽しむくらいでしょう。

諏訪さんがいない〈OFF〉の7日間のために僕らが何を用意し、〈ON〉の日のために何を設計したか。どちらの場合にもパーティが楽しめることは、すでにご説明しましたが、このあたりまでくると、日常の建築設計の検討と同じように、この場合はこうだからと明確に説明できる状態になっています。

赤松——ただテーブルが並ぶだけで一望のもとに全体が見えてしまうのでは、〈気配〉というのと違う。そこで、少しずつ隠しながら、パーティションを立てたり、穴をあけたり、ミラーを貼ったりして、向こうに見えるものが本当にあるのか、こちらが映っているだけなのか。また光がパーッと動いたりチラチラしたりするときも、ただ鏡に映り込んでいるのか、それとも実在するのかがわかりにくいのですが、虚実の重なるところでは視覚的に距離感がなくなるようにしました。人の〈気配〉につなげるために、L字形の壁を2枚立てて向こうとこちらを重ね、暗いほうに黒を重ねてわからないようにするなど、ものをつくりながら、ものを消していく設計を進めました。

「PARTY PARTY」展の平面図

Party Party exhibition plan drawing.

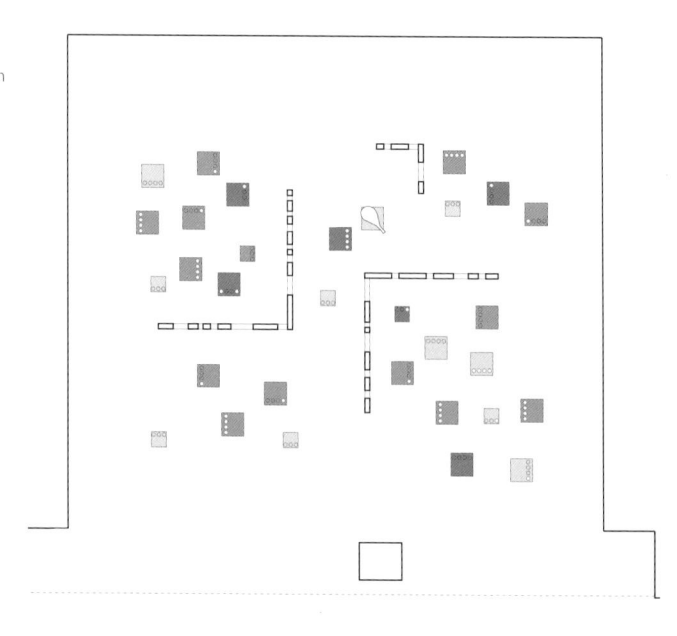

for ourselves. I think Suwa's work prioritizes senses that we don't use much as architects. Architects obviously use the five senses to experience our spaces, but we don't often describe our work in terms of taste or smell. We don't talk about "lickable" buildings, and the only smell we probably want to incorporate is the pleasant fragrance of wood.

Well, then, what to prepare for the seven "off" days when Suwa wasn't there, and what to plan for the "on" days? I already talked about how it was important to enjoy a party in either case, but once we finally had a clear understanding of the questions we needed to resolve, we were able to move forward and make decisions based on the effect that various approaches would have—just as we would when discussing our everyday architectural work.

Akamatsu — Just lining up tables in a way that the whole thing was visible at a glance wouldn't create much by way of intimation. So we set up partitions that would conceal things a little bit at a time, opening apertures in them and applying mirrors to create uncertainty about, say, whether what one saw over there was real or just a reflection of what was over here. With the lighting, too, when lights moved or flickered it could be difficult to tell whether they were real or just reflected in mirrors, but we tried to eliminate any sense of visual distance at the points where truth and fiction overlapped. In order to create intimations of the presence of people, we did things like putting up two L-shaped walls to create overlapping heres and theres, or layering blacks in the dark areas to make things less apparent, and in this way went about designing things in a way that both built and concealed.

Lighting was important here, so we worked with Okayasu to create a purposeful environment. I think our use of glass to catch the LED light in the shadows succeeded in creating just the sense of grown-up seductiveness that we were aiming for.

Kawamukai — Suwa, how did you go about overlaying your own food space in what the architects had created?

Suwa — I developed The Taste of Intimation, The Taste of Reverberation, and The Taste of Remembrance. Intimations and reverberations are invisible, intuitive things that occur, respectively, before and after something happens, while remembrances are things that remain in memory throughout the whole.

For The Taste of Intimation I created a red drink. During the "off" times, each guest was given a small bottle that they could pour into a glass

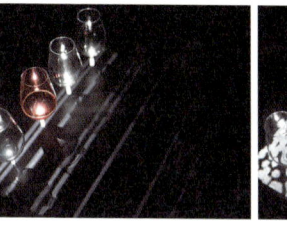

「PARTY PARTY」展より。会場のライティングの移り変わり

Party Party exhibition, showing lighting transitions in the venue.

ここでも光が重要でしたので、岡安さんに協力してもらって、意図した環境をつくり出しました。翳でLEDの光が当たるグラスが、〈大人の空間〉や〈艶〉を狙い通りに生み出していたと思います。

川向 — 諏訪さんは、建築家がそのようにつくった空間に、どう、ご自分の食の空間を重ねていったのですか。

諏訪 — 〈気配のテイスト〉、〈余韻のテイスト〉、〈記憶のテイスト〉をつくりました。〈気配〉は出来事が起こる前の、〈余韻〉はその後の目に見えない感覚的なもの、そして〈記憶〉は全体を通して記憶に残っていくものと考えました。

〈気配のテイスト〉として赤い飲み物をつくり、〈OFF〉のゲストに小さいボトルを1本お渡しして、会場にある好きなグラスに注いで飲んでいただきました。会場に飲みかけや飲み残しがあることで、〈気配〉が〈余韻〉になっていきます。〈余韻のテイスト〉としては、テーブルに大きな肉の塊を置きました。大きな塊も削られてだんだん小さくなり、その肉が〈記憶のテイスト〉になります。

全体的に赤いテイストにして、薄暗い空間の中でより〈記憶〉に残るようにしました。人間はどうしても肉とか血の色に本能的に突進していくので、人を惹きつける赤を多用しました。これらは〈ON〉の状態で出すのですが、その食べかけや食べ残しがテーブルの上に置かれることで〈余韻〉をつくり、また〈気配〉をつくります。そのほかの食べ物も〈ONとOFF〉の間に形状・状況がいろいろと変化して、〈気配〉、〈余韻〉、最終的な〈記憶〉に結びつく〈あじわい〉をつくり出しました。

〈ON〉は、会期中に3回ありました。基本的にはすべて同じでしたが、いらっしゃるゲストの顔ぶれが違うことで、おのずとパーティに違うテイストが出たように思います。

夜の〈雑木林的空間〉と浮かぶテーブル

川向 — 「PARTY PARTY」展の空間は、小嶋さんが書かれた『小さな矢印の群れ』（2013）に出てくる〈雑木林的空間〉だったのかなと思うのです。真っ平らで均質的な空間ではなく、見えたり隠れたり、何本かの〈木〉

of their choice in the venue and then consume. Having half-finished drinks around the venue transforms intimation into reverberation. For The Taste of Reverberation, I placed a large chuck of meat on a table. As it was carved away and grew smaller, the meat became The Taste of Remembrance.

I used a red tone overall that would stand out as more memorable in the dimly lit space. People cannot help but instinctively make a beeline for the colors of meat and blood, so I used a lot of that sort of color, which attracts people. I served these things during the "on" times, but the partially eaten bits left on the tables created reverberations, and then intimations. I also changed the shape and condition of other foods for the "on" and "off" times, conjuring a flavor that tied together intimation, reverberation, and ultimately remembrance.

There were three "on" times during the period of the exhibition. They were all generally the same, but the assembled guests were different each time so each party naturally seemed to take on a unique taste of its own.

Tables That Rise Like a "Thicket-like Space" at Night

Kawamukai — The space for the *Party Party* exhibition reminded me of the sort of "thicket-like space" that you talk about in your book *Chiisana yajirushi no mure* [A Swarm of Small Arrows] (2003)—not a flat, homogenous space but one filled with subtle changes that are

会場で提供された赤いフード
と赤いドリンク

The red food and red drink provided in the venue.

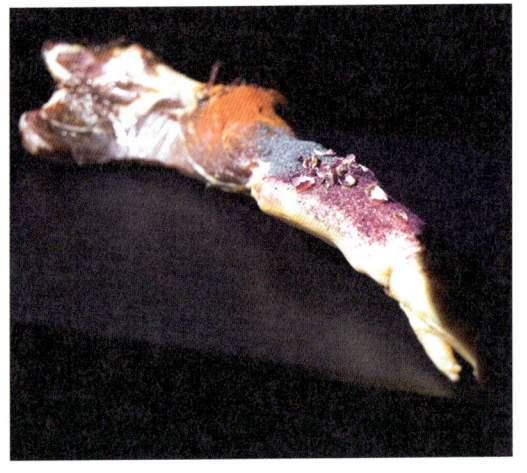

CHAPTER−3　Party Party　113

「宇土市立宇土小学校」の
ファーストスケッチ。〈雑木
林的空間〉の一例

First sketch of the Uto Elementary School, an example
of a thicket-like space.

に囲まれて、つながりつつも分かれたりと、微妙な違いを含んだ〈雑木
林的空間〉です。

小嶋 ─ありがとうございます。比喩としての〈雑木林的空間〉は、秋頃
の日差しが強い中、葉が落ちた雑木林をカサカサと音をたてて散策する
昼のイメージです。「PARY PARTY」展は、同じ雑木林でも真っ暗な新月
の夜に何が出てくるのかわからないイメージです。

赤松 ─諏訪さんからフードだけが浮かんで見えるアイデアを出していた
だいて、サーブする黒子が持つトレーと同じ鉄板のテーブルがフッと浮
いていたら面白いのではないかということになり、そこからテーブルの
厚みやサイズが決まりました。テーブルの間を巡り歩くのが木の間をさ
まよい歩くのに似た、場のつくり方になっていました。

川向 ─黒子がサーブするというのも、面白い、また重要なアイデアでし
た。普通の給仕係が会場に出入りしては、それだけで、普通のパーティ
会場に引き戻されてしまいますから。

諏訪 ─視覚的には、黒子の持つトレーがテーブルに見えることが特に重
要でした。中に入るとグラスの立つテーブルがあって、グラスを置こう
としたら、テーブルに見えていたトレーがフッとなくなったとか、食べ
物を取ろうとしたら急に動きだしたとか。人がいないはずなのに〈気配〉
を感じるとか、いたような気がしたけれどいなかったとか。〈余韻〉とか
〈記憶〉をつくるために、現れたり、動いたり、消えたりするトレーが必
要でした。皆さんの反応を見ながら、その動きを少しコントロールする
こともありました。

赤松 ─壁の後ろからスッとトレーが出てきたりと、会場の状況を見なが

114　第3章 PARTY PARTY

revealed and disappear, come together and move apart, in a way much like being surrounded by trees.

Kojima — Thank you. The metaphor of a thicket came from an image of walking through the woods on a sunny autumn day, kicking up a rustle of fallen leaves. For *Party Party*, I worked from an image of walking through those same woods at night under the light of a new moon, wondering what might appear.

Akamatsu — It was Suwa who came up with the idea of having it appear as if the food was floating in space. This made us think it might be interesting if the tables were made of the same steel plates as the serving trays and seemed to float in mid-air, and that's how we determined the thickness and size of the tables. The space was set up such that walking among the tables felt a lot like wandering among the trees.

Kawamukai — Having the wait staff dressed all in black with covered faces, not unlike *kuroko* stagehands, was a really interesting, and really crucial, idea. Had they been dressed in ordinary service uniforms it would have quickly pulled things back to the realm of a normal party venue.

Suwa — It was particularly important that the trays held by the *kuroko* be visually indistinguishable from the tables. Once inside, people saw tables lined with glasses, but when they went to set their own glass down they would find that what they had thought was a table was actually a tray and has been whisked away, or that

同じ仕様でつくられたトレーとテーブル。黒子がサーブするフードやテーブルが浮かんでいるかのように見える

Trays and tables made to the same specifications. The trays of food served by the *kuroko* and the tables seem to float.

「PARTY PARTY」展のDM。4
パターンのデザインで、展示
コンセプトを伝える

The direct mailing for the
Party Party exhibition came in
four variation that conveyed
the exhibition concept.

ら臨機応変にサーブされているのが面白いなと思いました。

川向 ── 空間が、特に翳の部分が生きているような感じでしたね。
ポスターとDMのデザインも、考えられていましたね。DMは、グラスの
中の赤ワインの量の違うものが数種類、制作されました。あんなに雄弁
なDMのデザインも珍しい。

赤松 ── ワインの量が違うデザインが4パターンありました。赤ワイン
の量が、これからパーティが始まる感じ、パーティが進行している感じ、
そして、飲み残された感じなどを伝えています。デザイナーの秋田寛さ
んも事務所のミーティングに参加して、議論が紆余曲折している最中に
「結局やりたいことは、こういうことじゃないの」と、あのデザインを出
してくださった。それで何か、展望が開けました。

小嶋 ── 秋田さんは素晴らしいデザイナーですし、さらに、デザインディ
レクションが素晴らしい。あのDMのデザインで、「PARTY PARTY」展で
感じ取ってほしい〈ONとOFF〉を実にうまく表してくれました。

家具と出来事

川向 ── さて、「PARTY PARTY」展から数年たちましたが、ここで試みら
れたことの、その後の展開についてお話しくださいませんか。

小嶋 ── 建築の仕事は、4年前と今で、そんなに変わるわけではないです
けれども、書籍や講演会で自分たちがやっていることを人に紹介すると
きの語り方が変わりましたね。

赤松 ── 普段、「学校では家具も重要な要素の1つ。ただ空間があるだけ
ではダメ」と言っていますが、人が集まるときに、家具と人をつなぐこ
とが、どういうことなのかと根本的に考えるいい機会を頂きました。建

when they go to pick up food the "table" has suddenly moved. They would sense someone's presence when nobody was around, or look up convinced someone was there only to find they were all alone. In order to create reverberations and remembrances, it was necessary for the trays to suddenly appear, and move, and disappear. There were times, too, when we controlled these movements a bit as we saw how people reacted to them.

Akamatsu — It was interesting to see how the servers responded flexibly to conditions in the venue, with trays suddenly slipping out from behind walls and the like.

Kawamukai — The space really seemed to be alive, especially its shadows. You gave a lot of thought to the design of the posters and the direct mailings, too, didn't you? You had a few different versions of the direct mailing, each showing more or less red wine in a glass. It was the kind of potent design not often seen in direct mailings.

Akamatsu — There were four patterns, each with a different volume of wine. The full glass suggested that the party was about to begin, a smaller amount that the party was underway, and even less that the wine had been left unfinished. Designer Kan Akita sat in on our meetings at the office and as the discussion was weaving this way and that he came up with that design and said, "Isn't this the kind of thing you're looking for?" Somehow, that really opened things up.

Kojima — Akita is a brilliant designer, and his design direction is outstanding, too. Your direct mailing was a keen expression of the sense of "on" and "off" that you hoped people would take away from the *Party Party* exhibition.

Furniture and Happenings

Kawamukai — Well, it's been a few years since the Party Party exhibition and I'm curious to know how your efforts then have developed since.

Kojima — Our architectural work hasn't changed all that much in the last four years, but I have changed the way I talk about what we do when writing or speaking to people.

Akamatsu — We often talk about the importance of furniture at schools, how just having the space alone isn't enough. The ODS-R exhibition was a great opportunity to think about what it means to connect people and furniture at times when people come together. Architecture has form, and it's powerful, but in the flow

築は形がある強いものですけれども、1 日なのか 1 年なのか 10 年なのか時間の流れの中で、そこで起きた出来事として人の記憶に残っていきます。出来事につながる漠然とした抽象的なものを具体的に落とし込んで、家具と一体化した空間をつくることの意義に、あらためて気づかされました。

川向 ── 先だって、「立川第一小学校 柴崎学習館 柴崎図書館 柴崎学童保育所」（2014）を拝見しましたが、シーラカンスの建築には特有の密度感がありますよね。好奇心旺盛な、育ち盛りの子どもたちが、たくさんの出来事に出合って体験できそうだと、その中を歩くだけでも感じられます。子どもたちがいなくても、子どもたちの笑顔や元気に動き回る姿が目に浮かんできました。〈気配〉、〈余韻〉、〈記憶〉に結びつくきわめて本質的なことが「PARTY PARTY」展の中に表現されていたことがわかりました。

小嶋 ── 昔、土居義岳さんに「シーラカンスの場合は、空間の中にエーテルが満ちている」と批評していただいたことがあるのですが、エーテルがただパンパンに満ちているのではなくて、スカスカしたところもないと、うっとうしいですし、何も表れてこないものをつくると失敗です。今、川向先生がおっしゃったことは僕らの特徴で、しかも、濃すぎない。そういう意味では、諏訪さんと〈コラボレーション〉することで濃すぎる部分も出せたのは、いつもはできないチューニングで、それが実現してよかったです。

赤松 ── 「PARTY PARTY」展のようなバーをつくりたい、という設計のオファーがないかと期待していますね（笑）。

「立川第一小学校 柴崎学習館
柴崎図書館 柴崎学童保育所」
（CAt、2014）

Tachikawa Daiichi Elementary School Shibasaki Study House, Shibasaki Library, and Shibasaki Afterschool Facilities (CAt, 2014).

〈あじわう〉ことでつくられる〈記憶〉

川向 ── 諏訪さんは、その後の 4 年間で活躍の場を世界に広げましたよね。

諏訪 ── 「PARTY PARTY」展を久しぶりに思い返してドキッとしたのは、このときのテーマが〈気配と余韻と記憶〉だったことです。この 4 年を

of time—whether one day or one year or ten years—people come to remember it as "something that happened." The exhibition was another reminder of how important it is to take something vague and abstract that leads to "happenings" and drop it into something specific to create a space that's in tune with its own furniture.

Kawamukai — Recently I had the chance to see your Tachikawa Daiichi Elementary School, Shibasaki Study House, Shibasaki Library, and Shibasaki Afterschool Facilities (2014), and I must say it sure has that distinctive Coelacanth sense of density. Just walking around I could imagine the growing children there, so full of curiosity, and how they were sure to encounter and experience all kinds of "happenings." Even though there were no kids there at the time, I could clearly see them smiling and running around energetically. I realized that in the *Party Party* exhibition you had expressed something really fundamental by tying together intimation, reverberation, and remembrance.

Kojima — A long time ago, Yoshitake Doi was describing our work and said, "Coelacanth spaces are filled with ether," but it's important that the ether not be dense everywhere—that it be thin in places so the effect isn't overbearing. If something doesn't reveal itself in what we build, then we've failed. What you've just described is a feature of our work, but it's one we hold in check. In that sense, collaborating with Suwa enabled us to cross the line—to really lay it on thick—and achieve a kind of recalibration that's normally not possible.

Akamatsu — I keep hoping someone will ask us to design a bar like the one at the *Party Party* exhibition. (*Laughs*)

Remembrances Created Through Taste

Kawamukai — Suwa, over the last four years your work has broadened internationally, hasn't it?

Suwa — What really struck me when thinking back on the *Party Party* exhibition for the first time in a while was the theme of "intimation, reverberation, and remembrance." The last four years have given me some insight into what I really ought to be aiming for, and ultimately I think it's creating remembrances. Rather than simply making materials into foods, what I should be aiming for is the memories that these will create. People have emotions and curiosity, and ultimately what I feel I want to make is unforgettable memories.

Kawamukai — I can remember re-reading a paper I wrote during

東京で行われた「ゲリラレストラン at ISETAN」(food creation、2014)

Guerrilla Restaurant at Isetan, held in Tokyo (Food Creation, 2014)

かけて、本来、自分が何を目指してやってきたのかが見えてきたように感じているのですが、それは、最終的に〈記憶〉をつくることだと思っています。単に食べ物としての物質をつくるのではなく、目指すところは、それが生み出す〈記憶〉です。人が感情や好奇心を抱き、最終的に忘れられない〈記憶〉をつくりたいのだなと感じています。

川向 ── 私も自分の書いたものを読み返す機会があって驚いたのは、ずっと昔に書いた大学の卒業論文に、建築に関する考え方が当時と今と同じように書いてあったことです。まったく変わっていないのです。

諏訪 ── 私もそうです。「ゲリラレストラン」というのを、ベルリン、パリ、シンガポール、香港、日本でやっていて、先日、金沢21世紀美術館でもやりましたけれど、実は、4歳から「ゲリラレストラン」と同じようなことをやっていたのです。能登半島の千里浜で野生児みたいに育ったのですが、当時はまさに想像のあじわいで、セミの抜け殻に花びらを詰めて花粉をふりかけるとか、トカゲのしっぽやくらげの死骸で「お料理」をつくって、新しいメニューができると友達を呼んで「レストラン」を開いていたのです。友達が驚く記憶に残るテイストをつくりたかったのでしょうね。人間ってそうそう変わらないです。

川向 ── 不思議ですね、本当に。

「ゲリラレストラン at ISETAN」
(food creation、2014)

Guerrilla Restaurant at Isetan
(Food Creation, 2014)

university—that was a long time ago—and being amazed that the views I expressed about architecture then were almost exactly the same as those I hold now. Nothing had changed.

Suwa — It's the same with me. I've been doing "Guerrilla Restaurant" performances in Berlin, Paris, Singapore, Hong Kong, and Japan, and just did one the other day at the 21st Century Museum of Contemporary Art in Kanazawa. But I've actually been doing the same sort of thing since I was four years old. I was raised as a kind of wild child in the Chirihama Beach area of Noto peninsula, and back then I really indulged my imagination, making "food" by stuffing cicada sloughs with flower petals and sprinkling them with pollen, or from lizard tails and dead jellyfish, and whenever I came up with a new recipe I would invite my friends to come visit my "restaurant." I suppose I wanted to create tastes that would be surprising and unforgettable. People don't change, do they?

Kawamukai — It's really incredible, isn't it?

CHAPTER —— 4

Boyoyong
ぼよよん

ARCHITECT
Jun Aoki

建築家
青木淳

ENGINEER, DESINGNER
Shinya Matsuyama

エンジニア・デザイナー
松山真也

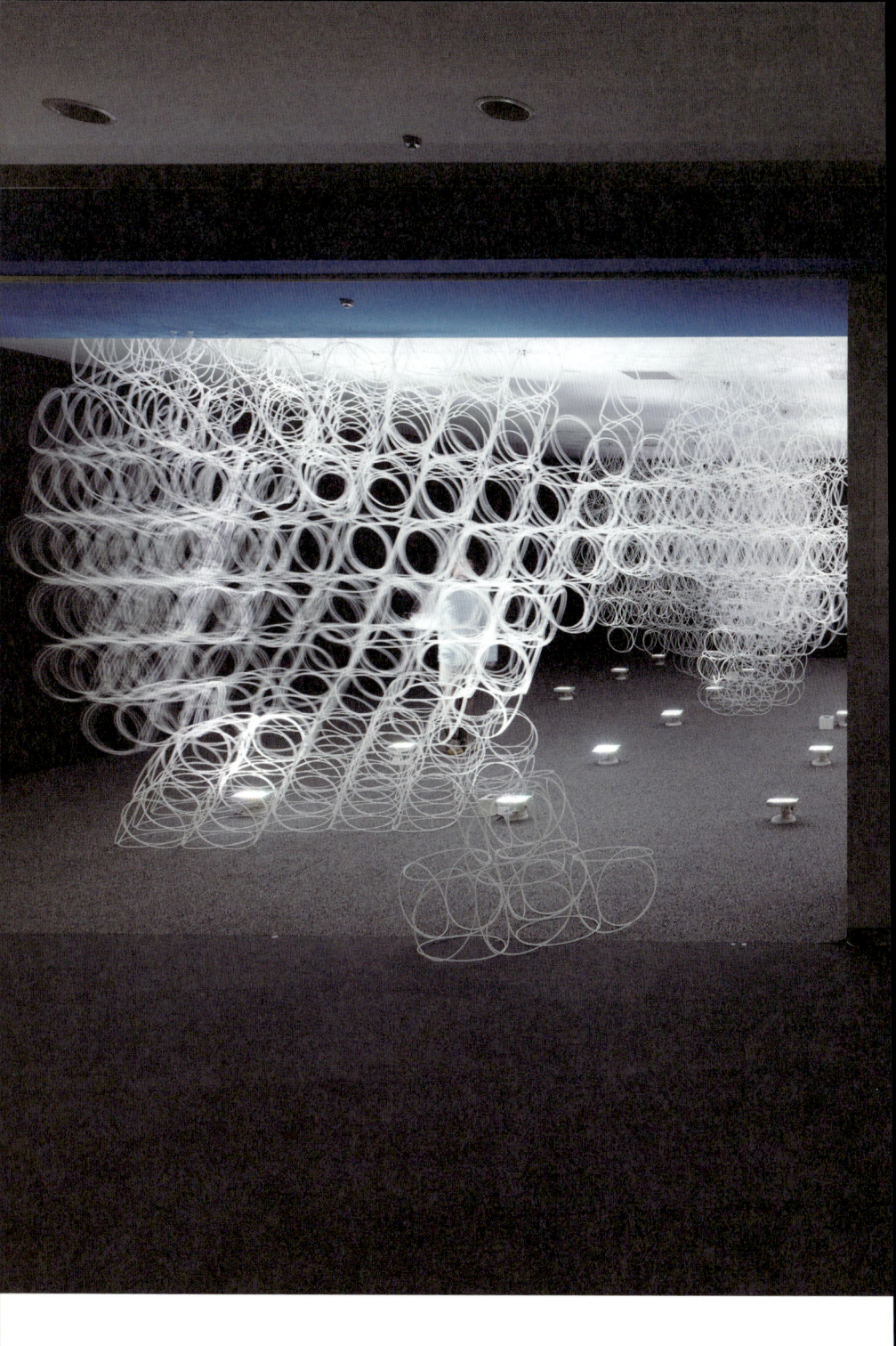

124　第 4 章　ぽよよん

CHAPTER−4 Boyoyong 125

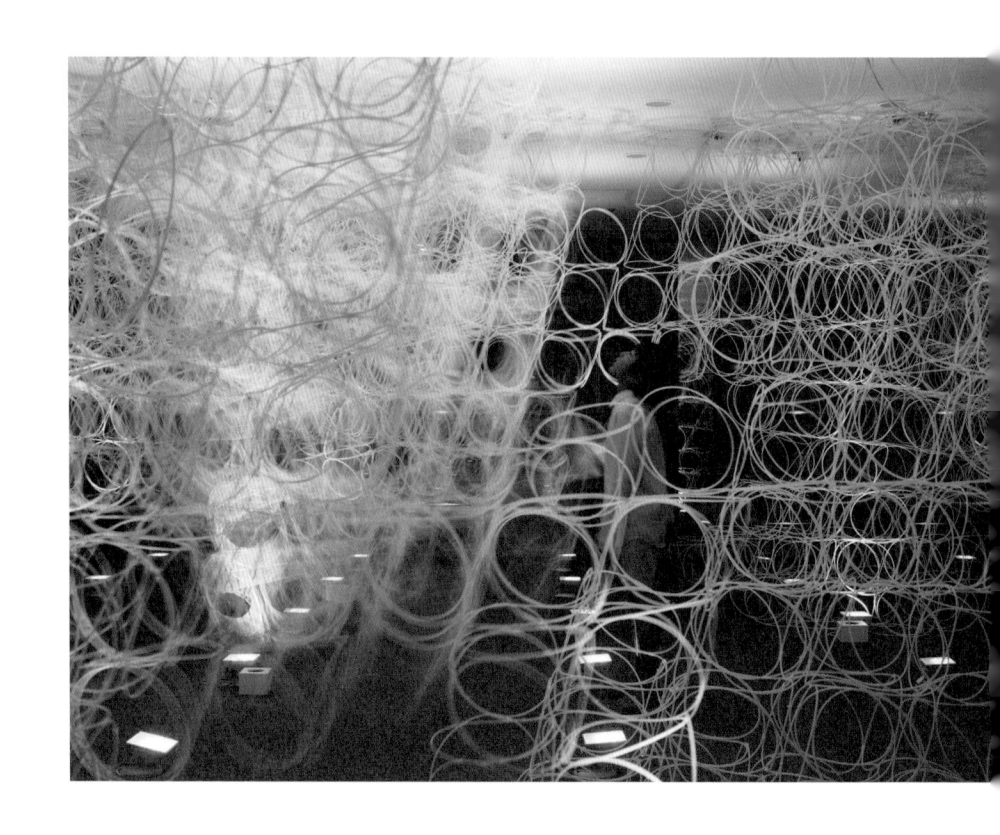

126　第4章　ぽよよん

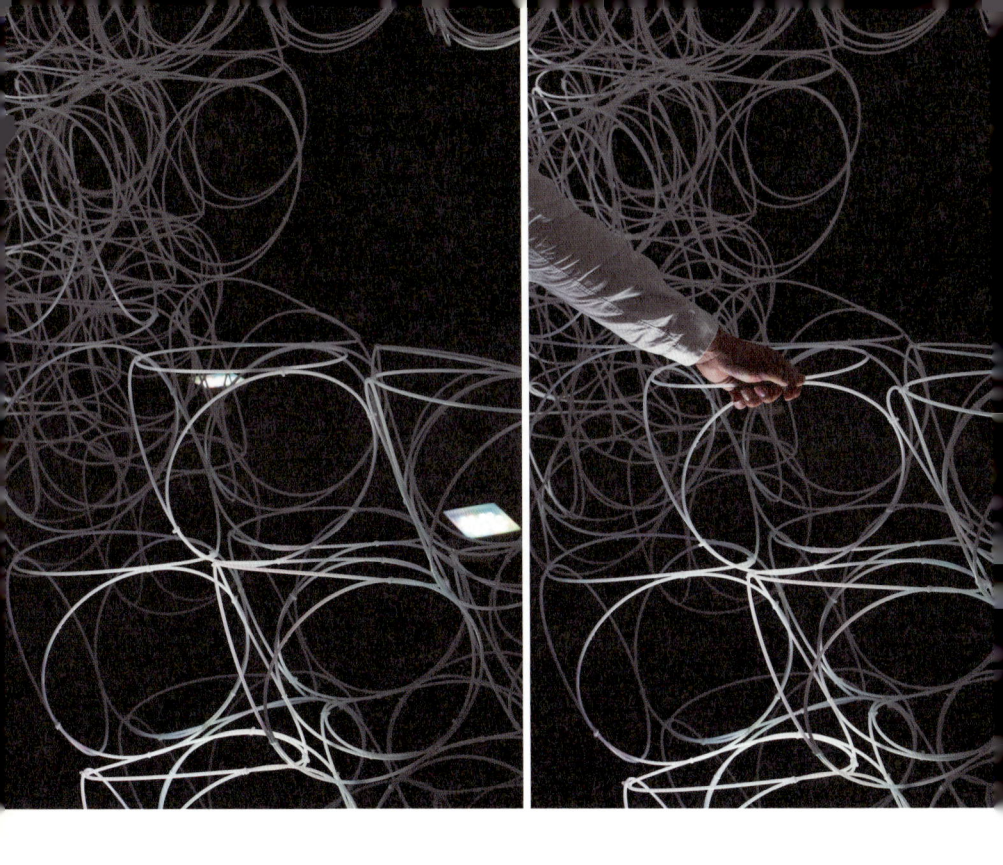

「ぽよよん」は、ゆれ、たわみ、きしみ、かしぐ
環境です。もし、堅牢堅固を前提とすれば、ゆれ、
たわみ、きしみ、かしぐことは、マイナスの現象
です。なぜなら、それはものや環境が壊れるとき
の前兆だからです。

しかし、3.11の大震災とそれに続く余震の連続の
なかで、どんなに堅牢堅固に環境をつくろうとも、
つねに想定以上のことが起きてしまうことを、世
界は、実は盤石どころか、生き物のように動いて
いるものであることを、私たちは、肌身をもって
知りました。私たちは、世界の堅牢堅固を前提に
できません。

では、生き物のように動いているこの世界に、素
直に呼応できる環境とはどのようなものなのだろ
うか。それを、仮に「ぽよよん」と呼んで、検証
してみようというのがこの展覧会の趣旨です。

約8,000個の、弾力性のある樹脂でできた300 φ
のリングが、立体的に組み合わさります。そうし
てできた「雲」が、ゆれ、たわみ、きしみ、かし
ぎます。それが人々に不安を与えるかわりに、安
心を与えることができる環境になるかどうかが試
されます。
（展覧会コンセプト文より）

128　第4章　ぽよよん

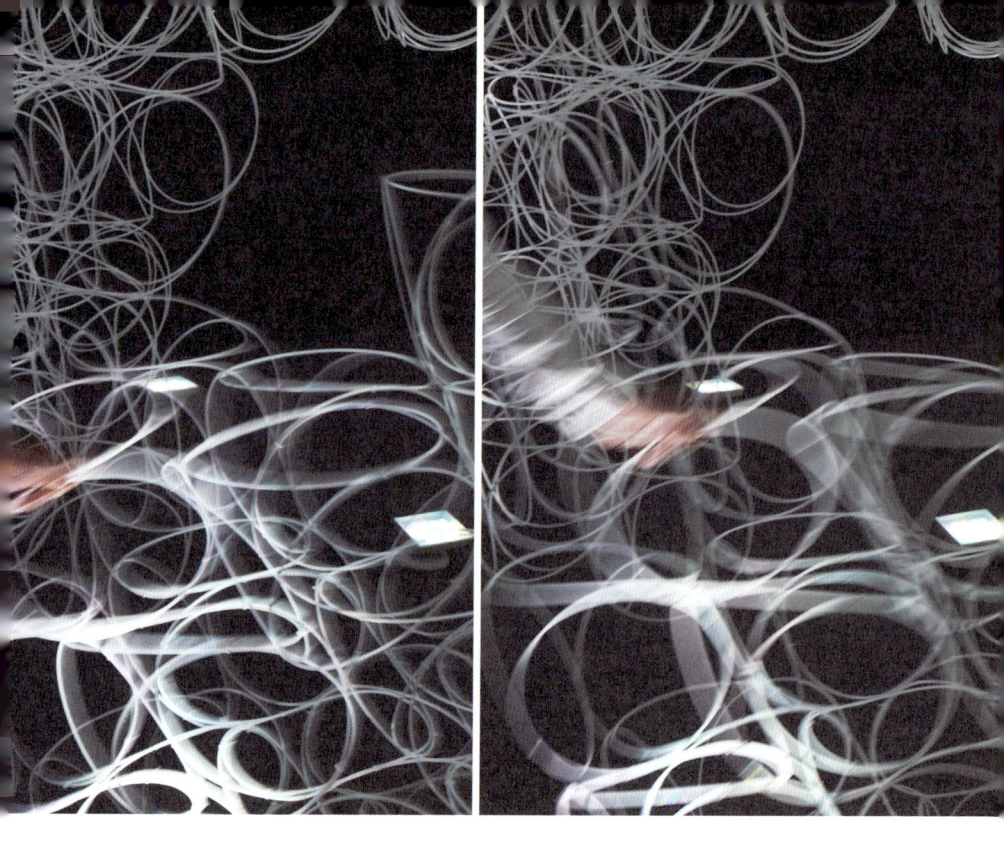

Boyoyong is an environment that shakes, sags, creaks, and leans. If creating something firm and solid is a positive, then shaking, sagging, creaking, and leaning are negatives. Why? Because such phenomena are often signs that an object or an environment is about to break. And yet, given the great earthquake of 3/11 and the constant aftershocks that have followed, we now have a visceral understanding that any environment, no matter how firmly and solidly made, can be subjected to forces that exceed assumptions—that the world is not a great rock but actually moves like a living thing. We cannot presume the world to be firm and stable. Well then, what kind of environment can respond without protest to this world of ours that moves like something alive? The aim of this exhibition was to examine that question, seeking what we provisionally called *boyoyong*. The exhibition is a sculptural assemblage of 8,000 rings composed of elastic resin, each measuring 300mm in diameter. The resulting "cloud" shakes, sags, creaks, and leans. The question is whether this creates an environment that puts the mind at ease despite the uneasiness such phenomena foster.

(Exhibition concept, July 2011)

〈ぼよよん〉という現象そのものを
組み立てる

青木淳
松山真也
川向正人

建築家
青木淳

1956 年 神奈川県生まれ。東京大学大学院工
学研究科修士課程修了後、磯崎新アトリエを経
て、1991 年 青木淳建築計画事務所設立。主な
作品に、青森県立美術館 (2006) ほか

ARCHITECT
Jun Aoki

Born in Kanagawa prefecture in 1956, Aoki
completed the master's course in architecture
at the University of Tokyo Graduate School of
Engineering. After working at Arata Isozaki &
Associates, he established Jun Aoki & Associates
in 1991. Major works include the Aomori Museum
of Art (2006).

川向 — 最初に、オカムラのショールームを使って、今、最もやりたいことに挑戦することと、どなたか建築家以外の表現者とコラボレーションすることの 2 つをお願いしました。それを受けて、どのようなことをお考えになりましたか。

安定から不安定へ〜〈ゆらぐ〉

青木 — 僕が展示をした 2011 年は、東日本大震災が起きるという、すごく特殊な年でした。もちろん、地震を予測していたわけではありませんが、1 月に提案したテーマは、まるで地震のあとに立てた企画のようでした。ちょうど「青森県立美術館」(2006) で、4 月から開催する展覧会「青木

Assembling
the Very Phenomenon of *Boyoyong*

JUN AOKI
SHINYA MATSUYAMA
MASATO KAWAMUKAI

エンジニア・デザイナー
松山真也

1978 年 富山県生まれ。2006 年より、MONGOOSE
STUDIO（2012 年で活動休止）のリーダーとし
て活動。「わくわくするためのテクノロジー」の
可能性を追求し、アーティストなどの多くの作
品に携わる

ENGINEER, DESIGNER
Shinya Matsuyama

Born in Toyama prefecture in 1978, Matsuyama
was active as the leader of Mongoose Studio
between 2006 and 2012, when it ceased
operation. Pursuing the potential for "technology
that excites," he is involved in the work of
numerous artists.

Kawamukai — We started out by asking you to do two things: to use
the Okamura showroom to take on some challenge in an area you
were interested in and to do so in collaboration with someone from
a creative field other than architecture. What did you think of this
request?

From Stability to Instability: Wavering

Aoki — My ODS-R exhibition took place in 2011, which became a
most unusual year marked by the Great East Japan Earthquake in
March. I certainly had no premonition that the earthquake was on

「青森県立美術館」（青木淳建築計画事務所、2006）

Aomori Museum of Art (Jun Aoki & Associates, 2006)

淳×杉戸洋　はっぱとはらっぱ」（震災の影響で中止）の企画も終盤に差しかかっていた時期です。「青森県立美術館」の5周年と東北新幹線が新青森まで延びることなど、明るい未来と平和がいっぱいの時期でした。しかし、僕たちは平和で確実な地盤の上に生きているのではなくて、実はどこか、もろくて危うい状況に生きているのではないかという思いがありました。ですから、杉戸さんと一緒に、平和に見える裏側に蠢く（うごめ）ゆがんでいるものに焦点を当てようと考えていました。僕は、ゆらぐ小屋をつくろうとしていたし、杉戸さんは、ゆがんだ家の絵ばかり描いていました。

ゆがんだものは普通、ネガティブなものだけれども、もしかすると、それは、美しいものなのかもしれないし、より快適なものなのかもしれない。〈ゆがむ〉とか〈動く〉ことで、堅固でない空間が実はすてきな空間だと思えるようになるかもしれない。このODS-Rでも、現象的にはまったく違うけれど、狙うところは同じでした。一番やりたいことをどうぞ、とお聞きして、僕が最初に思ったのはこういうことでした。

川向──面白いですね。私が今、研究している18世紀後半というのはやがてフランス革命が勃発する時代ですが、美術史上はロココ様式で、宮廷趣味を反映した繊細で優美な曲線的装飾が表層を飾る時代でした。迫り来る動乱、価値大変動の直前にあって、美に対立する概念として醜が問われるようになる時代でもありました。古典的な美しい輪郭を持つ以前の、むしろ怪奇で恐ろしげだが、一体的で個性と生命にあふれたものを求める時代です。

青木──時代性という点でいえば、1月に阪神淡路大震災、3月にオウム真理教の地下鉄サリン事件が起きた年であり、またWindows 95が発表

its way, but the proposal I submitted that January might as well have been conceived in the wake of that disaster.

Back then I was finishing up plans for a joint exhibition with Hiroshi Sugito at the Aomori Museum of Art (2006) called *Happa to harappa* [Leaves and Open Fields]. (Scheduled to open in April, it was cancelled as a result of the earthquake.) The event was planned to commemorate both the fifth anniversary of the museum's founding and the extension of the Tohoku Shinkansen line to Shin-Aomori Station; it was a peaceful time—one filled with thoughts of a brighter future. Still, even then I had a sense that we don't live on a placid, solid foundation so much as in a state of precarious fragility. So I decided to focus with Sugito on the twisted bits that wriggle beneath the veneer of tranquility. I set out to build shaky sheds while Sugito drew picture after picture of distorted houses.

Distortion is usually thought of as something negative, but I thought that twisted things might actually be more beautiful or more comfortable, and that creating unstable spaces through distortion or movement could result in something that seemed really wonderful. The piece for ODS-R was something completely different, but the aim was the same. And that's what I was thinking about when I heard I could do whatever I wanted.

Kawamukai — Very interesting. Right now I'm researching the second half of the eighteenth century, the period that sparked the French Revolution. In art history terms, it was characterized by the ornately decorated surfaces and elegant curves of the rococo style that reflected the tastes of the court. With upheaval on the horizon and a massive change in values fast approaching, it was also a time when people turned to ugliness as a conceptual alternative to beauty, seeking something grotesque and frightening, yet integral and brimming with personality and vitality, that preexisted the outlines of classic beauty.

Aoki — Speaking of points of time that mark epochal shifts, 1995 was also something of a landmark year, with the Great Hanshin earthquake in January and the Aum Shinrikyo cult's sarin gas attack on the Tokyo subway in March. That year also saw the launch of Windows 95, a huge leap forward in the computing world. The earthquake in 1995 made me realize that even though our world may seem to be rock solid, it actually isn't at all. I went to visit the affected area after the earthquake and on my way back, stepping off the shinkansen and out into Tokyo Station, I suddenly realized what a wasteland lurks just

されコンピュータの世界が大きく開けた年だった1995年も、大きな節目の年でした。僕も、この95年の阪神淡路大震災で、僕たちの世の中は盤石に見えるけれど、実はそうではないと気づかされたひとりです。震災のあと、被災地に行って、新幹線で東京駅に帰ってきたとき、突然、目の前の何でもない状況も一皮むけば廃墟なのだと思い至ったのです。その後、次第に危機感は薄れ、生ぬるい平和が続いて、2011年3月11日の大震災になります。

自己完結したフォルムを超えて〜〈雲〉

青木 ── もちろん、ずっとそんなパースペクティブで考え続けていたわけではありませんが、あとから振り返って考えてみると、結果的には〈雲〉とか〈歪んでいるもの〉とか、形を持っているように見えて、実は、その形が仮そめにすぎないものに関心を持ち続けていたようです。しかも、それをポジティブなものとしてですね。

川向 ── コラボレーターを選び、交渉する段階では、どのようなことをお考えになりましたか？

青木 ── すでに、ハイアット リージェンシー 大阪のチャペル「白い教会」（2006）で、鋼製リングを使った〈雲〉みたいなものをつくった経験がありました。構造形式としては立体トラスですが、単位部材にリングを使うことで、直線材ではなく曲線材の組合せになっています。リングの弓のような曲線のおかげで、弾性が生まれ、一般的なトラスと比べて、柔らかい構造になっています。もちろん、建築物なので動きませんが、その〈動〉という性格を拡張して、もっと大きくて柔らかいものが、時々、動いたらどうなるだろうかと考えました。

風が吹いたり人が触れたりすることで動くといいなと思ったときに、「MASAKI CLINIC」（2007）でインタラクティブなシステムの部分をつくってもらった松山さんを思い浮かべました。

「白い教会」（青木淳建築計画事務所、2006）。白く塗装された鋼製リングが立体的に組み合わさり、構造体となっている

White Chapel (Jun Aoki & Associates, 2006). The structure is composed of a three-dimensional assemblage of iron rings painted white.

beneath the ordinary and the everyday. After that the sense of crisis gradually faded, there was a period of mild tranquility, and then the massive earthquake struck on 11 March 2011.

Transcending the Self-contained Form: Clouds

Aoki — I wasn't always looking at things from that perspective, of course, but in hindsight I can see that I did sustain an abiding interest in things like clouds: things that are distorted, that appear to have shape but whose shape is only transient. And I looked at such things in a positive light.

Kawamukai — What were you looking for when it came time to select and negotiate with a collaborator?

Aoki — I had already used steel rings to create a cloud-like structure for *Shiroi kyokai* [White Chapel] (2006) at the Hyatt Regency Osaka. Structurally, the building is a space truss, but since I used rings as component units it is an assemblage of curved members rather than straight. The bow-like curves of the rings create an elasticity that makes for a softer structure than an ordinary truss. The building itself doesn't move, of course, but I wondered what it would be like if that structure's motive character could be expanded and turned into something bigger and softer that moved now and then.

As I was thinking about wanting to incorporate movement generated by the wind or by human touch, I recalled that Matsuyama had created the interactive system I used for Masaki Clinic (2007).

Kawamukai — Matsuyama, what did you think when Aoki approached you as a collaborator?

Matsuyama — After I heard about the project I went to see White Chapel. I was very interested in its sense of softness despite, of course, being a very solid building, and came up with ways that such softness might be conveyed effectively. For example, the ring structure could be hung horizontally from the ceiling and positioned like the surface of a body of water, offering the potential to generate ripple-like movement. Sensors could be used to detect such movement, which could be emphasized through the use of lighting to reflect even minute changes. From there I then further developed the idea of suspended rings.

川向 ── 青木さんから、そのような問いかけがあったときに、コラボレーターとして松山さんは、どのようにお考えになりましたか。

松山 ── 今回のお話を頂いて、「白い教会」を拝見し、固いはずの建物が柔らかいという点がすごく面白いなと興味を持ちまして、その柔らかさをうまく見せる方法を考えました。

例えば、リングの構造を水面に見立て、平面状に構成し天井から吊す。すると動きが波紋のように広がるのではないか。さらに、その動きをセンシングして光で強調していけば、微小な動きも見せられる。そこから吊すという方向に展開していきました。

インタラクティブな素材・空間・システム

川向 ── なるほど。古典的な静性もしくは安定性に対する問いかけでしょうか。青木さんのおっしゃる構想を受けて、人の身体の動きに合わせて変容するインタラクティブな素材や空間やシステムの探究へと進むわけですね。

青木 ── 木造家屋の2階は、身体を動かすと床がきしみ、微妙に建物が揺れますよね。あれを「気持ち悪い」と思うのか、それとも「気持ちいい」と思うのか。今の僕は「気持ちいい」と感じるのですが、前は、揺れるのが不安で「気持ち悪い」と感じていました。しかし安全面が確保されていることがわかっていれば、揺れることをポジティブに受け止め、楽しむことができます。ハンモックも、揺れることが楽しいですよね。揺れるものとか動くものも、ネガティブからポジティブに受け止める方向に変えることができるわけで。感覚をその方向に、もう少し先に進めたかったのです。

川向 ── それは、とても重要なお話です。まちづくりで、日本の古い木造家屋を残すか壊すかが、まさにそのポジティブに受け止めるか、ネガティブに受け止めるかに関係しています。固くて、びくともしない床や壁で、どこにも空気の抜け道がない完全密閉の空間を、われわれは無意識のうちに理想とするようになっています。長い近代化の歴史が、そういう身体感覚や意識をつくり上げたのです。そこから変えないと、建築的に見て素晴らしいと思う古い木造建築が、いとも簡単に壊されて、コンクリートの箱に置き換えられてしまいます。揺らぎ、メリメリもミシミシもあり、適当に隙間風もある。自然の中に、周囲に負担をかけない軽さと弱さで存在すること自体が、どれほど環境にとっても人間にとってもいいことかが理解されないと、本当の意味での環境問題は解決しません。私が青木さんのスタンスに共感するのは、われわれの近代化によって変容した身体感覚や意識のありように疑問を投げかけるところです。

Interactive Materials, Spaces, and Systems

Kawamukai — I see. You were, then, questioning classic notions of stillness and stability. You took Aoki's idea and moved ahead in a search for the materials, spaces, and systems that would transform it into something interactive that responded to people's bodily movements.

Aoki — If you move around on the second floor of a wooden two-story house, the floor creaks and the building moves slightly, right? The question is whether that sensation feels unpleasant or pleasant. For me, now, it's a pleasant feeling, but I used to find such instability unsettling. Once you feel confident there's no safety issue, instability can be seen as a positive, as something to enjoy. People like hammocks, which swing back and forth, right? It's possible, you see, to shift the impression left by things that sway, things that move, from something negative to something positive. I wanted to take this transformation of perception one step further.

Kawamukai — You make a very important point. When engaging in *machizukuri* (town building) activities in Japan, the decision of whether to retain old wooden structures or demolish them often comes down to the difference between positive and negative perceptions. Without ever realizing it, at some point we've adopted as our ideal these hermetically sealed spaces with floors and walls that don't budge an inch. It's a physical sensibility and awareness that has developed over the long history of modernization, and unless we initiate a shift at that level, it is all too easy to raze architecturally outstanding old wooden buildings and replace them with concrete boxes. I don't think we'll truly be able to address environmental issues until we understand just how much better these buildings are for the environment, and for people, precisely because—as shaky, groaning, creaking, and drafty as they may be—they have a lightness and delicacy that exists within nature without placing an undue burden on their surroundings. What I can relate to in your approach is the way you question how our physical sensibility and awareness has been changed by modernization.

The Phenomenon of *Boyoyong*

Aoki — I should note, though, that even when I talk of shakiness, I still presuppose some assurance of peace and safety. In the wake of

〈ぼよよん〉という現象

青木 —— ただ、揺れるとしても、平和で身の安全が保障されていることが前提ですよね。3.11の大地震を体験した直後だと、建物が揺れるとか動くということは、怖いことでしかない。だから、単に自分が立っている環境が動き揺れるということだけでなく、それをどう許容してもらえるようなものにできるか、いや、それ以上に、それを快適でポジティブなものにまで価値転換を引き起こせるか、というようなことを、〈ぼよよん〉で考えようとしたのです。

川向 —— 〈動く環境〉そのものの提案ですね。言葉でいうのは簡単ですが、動き方によって快適にも不快にもなります。不安をかき立てたり不気味だったりすることは避けたい。動いても揺れても、それが快適で、心地よいものでありたい。そこから〈ぼよよん〉という擬態語が考え出されたわけですね。誰もが気持ちよくポジティブに受け止める動き・揺れとしての〈ぼよよん〉。

青木 —— そうですね。日本語では擬態語を書き言葉でもよく使うけれど、英語ではあまりないですね。よく言えば、状況を感覚的に捉え、分析的にではなく、曖昧になってしまうかもしれないけれど、その感覚のまま伝えようとする姿勢が日本語にはあります。だから、日本語の擬態語には、言葉で説明してしまったら失われてしまうような感覚の微妙な差異が含まれます。「ぼよよん」と「ぼよよん」は違うし、「ぼよん」とも「ぽよん」とも違う。それで、松山さんが「ぼよよんとは何か？」と言い始めて、いろいろな材料を使って〈ぼよよん〉の映像を撮ることになりました。どう動くのが、〈ぼよよん〉なのか。〈ぼよよん〉という現象の分析に進むわけです。

松山 —— 映像をWebサイトで公開して、身の回りにあるもので〈ぼよよん〉

Webサイトに公開された「ぼよよん」の映像。こんにゃくを上から落としたとき（上）と、水風船同士をぶつけたとき（下）の挙動（Mongoose Studio、2011）

Boyoyong videos posted to the web site showing the behavior of konnyaku when dropped (above) and water balloons when bumped together (below) (Mongoose Studio, 2011).

experiencing the earthquake on 3/11, structures that shake or sway are just scary. So the question for me was not just about whether the environment in which one is standing is moving and shaking. I was also interested in how you get people to accept such conditions or—going even further—how to trigger a shift of values such that they see such conditions as enjoyable, as something positive. These are the sorts of things I wanted to think about with *Boyoyong*.

Kawamukai— So, your proposal was to create a "moving environment," which sounds easy enough but could end up either a pleasant or an unpleasant experience depending on the nature of the motion. You wanted to avoid stirring anxiety or making people queasy, and to aim for a kind of moving and shaking that was enjoyable and comfortable. And this led you to *boyoyong,* a mimetic word suggesting a kind of bouncy jiggle that everybody registers as pleasant or positive.

Aoki— That's right. Japanese incorporates a lot of evocative mimetic words in both the spoken and written language—something not so common in English. On the positive side, by doing this Japanese seeks to capture a given state directly, if perhaps a bit vaguely, through the senses rather than through analysis. Japanese mimetic words, therefore, incorporate fine variations in sensation that are lost when you try to explain them in other ways. *Boyoyong* conveys something different than *poyoyong* that isn't like *boyong* or *poyong*, either. Matsuyama started asking what I meant by *boyoyong* so we decided to film a variety of different materials and figure out what kinds of movement matched the word; we set out to analyze the very phenomenon of *boyoyong*.

Matsuyama— We posted the footage to the web and investigated what kinds of everyday things moved in ways that fit the word *boyoyong.*

Kawamukai— Rather than looking into functionality, or durability, or the character and performance of materials, you did a comparative analysis of the phenomenon of *boyoyong,* then, before deciding what to do.

Matsuyama— I thought there was something really unexpected about using *boyoyong* as the title of an exhibition done in collaboration with an architect. There was a certain idea I wanted to convey, and as naturally as possible. When Aoki was explaining things to me, he said, "Things that people call 'cool' really aren't all that cool. What is really cool are things that are just a little bit

に当たる動きとは何かを探っていきました。

川向 ── どう機能するかとか、どれぐらい耐久性があるかとか、物自体の性質・性能を調べるのではなく、〈ぼよよん〉という現象そのものを比較分析して、1つの案に決めるわけですね。

松山 ── 建築家とコラボレーションする展示に「ぼよよん」というタイトルが付けられることに、強く意外性を感じました。そこにある意図をできるだけ自然に伝えようと考えました。説明に際して、青木さんから「いわゆるかっこいいものは、あまりかっこよくない。むしろ、ちょっとかっこ悪いくらいが、かっこいい」というお話があって、それを示す言葉として〈ぼよよん〉は最適だと思いました。

自立した生命体のように～〈遅れ〉

青木 ── 普通、デザインは、スタイリッシュなもの、研ぎ澄まされたもの、一分の隙もなく完璧なもの、を目指します。ただ、そういうものに囲まれると、何か息苦しさを感じませんか。そうしたデザインには、ある1つの価値観というか美意識に収斂させていく力学があるからですね。僕はどうも、そういうタイプのデザインが苦手なのです。デザインされていない、というわけではないけれど、いろいろなあり方を許容してくれるデザイン。そういうデザインを目指したのが「青森県立美術館」でした。〈ぼよよん〉という擬態語は、予想とちょっと異なる、つまりルーズな復元の仕方をイメージさせます。押したら、バンッとかバシッとか、そのまま返ってくるのではなく、遅れて反応しているところがあったり、それが素直に反応しているところから引っ張られて、慌てて遅れを取り戻そうとしたり。これは、物理的にいえば、固有周期が3秒くらいの状況のようです。

川向 ── 固有の動きを持ち、自立性のある存在ですね。しかも、今回の展示は個人的体験も可能ですが、目指すところは集団的体験です。いろいろな感性を持った人々が〈ぼよよん〉を体験して、予想外の反応に驚き、その驚きを眺めながら、また自分も驚き、何か新たな快感と発見に出合う。多くの人々が集まりコミュニケーションを取り合う場の中に、建築とかアートが介在することによって、私たちの人とか物に対する感じ方が変わる。しかも包み込まれての驚きというか感動なので、すごく深いのです。

青木 ── 「ぼよよん」の場合、雲の中から見る視点と、雲の外から見るという視点があります。いわば寒天状の雲みたいなものを人が動かすと、その動きが勝手に伝播して、外から見ると、雲みたいなものと人と区別がつかない状態で、蠢いている感じになります。

川向 ── 自然現象のようで都市的現象でもありますね。個々の動きが全体

uncool." I felt like *boyoyong* was the perfect word for getting this idea across.

Like an Autonomous Organism: Delay

Aoki — Design typically aims for something stylish, something polished, something flawless and perfect. But doesn't being surrounded by such things feel kind of suffocating? The reason is that this kind of design all shares a dynamic that converges on a single sense of values or aesthetics. I have a hard time with that type of design. Not un-designed, but tolerant of many ways of being—that's the kind of design I was aiming for with the Aomori Museum of Art. The mimetic word *boyoyong* suggests something that returns to form in a way that defies expectation, that's a little bit loose. Instead of springing back with a snap or a click when pushed, it seems to give a partly delayed response, one that trails along after the initial reaction as if rushing to make up for lost time. In physics terms, it has a natural period of about three seconds.

Kawamukai — It has its own peculiar motion as well as a sense of autonomy, then. The *Boyoyong* exhibition was something that could be experienced alone, but you intended it to be a group experience, didn't you? The idea was that individuals of various personalities would experience the piece, be startled by the unexpected response, observe the surprise of others, and in one's own sense of surprise discover some new kind of pleasure. The intervention of architecture and art in a space where many people come together and communicate with one another can change the way we feel about people and about things. And the sense of surprise or emotional impact can be so deep when one is enveloped in that way.

Aoki — *Boyoyong* encompassed both the view from inside the cloud and the view from outside the cloud. When somebody moved the thing, like a gelatin cloud, the motion spread on its own. Seen from the outside, where the lines between the person and the cloud blurred, the thing seemed to wriggle.

Kawamukai — This is a natural phenomenon and yet also an urban one, too, isn't it? The movement of individuals causes movement of the whole, and from the outside the complex wriggling in the interior seems to happen of its own accord. Even though the *Boyoyong* exhibition presented something artificial assembled from ring-shaped parts, it moved less like a mechanism than an organism.

2点とも：「雪のまちみらい館」（青木淳建築計画事務所、1999）

Both: Snow Foundation Building (Jun Aoki & Associates, 1999).

の動きを呼び、外からだと、内部で蠢くような複雑な動きが、あたかも自動的に起こっているように見えます。「ぽよよん」展ではリング状のパーツを組み立てて人工的につくられたものであるにもかかわらず、機械ではなく生命体のように動きます。

〈その場の質〉の建築化と構成要素

川向 ── ODS-Rは月1回のペースで打合せを重ねますが、その第1回のプレゼンテーションで「青森県立美術館」を説明してくださいました。縄文時代の三内丸山遺跡のすぐ横にある建築として、周囲の環境と通じ合う雰囲気を醸し出していますね。同じ雰囲気、同じ気分です。単に形態や色を合わせたものとは全然違います。〈その場の質〉をそのまま建築化すると青木さんはよくおっしゃいますが。

青木 ──「青木淳 Atmospherics」展（2000）で、住宅の「B」（1999）と「雪のまちみらい館」（1999）を例にとって、〈その場の質〉ということを言いました。「アトモスファー」がムードとか雰囲気という意味なので、〈アトモスフェリックス〉というのはムードをつくる技法のことかとよく誤解されます。でも〈アトモスフェリックス〉というのはもともと気象用語で、無線電波に雑音を入れてしまう大気電流のことなのです。それで僕は、〈アトモスフェリックス〉という言葉で、その場の質を変える要因、あるいはその場の質をコントロールする方法を意味させたかったのです。実際には、この言葉の原義なんて、英語圏に行っても誰にも知られていないことがあとでわかったのですが（笑）。ともかく、〈その場の質〉のほうが構成・形式・造形より重要なのではないか、という視点を出したかったのです。

川向 ──「潟博物館」（1997）から「雪のまちみらい館」あたりの建築作品ではらせん状の動線を使い、それを〈動線体〉という言葉で表現していましたね。動きながら、多様に体験できることがポイントでした。〈動線体〉のあとは、空気感を建築化する方向に移り、その場の雰囲気、土地や空気の感じが全部そこに込められるようになって、〈ぽよよん〉に重なってきます。この変化については、ご自分でも『原っぱと遊園地──建

Atmosphere and its Component Elements

Kawamukai — We had meetings roughly once a month to talk about the ODS-R project, and at your first presentation you talked about the Aomori Museum of Art. The building is directly adjacent to the Jomon period Sannai Maruyama archaeology site and really seems at ease with its surroundings. There is a common mood, a common feeling. This is completely different than simply matching forms or colors. You often talk about trying to infuse your architecture with the atmosphere of a site, don't you?

Aoki — For the *Atmospherics* exhibition (2000), I talked about atmosphere, using the *B* residence (1999) and the *Yuki no machi miraikan* [Snow Foundation Building] (1999) as examples. In Japanese we use the English word "atmosphere" to mean the mood or feeling of a place, and Japanese people often misunderstand the word "atmospherics" to mean just techniques for evoking a particular mood. Originally, though, it was a meteorological term that meant electrical disturbances in the atmosphere that interfered with radio transmission. This is why I wanted to use the word "atmospherics" to mean factors that change the quality of a place as well as methods for controlling the quality of a place. Later on, of course, I realized that almost nobody in the English-speaking world knows the original meaning of the word, either. (*Laughs*) In any case, what I wanted to suggest was that atmosphere—the quality of a place—might be even more important to a work of architecture than its structure, style, or form.

Kawamukai — From the *Kata hakubutsukan* [Fukushima Lagoon Museum] (1997) through the Snow Foundation Building, you employed spiral-shaped circulation areas in your architectural works, which you described as "circulation bodies." The point was that they were spaces that could be moved around in and experienced in diverse ways. After this circulation area period you shifted in the direction of imbuing your buildings with atmosphere—incorporating the mood of a place, the overall feeling of the land and the air—which seems to have some overlap with *Boyoyong*. You've written about this shift yourself in *Harappa to yuenchi: kenchiku ni totte sono ba no shitsu to wa nani ka* [Open Fields and Amusement Parks: What, for Architecture, is the Quality of a Place?] (2004).

Aoki — Lying down and reading a book, having a drink, drowsing off—I don't think people's lives are really so easy to subdivide.

「潟博物館」（青木淳建築計画
事務所、1997）

Fukushima Lagoon Museum
(Jun Aoki & Associates, 1997).

築にとってその場の質とは何か』（2004）に書かれています。

青木 ── 寝そべりながら本を読み、お酒を飲んで、眠っちゃったり、人間の生活は本来、けっこう分節しにくいものだと思います。それを、「リラックスする」「本を読む」「食べたり飲んだりする」「眠る」と言葉できっちり分節して、それら個々に対応する部屋をつくるというのが、今の家の姿。それに違和感があって、いろいろな行為が〈未分化〉なまま形づくられた空間のほうがもっと自由なのではないか、と思ったのです。

それで昔の道のことを考えてみて、今の道が単に交通のための空間にすぎないのに対し、昔の道は、井戸端会議のように日々の生活の場であったり、市が開かれたり、祭りの場にもなったりと、つまり、道が未分化な行為に対応する空間だったことに思い当たりました。道の中に未分化な形で行為が溶け込んでいたのが、だんだんと道の脇に建物として分化・結晶化してきたのではないか、と思ったのですね。それで、もう一度、結晶化してできた機能ごとの空間を道なり、動線空間なりに戻して溶かし込んでやるのがいいのではないか。これが〈動線体〉のアイデアでした。建築で、都市における道に相当するのは廊下であり階段であり、「つなげられるもの」ではなく、僕が動線空間と呼ぶ「つないでいるもの」です。その「つないでいるもの」だけで建築ができないかと考え、自分の事務所を始めたごく初期のころ、住宅の「H」（1994）、「馬見原橋」（1995）と、目的を持った部屋をつくらないようにして、ずるずるとつながる道みたいな空間を試みていきました。建物を動線空間だけの系に還元してみました。その到達点となるのが「潟博物館」ですが、ここまでいくと逆に、歩かされているという気持ちが強くなり、結果的には、あらかじめ決め

Contemporary homes take the path of cleanly partitioning these activities with words—relaxing, reading, eating and drinking, sleeping—and constructing separate rooms for each. This didn't sit very well with me and I wondered if spaces that gave shape to a variety of activities without differentiating them might not afford greater freedom.

I also did some thinking about roads. Roads today are nothing more than spaces to facilitate transportation, but roads in the old days were living spaces where people gathered to gossip, where markets were set up, and where festivals were held. I realized that roads were once spaces that could cope with all sorts of undifferentiated activity. Actions that had once blended together in the undifferentiated middle of the road were shunted off to the sides over time and crystallized in the form of specialized buildings. I thought it would be good to take these crystalized, function-specific spaces and dissolve them back into the roads—into circulation areas. This was the idea behind "circulation bodies."

The parts of buildings that correspond to a city's roads are its hallways and stairways. These are not things that you link together, but circulation spaces that tie the whole together. I wondered if I could create entire structures made up of such spaces, and back in the early days after opening my own office I tried, both with the H residence (1994) and the Mamihara Bridge (1995), to avoid creating rooms with specific functions and to instead create spaces from extended, connecting paths. I wanted to reduce structures to just a system of circulation areas. The Fukushima Lagoon Museum was the culmination of that approach. I'm afraid, though, that taken to the extreme it ended up leaving the impression that you were being compelled to walk around, like being put on a roller coaster traveling between predetermined locations. This may still be enjoyable, but it doesn't inspire a sense of freedom.

It was the exact opposite of what I had set out to do. What I had really wanted to create was not so much an amusement park roller coaster as an open field in which activity could be undifferentiated and free, and everyone could play in the way they wished.

Kawamukai — Once you're returned things to the undifferentiated state of an open field, the question then becomes how to launch new architecture or new spaces there. Having swept away the concept and method of distinguishing between what does and does not constitute a circulation area—something of a functionalist relic,

られているところを動くジェットコースターに乗っている気分になってしまったと思いました。これは自由さが感じられない楽しみ方です。

僕がしたかったのは、それとは逆のことです。〈遊園地〉のジェットコースターではなくて、行為が未分化のままの自由がある、みんながそれぞれいろんな遊びを思いつくことができる〈原っぱ〉のようなものをつくりたかったのです。

川向 ── 未分化でもある〈原っぱ〉のような状態に一度戻りますね。さて、そこから新たな建築を、空間をどう立ち上げるか。そう考えるときに、動線部分とそうでない部分という、何となく機能主義の名残を感じさせる思想と手法を一掃して、青木さんは、その場の質そのものに向かいます。そして、質の把握と同時に、その構成要素を抽出する方向に進みます。

青木 ── そうですね。例えば「白い教会」の場合は、構成要素を検討する中で、リングを選びました。空間を密実に充填しているけれど、泡でできたような、軽いポーラス状の塊にしたかったからです。雲のような、不定形で、スカスカで、柔らかい空間。そのためには、直線状の部材ではなくリングが適切だと思いました。

〈ぼ・よ・よ・ん〉と光と音

川向 ── さて、リングという構成要素によって〈雲〉をつくるという基本構想が出てきたときに、松山さんは、どのような対応をされましたか。

松山 ── リングを揺らすとそれに反応して光や音が変化する。いくつかの構成原理を立てますが、今回は、これ以上の構成原理は立てずにシンプルに対応することにしました。もの自体が魅力的なので、触れてその面白さを味わってほしい。またいろんな角度から見て構造の魅力を知ってほしい。

そこで「触ると何か起きる」という仕組みを組み込みました。リングの上に一定の間隔で加速度センサーを取り付け、人が触れると力がリングを通じて伝播し、そのことで光を制御するシステムをつくりました。

当初は光の変化のみでシステムを考えていましたが、体験としての効果が十分かどうかを検討する過程で、音が加わったほうがより効果的だと気づきました。もともと〈ぼよよん〉という言葉自体がユーモラスで、多少青木さんご自身のお人柄も加味してユーモアのある表現を目指し、揺れる周期に合わせて「ぼ・よ・よ・ん」と聞こえるように開発しました。結果的に〈動く〉ことに関連しては、光はサブ的なものになりました。

川向 ── 夜、誰もいない、音もなく動きもない状態で光っている〈雲〉全体の姿が神秘的で美しい。それが昼間、子どもたちが入って揺すると、音を出し、光も発して、動くにぎやかな感じに切り替わります。私は、

「馬見原橋」（青木淳建築計画
事務所、1995）。橋の下がさ
まざまな活動の場となる
© 朝日新聞社

Mamihara Bridge (Jun Aoki &
Associates, 1995). The lower
deck is used for all sorts of
activities.
© The Asahi Shimbun Company

really—you moved in the direction of focusing on atmosphere, on the quality of a place. And while seeking to grasp the quality of a place you also sought to extract its component elements.

Aoki — That's right. With White Chapel, for example, when I was thinking about component elements I chose to use rings. I wanted to create a space that was densely packed but had a light and porous feel, as if made of bubbles—a cloud-like space that was irregularly shaped, permeable, and soft. I decided that using rings instead of straight members was a way to accomplish this.

Bo-yo-yo-ng and Light and Sound

Kawamukai — Okay then, Matsuyama, how did you respond once the basic concept of making a cloud from rings had been established?

Matsuyama — By making it so that shaking the rings would cause changes in light and sound. There were a number of different potential constitutive principles, but I decided to keep things simple this time. The objects themselves were appealing, so I wanted people to touch them and savor the fun. I also wanted people to be able to appreciate their structural beauty from a variety of angles. I incorporated a mechanism to ensure that something happened when the piece was touched, installing accelerometers at regular intervals above the rings and rigging up a system for controlling the lights using the energy ripping through the rings when they were touched.

At first I conceived of the system as only triggering changes in light.

この二面性がすごく好きでした。ただ、ニューオータニのこの場所ですので、音の量や質の問題が問われます。音を出すことに関しては、どのようなことに気をつけられましたか。

青木 ── 少し高めの音で、でも、うるさくない、風で木が揺らぐときの枝と葉っぱがサヤサヤする音の感覚に近いものを目指しました。

松山 ── 音の調整は、スピーカーも照明もセットした状態で、設営の場でプログラミングしました。単なる動きではなく、〈ぼよよん〉という概念を体感してもらう。このことがきわめて重要で、展示体験の短い時間に鑑賞者に概念にまで行き着いてもらうためには〈加速〉が必要になります。〈インタラクティブ〉な展示とするには、先ほど言いました〈遅れ〉のほかに、〈加速〉も必要です。

川向 ── なるほど。それによって体験が強められ、展示の意図が鮮明に伝わるようになりました。

それから今回の展示に関しては、オカムラ、ニューオータニ、近隣の小学生も巻き込むためのさまざまな試みがあったことも特筆すべきです。例えば、リングの製作に当たっては、オカムラから技術的サポートを得ました。

全員を巻き込む〜提案したいのは世界のあり方

青木 ── ものの製作という点では、工程やコストの調整の面でも、オカムラにサポートしていただきました。オカムラの工場で樹脂を扱っていて、協力してくださるというので、試作の型づくりをお願いして、ポリプロピレンの製作方法から、どのくらいのリングの太さ、径の大きさでいくかを決めていきました。

川向 ── ODS-R は、ポスター・DM のデザインも、オープニングパーティの趣向も、会期中のワークショップなどの内容と開催回数も、建築家に決定権を委ねていますが、青木さんは、すべて〈ぼよよん〉でいくという徹底ぶりでした。オープニングパーティの「ぼよよんの料理」は、あれ自体が創作料理として一級品でした。

青木 ── オープニングパーティの「ぼよよんの料理」は、ホテルニューオ

左・中：ホテルニューオータニのシェフが手がけた「ぼよよんの料理」が、オープニングパーティに彩りを添えた。
右：「ぼよよんの料理」を説明するシェフ

Left and Center: The *"boyoyong cuisine"* prepared by the chefs at the Hotel New Otani livened up the opening party. Right: The head chef explaining *"boyoyong cuisine."*

As I was testing out whether that made for a sufficient experience, though, I realized it would be more effective if sound was a factor, too. The word *boyoyong* is kind of humorous to begin with, and I wanted to find a way to spice it up further with a dash of Aoki's personality, so I tweaked the audio to sound like *bo-yo-yo-ng*, with each syllable synched to the cycle of the vibrations. In terms of effective "movement," then, light took on a subordinate role.

Kawamukai — At night, when no one else was there, the cloud as a whole, illuminated, silent, and absolutely still, was hauntingly beautiful. During the day, when children came in and shook the thing, triggering sounds and flashing lights, it transformed into something active and lively. I was very taken with this duality. The location of the exhibition in the New Otani, though, must have raised issues of sound volume and quality. What precautions did you take with regard to producing sound?

Aoki — I wanted a sound that was a bit high without being annoying, one that had the feel of a tree's leaves and branches rusting in the breeze.

Matsuyama — We programmed and adjusted the sound on site after setting up the lights and the speakers. The idea was to convey not just any old movement but the experience of *boyoyong*. This was extremely important, and leading visitors to this conceptual realization during a very short interaction with the exhibit required acceleration. Interactive exhibits need both delay, which I mentioned earlier, and acceleration.

Kawamukai — I see. This made the exhibition experience more evocative and ensured that its intent was conveyed with greater clarity. I think it's worth noting that the exhibition incorporated a lot of experimentation involving the Okamura Corporation, the New Otani, and even students from a nearby elementary school. You received technical support, for example, from Okamura when having the rings manufactured.

Get Everyone Involved: The World as it Should Be

Aoki — In terms of manufacturing, both process and cost, Okamura was very supportive. Okamura has factories that handle resin and agreed to help us out, so we had them produce test molds for us and worked together to determine everything from how to prepare the polypropylene to the thickness and diameter of the rings.

「ぼよよん」展の設営の様子。
ひとつひとつ、手作業でリン
グをつなげていった

Installation of the *Boyoyong*
exhibition. The rings were
connected by hand, one-
by-one.

ータニのシェフにつくっていただきました。〈ぼよよん〉のイメージをこ
ちらからは特に説明しなかったのですが、素晴らしい料理を何種類も並
べてくれました。

それから、〈雲〉を構成するリングは、大勢で一気に組み立てることが
できるようにデザインしてありましたので、この会場に来て、子どもた
ちにも一緒につくってもらいたいと当初から考えていました。ですから、
子ども向けワークショップを開催してみたのです。

川向 ── 大人も子どもも、全員が参加できるように設計されていたとこ
ろに、今回の展示の哲学を感じました。子どもの目線も十分に考慮され
ていて、どこか〈はらっぱ〉の思想にも通じるものがありました。実際、
リングを使って大勢で一気に〈雲〉が組み立てられていく光景は感動的
でした。

青木 ── 今回、ほとんど自分たちで施工しました。施工者に発注すること
を極力減らし、結束バンドによるジョイントとか、ほとんど手作りでで
きるように設計しました。撤去するときも、ぶどう狩りならぬ「ぼよよ
ん狩り」にして、結束バンドをペンチで自由にカットして持ち帰っても
らうことにしました。

川向 ── 本当に最後まで楽しませていただきました。さて、あの「ぼよよ
ん」展から数年がたちました。その後、〈ぼよよん〉がどのように展開し
たかについてお話しくださいますか。

真に完全な、安定した環境とは

青木 ──「ぼよよん」展の環境は、固定した環境ではなくて、揺らぐもの
でした。揺らすと光と音が出て変化します。ですが、揺らいで変化した
としても、全体のイメージは変わりません。リングが増えても減っても、
少々のことでは印象が変わりません。そういう意味では、繊細で弱くて
許容力もある環境だけれど、そういう性質を持つ点で、私自身、これが
すごく強固な環境だとも感じました。よく考えてみれば、自然の環境と

Kawamukai — For the ODS-R, the architect is given full discretion to decide everything from the design of posters and direct mailings, the planning of the opening party, the number of workshops to hold during the term of the exhibition, and what they should cover. Aoki, you were consistent in going with *boyoyong* for everything; at the opening party you even served "*boyoyong* cuisine," which turned out to be a first-rate dining experience.

Aoki — It was the chefs at the New Otani who put together the *boyoyong* menu for the opening party; I didn't give them any special directions about how to think about *boyoyong,* but they really came up with some amazing dishes.

Also, I designed the rings in such a way that the cloud could be assembled all at once by a large number of people so I was hoping from the outset that we could have some kids come to work with us on putting things together. That's one reason I chose to hold a workshop for children.

Kawamukai — The fact that things were designed in such a way that everyone could take part—adults and children alike— seemed to reveal the philosophy underlying the exhibition. The child's perspective was taken into consideration, and this seemed somehow consistent with the notion of an "open field." Indeed, it was impressive to see so many people come together all at once to put together the cloud.

Aoki — We did most of the construction ourselves this time. The project was designed to be almost entirely handmade, and to reduce outsourcing as much as possible. We used zip ties, for example, to connect the rings. Then, when we took down the piece, we used the "pick-your-own" model, letting people clip the zip ties with a pair of pliers and take home as much *boyoyong* as they wanted.

Kawamukai — Yes, it was great fun all the way to the very end. Well, it's been a few years now since the *Boyoyong* exhibition. Could you talk a little bit about where *boyoyong* led?

左：「ぼよよん」のリングを
つくる、子ども向けのワーク
ショップの様子。右：ワーク
ショップのときだけ、揺れに
連動して会場がカラフルに
輝くようにした

Left: A *boyoyong* ring-making workshop for children. Right: Just for the workshop, colorful lighting in the venue was linked to the shaking of the rings.

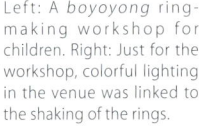

CHAPTER-4   Boyoyong   **151**

「杉並区大宮前体育館」（青木
淳建築計画事務所、2014）

Omiyamae Gymnasium in
Suginami (Jun Aoki & Associates, 2014).

いうのはそもそも、そういうものですね。

実際の建築を設計する中で、いろいろなことが起きても許容できる〈完
成しない強さ〉を考えることが多くなりました。「杉並区大宮前体育館」
（2014）では、できた後にポスターとか注意書きがたくさん貼られていく
のですが、それでも変わらず、大丈夫だという環境のあり方を考えました。
設計者としての自分の手を離れて、いろいろなことが起きてもその場の
質が維持される環境の追求は、〈ぽよよん〉から発展したものです。

その実現のためには方法論が必要だと思いますが、今のところ、それを〈解
像度〉の違いから考えてみようとしています。解像度を変えると、見え
る姿が変わってきます。バラバラを許す解像度と、バラバラを許さない
解像度があるわけですが、そういう解像度の異なる姿をミルフィーユの
ように重ねていけないかと思うのですね。

建築の許容度を上げる方法として、まず思いつくのは、インフラとイン
フィルに分けるということです。どんなインフィルも許容できるインフ
ラをどうつくるかという問題設定です。この場合は解像度の層が2層で
すが、もっと層を重ねられないか。層を重ねたのがミルフィーユです。

川向 ── 松山さんのその後は、いかがですか。

西洋的・東洋的な美の感覚

松山 ── KAPPES というチームで「MOMENTum」（2014）という作品をつ
くりました。縁から水が出てきて玉状になり、水の粒が模様を描いては、

What's a Truly Safe and Stable Environment?

Aoki — The environment for the *Boyoyong* exhibition was not a stable environment but one that shook. Shaking the cloud caused changes in light and sound, but even when it was shaking and changing the overall impression remained the same. Making modest changes like increasing or decreasing the number of rings wouldn't really have changed the piece at all. In this sense it was a delicate, weak, and tolerant environment. Having this temperament, I think, made it a very powerful one. When you stop to think about it, that's really the essence of a natural environment, isn't it?

When designing actual buildings, I've come to think a lot about a kind of "strength in incompleteness" that can cope with all sorts of things that might happen. All sorts of posters and announcements are likely to be put up at the Omiyamae Gymnasium in Suginami (2014), but I conceived of an environment where that would be okay, where it wouldn't make any real difference. My pursuit of environments that maintain their quality of place even after they leave my hands as an architect—even after all sorts of things occur—is something that developed out of *Boyoyong*.

I think achieving such environments requires a methodology, and for now I'm trying to think about it as a matter of resolution. Changing the resolution alters the way things appear. There are resolutions that tolerate inconsistency and resolutions that do not, and I've been wondering if I could layer the appearances that result from these varying resolutions like in a *mille-feuille* pastry.

As a means of raising a building's tolerance, the first thing that comes to mind is dividing it into infrastructure and infill. You define the problem as being how to build an infrastructure that can accept any sort of infill. That makes two layers of resolution, but I wonder if I can add more layers, and end up with something like a *mille-feuille*.

Kawamukai — And Matsuyama, what projects have you been working on since then?

Western and Eastern Aesthetics

Matsuyama — I created the MOMENTum (2014) installation as part of the Kappes creative team. Beads of water come out from the edge of a basin, forming patterns as they fall and disappearing down an aperture at its center.

「MOMENTum」（KAPPES、2014）

MOMENTum (Kappes, 2014)

真ん中の穴に消えていきます。

川向 ── 水の粒の動く様子が、幼稚園の園庭を駆け回る子どもたちみたいじゃないですか。

松山 ── 水の混沌とした感じを引き立たせるために、対照的に、規則的に水の粒を出しています。本来は整わないはずの水を粒々にして規則的なパターンにねじ伏せ、このように秩序づけて魅力を感じるのは、西洋的な美の感覚だと思うのです。不規則で制御できない状態にも美を感じるのは、東洋的な感覚だと思います。この二極にある美の感覚を最近考えていました。「ぼよよん」はこの中間なのか、両者の融合なのか。いずれにしても、これは、あの延長線上にあります。

アートよりは家具としてやってみたいので、「MOMENTum」はテーブルにしています。自分がつくった作品は暮らしの中で日常的に味わってほしいという気持ちを以前から持っていました。日常に入り込むには、建築と一体になって何かできれば面白いなと思っています。その意味でも「ぼよよん」は、いい経験になりました。

川向 ── 広い意味でのシステム設計が、建築でも求められていますが、まさに〈ぼ・よ・よ・ん〉的な、ユーモラスで、緩めのシステムを松山さんには、いろいろと考えてもらいたいですね。

松山 ── 可能性は、まだまだあります。例えば、「MAKE HOUSE 木造住宅の新しい原型展」（2014）で、建築家・吉村靖孝さんのプロジェクト「アプリの家」のために、自分で設計でき、すぐ値段がわかるアプリ「House Maker」（2014）をつくりました。最終的に建築に組み込まれるシステムではなく、設計段階での思考のためのツールをつくるという、建築家とのコラボレーションもあり得るかなと思っています。

川向 ── 誰にでも使える思考ツールというところがいいですね。どうも、ありがとうございました。

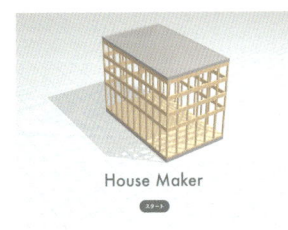 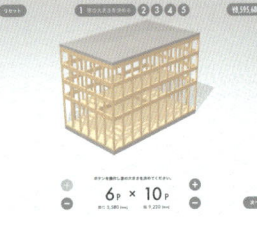 

House Maker

6ᴘ × 10ᴘ

アプリ「House Maker」(松山
真也、2014) の操作画面

Operation screen for the
House Maker app (Shinya
Matsuyama, 2014).

Kawamukai — The movement of the water droplets is a lot like that of children running around a kindergarten playground, isn't it?

Matsuyama — In order to highlight the chaotic feel of the water we had the water droplets emerge, by contrast, at regular intervals. Twisting water, which resists tidy alignment, into droplets that form regular patterns—imposing an appealing order—reflects, I think, a Western aesthetic. Finding beauty in the irregular and uncontrollable, meanwhile, reflects an Eastern aesthetic. I've been thinking a lot recently about these two opposing aesthetic sensibilities, and whether *Boyoyong* stood between them, or merged the two. In any case, MOMENTum is an extension of the same idea.

I am more interested in creating things that function as furniture than as works of art, so I made MOMENTum in the form of a table. For a while now I've wanted the things I make to be enjoyed as part of everyday life. I am interested in getting involved in the everyday through integration with architecture, and in this sense, *Boyoyong* was a good experience.

Kawamukai — System design broadly is something that architecture needs, too, of course, and I hope you'll come up with all sorts of systems that share that same humorous, *bo-yo-yo-ng* looseness.

Matsuyama — There are still lots of possibilities. For example, I designed the House Maker application, which enabled users to design their own houses and immediately get a price estimate, for architect Yasutaka Yoshimura's App House project at the Make House exhibition (2014). This made me realize the potential for collaboration with architects not just through systems integrated into final works of architecture but also through tools for thinking that are used during the design phase.

Kawamukai — I like the idea of tools for thinking that anyone can use. Thank you very much.

CHAPTER–4 Boyoyong 155

CHAPTER —— 5

Flow_er

ARCHITECT
Akihisa Hirata

GARDEN PLANNER / FLOWER ARTIST
Yuichi Tsukada

建築家
平田晃久

ガーデンプランナー／フラワーアーティスト
塚田有一

158　第 5 章　Flow_er

CHAPTER-5　Flow_er　159

160　第 5 章　Flow_er

CHAPTER-5 Flow_er 161

私たちのからだの大半は水でできている。地表面に水が流れているのと同様、私たちのからだの中にも、水が流れている。

植物の中にも、水が流れている。というよりむしろ、植物の形そのものが、水の流れである。「みどり」という言葉が「みず」と同様の語源を持つのも、全く自然なことだ。

近代的な建物の中にも、水が流れている。しかしそこでは水という自然が、人工的な配管のシステムの中にほとんど完全に制御されている。そんな中で日々を過ごす私たちも、自分たちが水という自然に貫かれていることを、忘れている。

ここでは近代的なオフィス空間のただ中に、水と構造体と植物がからみ合った、庭とも建築ともつかない光景をつくろうとした。中央にあるアクリルの構造体を伝って、水が一枚の花のようにひろがりながら、流れ落ちる。この水の流れと、様々な植物がからみ合う。人は、この奇妙な混ざり合いの中に入り、目に見える、あるいは見えない様々な流れに、耳を澄ます。これは、庭師の思考に導かれながら、建築のかたい殻を、水の流れの中に解き放つ試みであり、私たちのからだを、変化する水の様態の中に解き放つ試みである。

（展示コンセプト文より）

162 　第5章　Flow_er

CHAPTER-5 Flow_er

Our bodies are made up mostly of water. Just as water flows beneath the surface of the ground, so water flows within our bodies. Water flows within plants, too. Or rather, the very shape of plants is that of the flow of water. It is completely natural that Japanese word *midori* (greenery) should share etymological roots with the word *mizu* (water). Water flows, too, within modern buildings, although this natural element is managed almost completely within a system of manmade plumbing. Living in this midst, we forget that we ourselves are run through with water. Here, right in the middle of a modern office space, we tried to create a space that was neither garden nor building but a tangling of water and structure and vegetation. Water conveyed from the acrylic structure in the center spreads like a flower, then falls and flows. This flow of water is entangled with many plants. People enter this strange mix and listen carefully to various seen and unseen flows. Following the mindset of a gardener, this is an effort to open the hard shell of architecture in the flow of water, to open our bodies to the changing state of water.

(Exhibition concept, July 2012)

水と花で、
〈からまりしろ〉を生体化する

平田晃久
塚田有一
川向正人

建築家
平田晃久

1971 年 大阪府生まれ。京都大学大学院工学
研究科修了後、伊東豊雄建築設計事務所を
経て、2005 年 平田晃久建築設計事務所設
立。主な作品に桝屋本店 (2005)、alp (2010)、
Bloomberg pavilion (2011) ほか

ARCHITECT
Akihisa Hirata

*Born in Osaka in 1971, Hirata completed his
postgraduate studies at the Kyoto University
Graduate School of Engineering. After working at
Toyo Ito & Associates, Architects, he established
the Akihisa Hirata Architecture Office in 2005.
Major works include Masuya (2005), Alp (2010),
and the Bloomberg Pavilion (2011).*

川向 ─ オカムラのショールームを使っての、建築以外の表現者とのコラ
ボレーションをお願いしましたが、この依頼を受けて、最初にどんなこ
とをお考えになりましたか。

〈からまりしろ〉

平田 ─ 今、一番関心のあることをやりなさい、というお題がありまし
たから、生きている世界と建築をつなげる方法を考えたいと思いました。
もともと生き物の世界に関心があって、生物学者になりたいと思ったこ
ともありました。人間という生き物のつくる建築が、その根本のところで、
生物の世界に近づくことは自然だと考えています。20 世紀の近代建築は、

Bringing Alive
a "Tangled Place" of Water and Flowers

AKIHISA HIRATA
YUICHI TSUKADA
MASATO KAWAMUKAI

ガーデンプランナー／フラワーアーティスト

塚田有一

1991 年 立教大学経営学部卒業後、草月流家元
アトリエなどを経て独立、「温室」を主宰。花
活けやイベントのディスプレイなどのグリーンデ
ザインを多数手がける。 庭や花のデザインを通
して、人と自然の経路を開くことを試みる

GARDEN PLANNER / FLOWER ARTIST

Yuichi Tsukada

After working at a number of places including
the atelier of the head of the Sogetsu school of
ikebana, Tsukada became independent. As head
of Onshitsu, he engages in flower arranging and
numerous other forms of green design including
events and displays. Through the design of
gardens and flowers, he seeks to open channels
between man and nature.

Kawamukai — We asked you to use the Okamura showroom for a
collaborative project with someone from a creative field outside
of architecture. What were your first thoughts when you heard this
request?

Tangled Places

Hirata — When I heard that the "assignment" was to do whatever
I was most interested in at the time, I decided I wanted to explore
methods for connecting architecture and the living world. I've
always been interested in the world of living things; there was a time

自然や環境と切り離し、独立した秩序をつくることを理想としていましたが、21世紀には異なる理想が掲げられるべきだと思います。建築も生物世界とつながっているという考え方から生まれる本当の意味でエコロジカルな建築をつくろうとするならば、20世紀とは違う概念によってアプローチしなければならない。僕は、この21世紀の新しい課題に正面から取り組みたい。

20世紀の近代建築が「空間」をつくり、それを人工的にコントロールすることを目指したとすれば、僕は、例えば、1本の木に小動物が暮らし、鳥が巣をつくり、そこに植物が生えたりして、さまざまな生き物がからまっていくように、さまざまな〈からまりしろ〉をつくることを目指したいのです。〈からまりしろ〉が最大化していくような建築が生き物の秩序に近いのではないかという仮説を立てた本『建築とは〈からまりしろ〉をつくることである』(2011)も書きました。

川向 ── 平田さんにお願いしたのは、〈からまりしろ〉という概念が、大きな環境から建築、インテリア、そして私たちの身体に近いところまで、いくつもの次元に共通する現象を捉えていて、これが、これからの建築全般にとっても、このODS-Rの企画構想にとっても、とても大切だと思ったからです。

平田 ──ありがとうございます。「Flow_er」展が行われた2012年は、東日本大震災の翌年でもあり、より根本的なレベルで〈からまりしろ〉の問題を考え直そうとしていたときでした。建築を、単に内部機能の充足のための器械としてではなく、例えばその屋根ひとつにしても、雨水が流れてできる自然地形に近い、まさに〈からまりしろ〉として考えるならば、人間と自然のどんな新しい関係が生まれるか。屋根を流れた雨水は、やがて自然地形の上を流れていきます。人工物と自然がさまざまなレベルでからまり合い、つながることによって、水の流れ、空気の流れ、人やほかの生物の動きが成り立っています。さまざまなものが、互いに、からまり合う。これが生き物の世界であって、建築もその一部だと考え

〈からまりしろ〉の建築。「architecture farm」(平田晃久建築設計事務所、2009) ダイアグラム(左)と模型(右)

"Tangled place" architecture as seen in a diagram (left) and a model (right) for *Architecture Farm* (Akihisa Hirata Architecture Office, 2009)

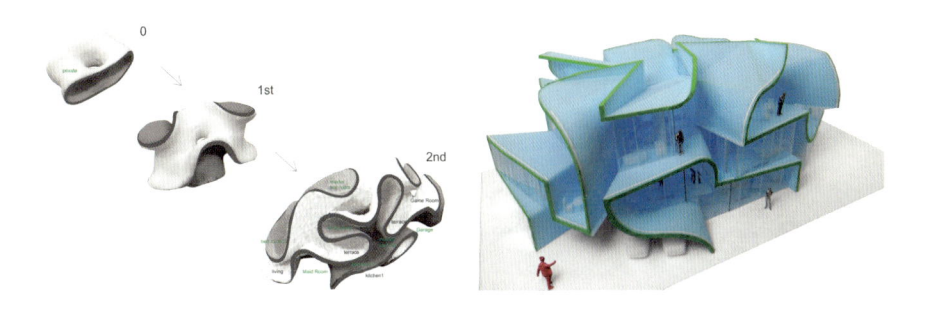

166　第5章　Flow_er

when I even hoped to become a biologist. I think it's only natural that architecture—which is built by living humans, after all—seeks to draw closer to the living world in some fundamental way. The modern architecture of the twentieth century sought to separate itself from nature and the environment, to impose some autonomous order, but I think we must raise a different banner in the twenty-first century. If we want to make architecture that's ecological in the truest sense— that's grounded in the notion that architecture is linked to the living world—then we have to take a conceptual approach unlike that of the twentieth century. I'd like to tackle this new, twenty-first century challenge head-on.

If the modern architecture of the twentieth-century aimed to build "spaces" that could be artificially controlled, then I aim to create "tangled places"—great jumbles of living things like trees inhabited by small animals, and in which birds build nests, and on which plants grow. I even wrote a book laying out my hypothesis that architecture that maximizes "tangled places" may best approximate living systems: Kenchiku to wa <karamarishiro> wo tsukuru koto de aru [Tangling] (2011).

Kawamukai — The reason we approached you was that we felt your concept of tangled places captured a number of phenomena common across multiple dimensions from the greater environment to architecture, interiors, and even our very bodies, and that it was important not only for the planning and conception of the ODS-R exhibition but also for the whole field of architecture going forward.

Hirata — Thank you. The Flow_er exhibition was held in 2012, the year after the Great East Japan Earthquake, at a time when I was thinking about fundamentally reevaluating the idea of "tangled places." What new relationships would be formed between man and nature if we could think about buildings not simply as instruments for satisfying interior functionality but rather as tangled places—seeing roofs, for example, as things that approximate the natural features formed by flowing water? The rainwater that flows across a roof eventually flows across natural features. It is through the multi-layered and complex interweaving and inter-connection of the artificial and the natural that the flow of water, the flow of air, and the movements of people and other animals take shape. All sorts of things are all tangled up together. This is the world of living things and I try to think of architecture as a part of it. For the ODS-R exhibition I was thinking about creating an installation that expressed the idea of tangled

ようとしています。ODS-R でも、この〈からまりしろ〉、特に建築と水の流れ、植物の関係にフォーカスしたアイデアをインスタレーションで表現することを考えました。

そして当時、実際の建築の仕事でもコラボレーションし始めていた塚田さんに、ODS-R のコラボレーターをお願いすることにしました。

コラボレーション〜水と緑の世界へ

川向 ── われわれの生きる〈世界〉のあるべき姿を、その内部に入って実際に体験できる建築とかインスタレーションによって示す。この〈世界〉の構築には、塚田さんのような異種の知識・技術を持つコラボレーター、つまり、最終的に目指すところは同じだが、異なるアプローチをとるがゆえに互いに触発し合い、啓発し合えるコラボレーターがいたほうがいい。それが平田さんの場合は、塚田さんです。実際の建築設計でも、またこの ODS-R でも、塚田さんをコラボレーターに選ばれた理由をもう少し説明してください。

平田 ── 塚田さんとは、言葉に対するアプローチが正反対といってもいいほど違うのです。たまに、思ってもみなかったような言葉のつながりに気づかされて、刺激を受ける。特に、塚田さんが「みづ（旧かな遣いでは水を「みづ」と表す）」と「みどり」の語源は同じだし「緑は水の一形態なんだよね」とおっしゃったのはとても印象的でした。そう言われて、川を上から見ると、なるほど、樹形になっています。植物は根から幹へと吸い上げた水を枝分かれさせ、最後に空中に解き放ちます。川や植物が水に形態を与えているのです。そんなところからアイデアの原形が少しずつ見えてきました。

空気中の 1 点から水を落とすと、何も抵抗のない場所では、まっすぐに落ちていきます。〈からまりしろ〉がない状態だといえます。「Flow_er」展では逆に〈からまりしろ〉を設けて、植物の幹から枝へと分岐するように水が広がりながら、ゆっくりと時間をかけて少しずつ落ちていきます。どうしたらできるだけ滞空時間を長くすることができるかを考えました。山に雨が降り、ゆっくりしみ込んで地下水となり、川となって流れていく。あるいは木が根から雨水をゆっくり吸い上げて、細かくして空気中に放つ。この水の変形過程の途中に、緑があり、人間の身体があり、さらに建築がある。そんなことを、ODS-R でやりたいなと思いました。

川向 ── これらの話を受けて、塚田さんは、どんな構想を持たれたのですか。

塚田 ── 平田さんの〈からまりしろ〉という考え方に共鳴しました。立て花は「依り代」が原形ともいわれています。「しろ」は依り代とか、糊代ともいうように余地のある場所、何かを受け入れる空いた場所、そんな

places, focusing in particular on architecture and its relationship to plants and the flow of water.

At the time I was starting to work with Tsukada on architectural projects so I decided I would ask him to collaborate with me on the ODS-R, too.

Collaboration: A World of Water and Greenery

Kawamukai — Creating an installation or a work of architecture that, when actually entered, makes it possible to experience the way the world we live in really ought to be—constructing such a world is a lot easier if you have a collaborator equipped with different knowledge and different skills, someone with whom partnering leads to cross-stimulation and enlightenment precisely because you approach things in different ways. In your case this was Tsukada. Could you explain a bit more about why you chose to collaborate with him both for actual architectural design projects and for the ODS-R?

Hirata — Tsukada approaches language in a way that is perhaps the exact opposite of the way I do. Sometimes he notices relationships between words that I had never considered, and in a way that's thought provoking. It left a real impression, for example, when he pointed out that the Japanese words for water (*mizu* or, in the old days, *midzu*) and greenery *(midori)* have a common etymology and said, "Greenery is really just water in another form." This made me realize that a river seen from above takes the shape of a tree. Plants draw water through their roots to their trunk, divide it among their branches, and then ultimately release it into the air. Rivers and plants give shape to water. This is the sort of thing that, little by little, revealed the germ of an idea.

If you release a drop of water in midair in a space where there is no resistance, it will fall straight down. This might be called an untangled state. For the *Flow_er* exhibition, though, we set up tangled places where water fell slowly, over time, bit by bit, spreading in the same way that it diverges from trunk to branches. We tried to think about how we could extend the water's "flight time" for as long as possible. When rain falls in the mountains, it soaks slowly into the soil, becomes groundwater, and then flows on as a river—or perhaps is slowly drawn up by the roots of a tree, made microscopic, and released into the air. In this process of water's transformation, there is greenery, there is the human body, and there is architecture. This was

意味を持つと思います。そこには植物や鳥の声がからんでいく。そんな場所とからむことで生命体が根を張り、場所が生き生きする。

平田さんがおっしゃったように、水と緑の話をしました。「みづ」と「みどり」は語根が一緒です。水もまた、からまり、しみ込み、満ちていくわけですが、何より命の源ですよね。植物から水が抜ければしおれ、やがて枯れる。それは命が「離れる」ことでもあります。しかし、枯れると乾いて軽くなって、次の命の生まれる場所になります。また緑は、水の循環装置であり収集装置でもあります。

震災後ということもありまして「風土」のことを集中的に考えていた時期でもありました。水がからまってできるこの透明な風景は山であり、水に浮く島であり、まさに日本列島の模型でした。日本の作庭に見られるように水のもたらす情緒を反映させたものにしたいと思いました。水がからまりつつ落ちていく風景が、精神的な意味を帯びた〈山〉となり、同時に〈島〉にもなるようなストーリーを考えたい。それは複雑な地形を持ち、海に囲まれた日本列島の原型のようにも見え始め、同時にそこに多様な植物がからんできます。この水と緑の風景づくりには、生け花や庭づくりの手法を敷衍して使えるのではないかと考えました。

からむことで、ゆっくり流れる

川向 ── 平田さんの構想の中心に、広がり、からんで、ゆっくりと時間をかけて流れる水のイメージがあります。緑の内部にも、水は広がり、からみ、ゆっくり流れる。

平田 ── 流れているものを取り出して、顕在化させることを今、「（仮称）

「（仮称）太田駅北口駅前文化交流施設」（平田晃久建築設計事務所）。模型

Model for the provisionally named Ota Station North Entrance Center for Culture and Exchange (Akihisa Hirata Architecture Office) the sort of thing I wanted to do for the ODS-R.

Kawamukai — Tsukada, what did you think when you heard about the project?

Tsukada — I was really taken with Hirata's idea of tangled places (*karamarishiro*). Japanese flower arranging is said to have roots in the concept of *yorishiro*, places where the divine is revealed. Hirata's *shiro* seemed to recall this—as well as *norishiro*, the edges on a piece of paper left open for the application of glue—that is, it suggests a place with room to spare, open and ready to accept the arrival of something else, like plants or the chirping of birds. When entangled in such a place, living things set down roots and the place comes alive.

As Hirata mentioned, I did talk about water and greenery. *Midzu* and *midori* do share the same etymology. Water, too, becomes entangled, and seeps, and fills, but most of all it is the source of life. In the absence of water, plants fade and wither. To wither *(kareru)* means the withdrawal (*kareru*) of life. Yet when something withers it dries out, and grows lighter, and becomes a place for the next life to emerge. Greenery is also a mechanism for circulating and storing water.

In part because it was after the earthquake, I was spending a lot of time back then thinking about the idea of *fudo* (the climate and natural features of a place). Our transparent, water-entangled landscape was a mountain, a floating island—really the Japanese archipelago in miniature. I wanted to do something that reflected the kind of water-generated atmosphere you see in the construction of Japanese gardens. I wanted to develop a story in which landscapes of tangling, falling water became mountains—and at the same time islands, too—that were charged with a spiritual significance. I began to envision a kind of primal Japanese archipelago, surrounded by the sea, with complex natural features, and that was entangled with a diversity of plants. In creating this landscape of water and greenery I also felt I might be able to stretch the methods of ikebana flower arranging and garden construction.

Flowing Slowly by Becoming Entangled

Kawamukai — Hirata, your concept was built around an image of water spreading, tangling, and flowing slowly over time. Even within the greenery, the water would spread, and tangle, and flow.

Hirata — I'm working on a project now, tentatively called the Ota Station North Entrance Center for Culture and Exchange, that tries

太田駅北口駅前文化交流施設」で試みています。ここでは主に人の流れ
がテーマになっています。群馬県太田市ではほとんどの人が車に乗って
移動するので、駅前は閑散としています。車で目的地から目的地に移動
し、郊外型ショッピングセンターの中だけを歩きます。町を歩く人がいて、
からまることで初めて市街地もにぎわう。ところが現実は逆で、人は速
いスピードで通り過ぎ、からみ合っていない。そういう状況に一石を投
じようとしています。

川向 ── ただ流れるのではなく、からみ合って、ゆっくり流れることに、
意味があるということですね。私がまちづくりに参加している長野県小
布施町の場合も、車社会になってしまって、何事をするにも、住民は車
で表通りを移動します。昔は、どこに行くにも人々は、田畑のあぜ道や
町の路地を、時には近道しながら歩いて移動したものです。だから、あ
ちこちに人の姿があって、町も村も全体に活気がありました。
もう一度「Flow_er」展に戻りますと、水の〈からまりしろ〉は、具体的
にどうつくられたのでしょうか。

〈襞〉をとること～関係と奥行き

平田 ──〈からまりしろ〉をつくる方法として考えたのは、〈襞〉をとるこ
とです。以前から、表面積を増やすことでできる形態をいろいろと研究し、
建築に応用することを試みていました。今回はアクリル板を使いました
が、同じ容積であっても、アクリル板を折り込んで〈襞〉をとっていくと、
表面積が増えます。増えたアクリル板の表面に薄く水をためつつ少しず
つ流すことで、広げ、からませ、ゆっくりと時間をかけて、水が落ちて
いくという状態が実現できたように思います。

川向 ── 建築の場合、空間境界に〈襞〉をとるということは、その内部か
ら見れば外部との接触面が増え、内部に外部が織り込まれて入ってくる
ことを意味しますね。

平田 ── はい。表面積が増えていきます。そもそも人間が建物を建てたり
都市化したりするのは、自分が扱える表面積を増やすためだということ
ができます。内部の床面積が同じでも、外部の都市や自然との接触を増
やすことで、建築が人間に与えるものがはるかに豊かになります。

川向 ── ええ。関係が豊かになります。〈襞〉の導入の仕方によって、内
と外だけではなく内と内、表と奥など、いろいろな関係が生まれてきます。

平田 ──〈奥行き〉が発生しますから、内と外という単純な分割ではなく
なります。現行の不動産価値の指標やいわゆる省エネルギーを軸にした
エコ建築は内外を単純に分割するから、閉じた内部を前提にしたエネル
ギー効率、内部の床面積だけに特化した話に終始する状況が生まれてい

to extract something that flows and make it tangible. In that case, the main concern is the flow of people. Almost everyone in Gunma prefecture's Ota city moves around by automobile, so the area in front of the station is pretty quiet. People move from destination to destination by car and only walk within suburban shopping centers. A city only really comes to life when people walk around and get tangled up in its streets. But the reality now is that people zip through at high speed without getting tangled at all, so I wanted to try and shake things up a little bit.

Kawamukai — So it's not only flow that's important, but also the fact that the flow moves slowly and entails entanglement, right? I'm involved in local community building efforts in the town of Obuse in Nagano prefecture, and local residents there, too, do most of their moving around using cars on the main roads. In the old days, though, people had to walk to get anywhere, following footpaths through the fields and back alleyways, taking an occasional shortcut along the way. There were people all over the place, and both the urban center and the outlying agricultural areas were part of a single, vital whole. Getting back to the *Flow_er* exhibition, how, in concrete terms, did you make "tangled places" using water?

Pleating: Relationship and Depth

Hirata — The method I came up with for creating a tangled place was what I call "pleating." I've researched shapes that increase surface area before, and applied them to my architectural work. We used acrylic sheets for the exhibition, so folding the acrylic back on itself made it possible to increase the surface area within a given volume. The acrylic sheets then captured a thin layer of water over that much greater an area, creating conditions where it could be shed, and spread, and tangled, and fall, more slowly, over time.

Kawamukai — For architecture, making pleats in spatial boundaries means, when seen from within, increasing the scope of the interface between interior and exterior while also bringing the outside inside.

Hirata — Right. It increases the surface area. You know, I think the whole reason people build buildings or create cities at all is to increase the surface area they can make use of. Even if the interior floor area is the same, increasing surface contact with the city or nature outside leads to architecture that gives people a much richer experience.

Kawamukai — Yes, richer relationships. Depending on how you

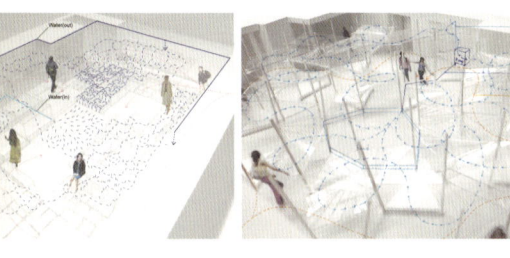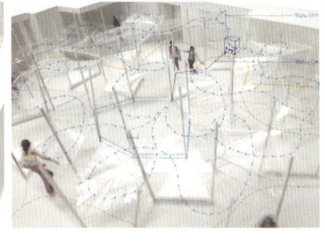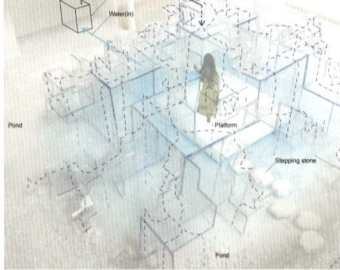

「Flow_er」展、水の流れのダイアグラム。左から2月、3月、5月時の提案。5月に山の形が現れた

Diagrams of proposed water flow at the *Flow_er* exhibition submitted in (from left) February, March, and May (when the mountain first appeared).

るともいえます。おっしゃるように、大切なのは関係の豊かさであって、奥行きとかグラデーションを伴う〈襞〉のある空間が求められるようになっていくと思っています。

襞のある〈山〉、〈島〉

川向 ── 同じ容積でも〈襞〉という概念を導入すると、まったく別の空間形状あるいは内部構成が生まれ、それによって風景ががらりと変わる可能性があるわけですね。

「Flow_er」展でも何回か打合せを重ねる過程で、最初はだんだんと下がってくるカスケードのような形状だったものが、〈襞〉を含む、全体としては山のような形状に変わっていったのが、すごく大きな変化だと思いました。

平田 ── ゆっくりと水を下ろすアクリルの面をどう折り畳むかをスタディしていたわけです。当初は、スパイラル状に下がっていくカスケードの案も検討しました。しかし、最終的にはもっと多様に分岐して広がる水の流れを生み出す、襞状の形態に落ち着きました。また、少し距離を置いて眺めたときの全体形状とか、内側に入っての体験可能性といった観点を加えて、最終的には、大きな山あるいは島のような塊にしたほうがいいと判断しました。あの全体構成の転換は、今回の構想が大きく展開する、ある種のブレークスルーだったと思います。

川向 ── 全体の姿が山に見えてきたとき、塚田さんは、ここから次に大きく展開しそうだなという印象は持ちましたか？

〈奥〉と〈間〉の発生〜内面の世界へ

塚田 ── 〈奥〉とか〈間〉があることで、もっと遠くまで想像力を膨らませることができます。昔の日本建築では、軽く遮られた〈間〉があるこ

introduce the pleats or folds, you can create relationships not only between interior and exterior but also among interiors, or between what's out front and what lies within.

Hirata — Yes, they create an element of depth that makes it impossible to divide things simply into inside and out. The current indices for assessing real estate or evaluating "eco-housing" based on energy efficiency just divide things into inside and outside, which is why they go no further than talking about interior floor space and the energy efficiency of closed-off interiors. As you've said, the important thing is the richness of the relationships, and I think people will more and more come to demand "pleated" spaces that offer depth and shading.

A Pleated "Mountain" or "Island"

Kawamukai — Incorporating pleats into a given volume creates entirely different spatial forms or interior compositions that have the potential to completely transform the scenery. It struck me as a real metamorphosis when, in the course of our many meetings leading up to the *Flow_er* exhibition, what began as a gradually descending cascade changed over time to become, in its totality, a stepped, pleated mountain.

Hirata — I was making a study of how to fold the acrylic surfaces in a way that would spill the water slowly. Initially I considered using a cascade that followed a descending spiral, but ultimately settled on a stepped, pleated form that led to more varied branching and spreading as the water flowed. In the end I decided it would be better, in terms of the shape of the whole when seen from a distance, and in order to leave open the possibility of entering the piece and experiencing it from the inside, to create a mass that was reminiscent of a mountain or an island. That shift in thinking about the overall composition was the kind of breakthrough that really took the concept to the next level.

Kawamukai — Tsukada, when you saw how the shape of the whole was starting to look like a mountain, did you have the sense that things would really take off?

Creating Depths and In-betweens: Interior Worlds

Tsukada — Having depths and in-betweens inspires the imagination

とで〈奥〉の存在を感じていたと思うのです。花や庭も同じで、「ここではないどこか」を引き寄せる技術だと思っています。庭があって季節のうつろいを見たときに、遙かなものに想いを馳せます。例えば、山の奥に「桃源郷」を、海の果て（＝沖）に蓬莱山とかニライカナイとか、いわゆる仙境を思い描きます。今回のインスタレーションでは、水の滴る山の形状の出現によって、この両者が１つになったところが、すごいと思いました。

〈襞〉についていうと、通常、植物をこれくらい使うだろうという量の倍ぐらいを用意したのですが、その量があっさり入ってしまいました。それだけ表面積が増えていたのです。〈襞〉がある空間は、次々と奥が生まれ、その分、関係性も増えることを体験できました。多層なものに包まれている感覚は、森などの中にいても感じるものですね。

川向 ── 内部へ、奥へと引き込んで、包み込む。私も、〈襞〉の効果には驚きました。

平田 ── 表面積が何倍にも増えていたと思います（笑）。同時に「築山（つきやま）」みたいなものになった瞬間に、外側から見る、内部で体験する、さらに〈襞〉によって内外が混ざるといった概念的な多重性が生まれてきました。塚田さんの蓬莱山の話など、それまでとは違う次元もからまってきたので、これは面白いなと感じました。

〈庭〉～１つの世界を内から体験する

川向 ── ODS-Rの企画展も回を重ねてきましたが、このショールームの一角を使いこなすには、内からの視点と外からの視点の両方を達成する必

塚田氏が描いた植物のレイアウトスケッチ

Plant layout sketch by Tsukada.

to reach further. In ancient Japanese architecture, lightly interrupted in-betweens created the sense of something beyond. As with flowers or gardens, this is a technique for drawing people toward "a somewhere other than here." When you observe the changing of the seasons in a Japanese garden, you imagine far-off places and enchanted lands, an earthly paradise deep in the mountains or a heavenly island across the sea. For this installation, the appearance of a mountainous form that was dripping with water seemed to combine both of these ideals in the most amazing way.

On the topic of pleats, I prepared twice as many plants as I thought I would need to use, but then ended up fitting them all in without any trouble. That's how much the surface area had increased. I was able to experience for myself the way a pleated space generates layers of depth and more relationships. The sense of being enveloped by something multilayered is a lot like the feeling of being in a forest.

Kawamukai — I was also surprised at how effective the pleating was in drawing people deeper into the interior and enveloping them there.

Hirata — I think the surface area must have multiplied many times. (*Laughs*) At the same time, from the moment it became something like a miniature *tsukiyama* mountain in a garden,, it generated a conceptual multiplicity in being seen from the outside, experienced from within, and then mixing inside and outside as a result of the pleating. I was really pleased with the way the piece became tangled up in new dimensions, like the earthly paradise Tsukada spoke about earlier.

Gardens: Experiencing One World From Within

Kawamukai — The ODS-R exhibition series has been running for a while now, and we've seen that making full use of that corner of the showroom really requires achieving both an outward-directed perspective and an inward-directed perspective. So far, none of the exhibitions have ever sought to rely only on viewing from a distance; all have prioritized experiencing the exhibition from within.

In the earliest stage it was important to think about how to entangle water and greenery with the acrylic structures that would become a "tangled place," but gradually the focus of discussions turned to the exhibition space itself, that is, how to get the work tangled with the space. Needless to say, relying on the walls and columns of the showroom wouldn't do at all; there was a need, even while meshing

要があるようです。これまでも、ただ遠くから眺めるだけというものは
なく、どの回も必ずといってよいほど、内に入っての体験を重視してい
ました。

最初の段階では、〈からまりしろ〉となるアクリルの構造物にどう水や植
物をからませるのかが重要でしたが、次第に議論の重点が、この展示ス
ペース、つまり場所自体へのからませ方に移っていきましたね。言うま
でもなく、ショールームの壁や柱に頼るような〈からまり〉ではダメで、
どこかで現実の場所にからみつつも自立した世界でなければならない。
このような意味で、ショールームという場所に根を下ろしつつ、次第に
自立した世界が立ち上がってくる過程は、感動的でした。

もう少し具体的にいえば、日本の作庭にある、奥に滝をつくり、その落
水が川となって手前に向かって流れてくるという手法が導入されたよう
に感じましたが。

塚田 ─ そうですね。山の形がだんだん見えてきて、京都の無鄰菴（むりんあん）を思い
浮かべました。そして無鄰菴に倣って、水の音の効果も取り入れること
にしました。下の建物の位置から眺めても、上の奥にある滝はほとんど
見えません。天気がいい日には、木の葉の裏に水からの反射光がきらめ
くのが、下からも眺められます。さらに、渡る風の音や訪れる鳥の声が
重なって聞こえてきます。流れには、ポリフォニックな音を響かせる仕
掛けがあります。水が落ちるときの落差、落ちた場所の水の深浅、流れ
に沿う石の配置、その水底に敷かれた砂利の大小などによって、音はさ
まざまに変わるのです。

平田 ─ 生き物のように広がる感じも出したかったのです。そのために、
ご指摘のように、既存の柱や壁に依存して寄りかかるように〈からまる〉
のではなく、それ自体が自立して生命力を感じさせるものでありたかっ
たのです。

〈建築〉～自然と人工の境界を秩序づける

川向 ─ さて、全体の姿が山あるいは島のようになりましたが、これで終
わったわけではありません。アクリル板の上に水を広げつつ、からませ、
しかも自然に見えるように落とすための検討作業は、さらに続きます。
あの検討作業の内容をご説明いただけますか。

平田 ─ ある流体の容積を薄く水平方向に延ばすことは、数学的には簡単
に考えられますが、実際の水の流れは違うもので、なかなかアクリル面
に沿って自然に広がってはくれないのです。われわれは、水の流れとい
うものをいったん抽象化して建築的仕組みに置き換えていくわけですが、
根本のところにギャップがあります。それは建築と自然の間にあるギャ

with the real world at some point, to create a world that stood on its own. In this sense, the process by which the piece, even as it set down roots in the showroom, gradually emerged to be independent of it, was impressive to see.

Being more specific, you seemed to incorporate a technique drawn from Japanese garden design, with a waterfall constructed in the back whose falling waters became a river that flowed toward the front.

Tsukada— That's right. As the mountain gradually took shape I was reminded of Murin-an Villa in Kyoto. I decided to follow the example of the Murin-an garden by incorporating the sound of water as an effect. At Murin-an, from the building below you can barely see the waterfall located above and to the back. On days with nice weather, though, you can see the sunlight reflected on the backs of the leaves from the water behind the trees. You can also hear the sound of the wind and the chirping of visiting birds. The flow is configured in a way that produces a polyphonic symphony; the height of each tier of the waterfall, the depth of water at each basin, the placement of rocks along the flow, and the size of the gravel over which the flow travels are all designed to produce a changing variety of sounds.

Hirata— I wanted the piece to conjure a sense of expansiveness as if it were a living thing. To do that, as you say, it was important not simply to rely on tangling with the existing walls and columns but rather to ensure that the thing itself had a sense of autonomy and vitality.

Architecture: Establishing Order at the Boundary Between Nature and the Man-made

Kawamukai— Well, even after the shape was established as a mountain or an island, your work wasn't done, was it? You still had to work out how to spread the water over the acrylic sheets and ensure that it fell in a way that was both entangling and appeared natural. Could you describe how you went about this?

Hirata— It's easy enough to think mathematically about spreading a given volume of liquid over a horizontal area, but a different matter altogether when dealing with actual water, which was not very cooperative in spreading naturally over the acrylic sheets. We approached the flow of water as an abstraction, as part of an architectural framework, but there was still a fundamental gap— perhaps the very gap that separates architecture and nature. The trick was not to simply understand water in the abstract and try

「Flow_er」展より。アクリルにあいた穴から均等に水が流れ落ち、たまり、植物の居場所をつくる

Flow_er exhibition. Apertures in the acrylic enabled the water to flow down evenly, pool, and create a place for plants.

ップそのものかもしれません。そこで、単に流水を抽象的に捉えて、そこで得られる秩序とか法則にすべてを押し込めるのではなく、逆に庭とか生け花の持っている秩序を尊重して、自然の中で建築をつくる感覚に近い、ギリギリの均衡を探ろうとしたわけです。

そのために、目の前の現象を徹底的に分析しました。水を大量に速く流すと、勢いよく流れすぎて、広がる前に水のスジがついてしまう。水をゆっくり少量ずつ流すと、流れているのかどうかがわからない。そばにいて人が水の流れを感じることができるようにしたかったので、水が止まっている感じは避けたい。そこで、絶妙の間隔でアクリルに小さな穴をあけ、広がりつつ流れ落ちるものをどうつくるかと、いろいろな水の落とし方と穴の大きさなどを試して、実にアナログ的に、泥くさくやりました（笑）。

to make it fit within some abstract order or principle, but rather to respect the order found in gardens and ikebana and adopt a process that felt more like designing in the natural world, like seeking a delicate equilibrium.

To achieve this, we thoroughly analyzed what was happening before our eyes. Quickly releasing large volumes of water led the water to flow too fast, forming rivulets before it had a chance to spread out. Slowly releasing water just a little at a time, though, made it difficult to see if it was even flowing.

Since we wanted people who were close to the water to be able to feel that it was flowing, this sense of motionlessness was something we wanted to avoid. So we opened small apertures in the acrylic at just the right intervals to make the water spread as it fell, something that took a lot of very analog, trial-and-error tinkering with ways of making the water fall and with different sized holes—really crude stuff. (*Laughs*)

Kawamukai — That seemed extremely architectural, though. Even when the object of study is something so minute as to even seem trivial, to step into that boundary region between the natural and the artificial and seek an equilibrium that produces the desired result is really the very essence of architecture. Changing the diameter or the pitch of the holes, not resting until the water was performing as you wanted, seemed like the sort of path our predecessors must also have traveled as they sought to cultivate from nature a kind of man-made beauty.

You also had to contend with the issue of acrylic sheets that sagged under the weight of the water and plants that they supported.

Shallow Layers of Flowing Water as a Material

Hirata — The raised edges determined the depth of the water while also serving as support beams. I wanted everything to seem thin, so instead of thinking about acrylic on its own I understood my material to be acrylic with water constantly flowing over its surface, assembling something three-dimensional and architectural that we then entangled with plants. Greenhouse architecture was the first to combine plants and glass, and took advantage of glass's unique properties, but I wanted to try something different. I wanted to create something that revealed the essential liquidity of water.

Kawamukai — I think it's a wonderful idea to understand the

「Flow_er」展より。ショー
ルーム内に池が出現した

The pond that appeared
in the showroom for the
Flow_er exhibition.

川向 ── 私は、そこがきわめて建築的だと感じました。対象が微細であっ
て、ささいなことに思われるかもしれませんが、自然と人工の境界領域
に踏み込んで、望ましい現象を得るためにギリギリの均衡を探っていく
のは、まさに建築の神髄です。穴の径とかピッチを変えて、望ましい水
の現象を獲得するまで探究の手を緩めない。自然を相手にして人工的な
美にまで高めるときに、先人たちも必ず通った道のように思えます。
上に載ってくる水や植物の量で、アクリル板のたわみの問題も出てきま
すね。

流れる薄い水の層こそがマテリアル

平田 ── 立ち上がり部分が水のたまる深さであって、梁成^{はりせい}でもあります。
すべてを薄く見せたいので、アクリルを単体で扱うというより、アクリ
ルの表面に常に水が流れている状態をマテリアルと捉えて、建築のよう
に立体的に組み立てました。そこに植物をからませます。植物とガラス
を最初に組み合わせたのは温室建築で、ガラスの特性を生かしたもので
すが、それとは違うものを試みたいと思いました。つまり、水の持つリ
キッド感が見えている状態をつくりたかったのです。

川向 ── アクリル板でもガラス板でもなく、流れる薄い水の層そのもの
が、空間を構成するマテリアルだというのは、素晴らしいアイデアです。
言われてみれば、われわれは、自然の滝や小川でも、無鄰菴の流水でも、
流れる薄い水の層そのものに魅せられているのかもしれませんね。アク
リル板だけで〈からまりしろ〉を構築して、そこに水や植物をからませ
るのではなく、アクリル板と水の層で〈からまりしろ〉を構築して、そ
こに植物をからませようとしていたわけですね。その実現は試行錯誤の

material by which you structured the space not as glass or acrylic but as shallow layers of flowing water. Come to think of it, such shallow layers of flowing water really exert an almost magnetic pull on us, whether natural waterfalls and creeks or the flowing waters at Murin-an. Rather than build a tangled place made of acrylic alone and then entangling it with water and plants, you built a tangled place made of acrylic and layers of water and only then entangled it with plants. Making it happen required a series of trial-and-error experiments, but the addition of the liquidity of water created a truly soft and gentle landscape that had depth without becoming heavy.

Hirata — Yes, the flowing water invested the piece with a distinctive texture.

Creating and Maintaining "Nature"

Kawamukai — There were also landscapes with pooled water, places reminiscent of ponds or swamps that one could imagine teeming with microorganisms. These created a natural atmosphere. How did you go about devising such scenery?

Tsukada — There were places in the flow where water pooled. There are actually only a limited number of kinds of plants that can be placed in very shallow water, so we created places that would hold larger volumes. Ease of maintenance was also a factor.

Kawamukai — Did you include plant species from overseas as well as those native to Japan?

Tsukada — We did. I wanted to create a space that looked natural but was unlike anyplace else. Creating other worlds is the essence of ikebana. I made a point to gather many kinds of plants that are readily available in big cities. For example, I gathered more than thirty varieties of aquatic plants used in aquariums like *marimo* round algae and *tanukimo* bladderwort.

Then, after seeing the exhibition site, I discussed things with Hirata and we decided to illuminate the piece only from the east, where natural light came in. In placing the plants, too, I put gentle spring grasses and white birch on the east side to create a spring-like brightness while on the west, where the plants would be backlit, I used plants with leaves of deeper green or yellow to suggest autumn. It's easy to lose your sense of the seasons and sense of direction when inside, so as soon as the mountain shape took form I decided to vary the placement of plants in accordance with their direction.

連続になりますが、水のリキッド感が加わり、厚みはあるが重たくはない、実に柔らかい風景が誕生してきますね。

平田 — はい。水が流れるときの独特の質感が加わります。

〈自然〉をつくり、維持する

川向 — 水がたまっている風景もありました。池とか沼のように微生物がいそうな場所もあって、ある種の自然な感じが生まれていました。その辺の工夫は、どのようにされましたか。

塚田 — 流れの中にも、たまりが生じていました。実際あまり薄い水では入れられる植物が限定されてしまいますので、水が多めに入る場所もつくってもらいました。手入れのしやすさも考慮に入れて。

川向 — 植物は日本のものだけではなくて、海外の品種もあったのですか。

塚田 — そうしました。自然に見せるけれども、どこにもない場所をつくりたいと思いました。別の世界をつくるということは、生け花の醍醐味でもあります。大都会だからこそ集められる植物を、あえて大量に入れました。例えばマリモとかタヌキモとか、アクアリウムで使う水生植物だけでも30種類以上使いました。

その上で、展示空間のオリエンテーションから平田さんと相談して、自然光の入る東からのライティングだけにしました。植物の配し方も、東側は春っぽく明るくしようと、春のやさしい草や白樺を入れて、西側は逆光になるので、濃い色の葉や黄色系の葉を入れて秋を表現しました。屋内にいると季節感とか方位の感覚もおかしくなりますから、山の形が出てきたので、方位に合わせて植物を配置することを考えました。

川向 — 会期中、毎朝会場にいらして手入れされていましたね。

塚田 — やはり、更新し、死んでいく部分があるのです。それらを片づけないと濁っていきます。水替えもしましたし、一部植物を差し替えたりもしました。

川向 — 会期中も、時間とエネルギーのかかる展示でした。大量の植物と水で生態系をつくっていたので、維持するのが並大抵ではなかったですね。ところで、真ん中に山ができ周囲に水が張られて島のようでもありましたが、水際は、どう仕上げたのですか。

平田 — 砂利を入れ、それを自然な岸になるように使いました。このオフィス空間に水がたまっていることが異常です（笑）。ですが、あくまでも自然に、1つの風景が突如そこに発生した感じを出そうとしました。実際は防水シートを敷いていますが、それをぼやかし、池がここに湧いて出たという感じになればいいなと思いました。

川向 — あの水は循環していたわけですが、思わぬ挙動をするかもしれな

Kawamukai — You visited the site every morning during the exhibition to tend the plants, didn't you?

Tsukada — Inevitably there are plants that die and need to be replaced. If these aren't cleared away it can create cloudiness in the water. I changed the water and also switched out plants as needed.

Kawamukai — It was an exhibition that required a lot of time and energy while it was up. You created an ecosystem of water and a great many plants and I can only imagine that maintaining it must have been quite a task.

But tell me, with a mountain in the middle surrounded by water that created the appearance of an island, how did you handle the water's edge?

Hirata — I added gravel to create the appearance of a natural shoreline. It was a bit odd seeing a pool of water in an office space. (*Laughs*) But I really wanted to create the impression of a decidedly natural landscape that had suddenly appeared. We laid down waterproof sheeting, of course, but I wanted to make its presence ambiguous in the hope that it would appear almost as if spring water had welled up in the spot.

Kawamukai — The water circulated but there was certainly the potential for the unexpected. Did you get through the exhibition without any accidents?

Hirata — I was very worried for about a week. At the same time, it would have been impossible to hold the exhibition had we decided that water was out of the question because of all the things that could go wrong. Using water, which has a life of its own—and moving water, to boot—is easy enough to talk about but when it comes to actually making things happen I was scared even though I had designed the piece, so I really appreciate how tolerant the folks at Okamura were.

Workshops: Narrative and the Sound of Water

Kawamukai — You ran two workshops during the term of the exhibition. Could you talk about them a little bit?

Tsukada — The two workshops were, respectively, *Meguribana* and a performance by Noh actor Noboru Yasuda called *The Sound of Water.*

The *meguribana* workshop, which involved audience participation in creating a collaborative arrangement by placing flowers in turn, was

左：ワークショップ「廻り花」。参加者は裸足になって水に入り、花を生ける。右：会期中に同じ会場で行われた能楽師 安田登氏の公演「水の音」

Left: *Meguribana* workshop, at which participants stepped barefoot into the water to arrange flowers.
Right: *The Sound of Water*, a performance by Noh actor Noboru Yasuda held at the venue during the period of the exhibition.

かった。事故もなく終わってよかったですね。

平田 ── 1週間くらいは、毎日心配でした。とはいえ、何かが起きることを心配して「水はダメだ」ということになったら、展示が成立しません。水という生ものを持ち込み、しかも動いている状態をつくる。言うのは簡単ですが、実際にやるのは設計者本人も怖かったくらいですから、オカムラの方々の懐の深さに感謝します。

ワークショップ～〈物語〉と水の〈音〉

川向 ── 会期中に2度、ワークショップを試みましたね。その話をお願いします。

塚田 ── ワークショップは「廻り花」と能楽師の安田登さんの公演「水の音」です。

「廻り花」は、旧暦の七夕の日に行いました。七夕なので花は七種類ずつ、東西南北の方位に合わせて花を選びました。都市で暮らしているからこそ、風習や風土、あるいは宇宙のことを考えるワークショップをやってみてはどうかと平田さんに相談しました。七夕なので例えば天の河のように、宇宙の水をイメージさせることができます。そもそも、水の中に入って花を生けることはめったにないでしょう。

安田さんは打合せですぐに『死者の書』（折口信夫著）の朗読を提案してくださいました。あの内なる空間が、死者がよみがえるという書の冒頭を想起させたのだと思います。安田さんは能のワキ方ですが、芸能にはそもそも土地の魂を鎮めるという鎮魂のほかに魂振りの意味があります。そういう意味で、あそこに誕生した場所を言祝ぐための1つの物語を演じてもらえば、声と水の響き、演者の身体、つくられた自然が一体化して、面白くなるのではないかと考えました。

平田 ── 会場を暗くして、わずかな光の中で安田さんが動きながら声を発

held on the date of the Tanabata star festival (7 July) under the lunar calendar. Since it was Tanabata, I chose seven types of flowers for each of the four directions. I had discussed with Hirata how I wanted to do a workshop that gave city dwellers an opportunity to think about customs and climate and the cosmos. Holding the event on Tanabata created the opportunity to imagine the water as a kind of cosmic river like the Milky Way. And it isn't often that I have the chance to do ikebana while standing in the water.

When we were discussing the project, Yasuda immediately proposed incorporating the novel *Shisha no sho* [The Book of the Dead] as read by the author, Shinobu Origuchi. I think the inner space of the exhibition must have reminded him of the part at the beginning of the book where the dead come back to life. Yasuda is a *waki-kata* (supporting actor), but Noh is grounded in rituals for both appeasing the spirits of the land and bringing them back to life. In this sense, I thought it would be interesting to have Yasuda perform a narrative to celebrate the place that had been created, integrating the sounds of voice and water, the body of the performer and fabricated nature.

Hirata — Darkening the venue so that Yasuda was moving, and vocalizing, in only the barest minimum of light also left a powerful impression.

Tsukada — As in the opening to *The Book of the Dead*, we decided to stop the water momentarily, and then let it flow again after a short pause. We started with the drip, drip of falling water, which Yasuda later said he thought had been a very effective piece of stagecraft.

Kawamukai — The inclusion in the performance of water sounds that were not ordinarily part of the exhibition was very effective. It was fantastic how we could hear even the subtlest of changes in the soundscape.

Opening Party and Direct Mailings

Hirata — For the opening party, Natsumi Toyama from Horo Kitchen treated everyone to soup. Soup was the only food that we served, the idea being that it's a kind of water consumed by the body. We also placed the soup within the exhibit, trying to entangle everything with the piece itself.

Tsukada — Colorful and beautiful to look at, the soup made an effective addition to the piece. Toyama has been pursuing a project of "travel through soup." Apparently it was something she began

している様子は、ものすごく印象的でした。

塚田 ──『死者の書』の冒頭のように、水もいったん止め、しばらくして
また出していく方法をとりました。最初、シタシタと水の滴るところか
ら始まったので、あとで安田さんもおっしゃっていましたが、とても効
果的な舞台演出になったと思います。

川向 ── 通常の展示にはなかった水の音という要素も、公演では実に効果
的に使われていました。非常にかすかな音の変化まで聞き取れたという
のが、素晴らしかった。

オープニングパーティとDMへの広がり

平田 ── オープニングのパーティでは、HORO Kitchen の遠山夏未さんが
スープを振る舞ってくれました。体内に取り入れられる水分というコン
セプトで、フードもあえてスープだけにとどめました。しかも、そのス
ープを展示の中に置きました。すべてを展示本体にからめようというこ
とで。

塚田 ── スープがカラフルできれいでしたから、緑が多い中で花のようで
した。展示品としての効果もありました。遠山さんは「スープで旅する」
プロジェクトなどを行っています。一緒に旅行していた方が旅先で身体
を壊したときに、その土地のスープを飲んだらすごく元気になったこと
から、このプロジェクトを始めたのだそうです。スープはエネルギーの
凝縮された薬みたいなものですね。

平田 ── 水のきれいなイメージといえば、SUIMOK DESIGN の 松田沙織さ
んがデザインしてくれたポスターは美しかったですよね。

塚田 ── そうですね。花の咲いた木の下に鏡を置いて空と木と花を映し、
そこに水滴を垂らして撮った写真を加工してグラフィックにしてくださ
いました。建築と植物の新しい関係が浮かび上がったようで、とても気
に入っています。

その後の展開

川向 ── さて、「Flow_er」展から数年たちましたが、その後の展開につい
て、お話しくださいませんか。

平田 ── 今、まさにやっている「（仮称）太田駅北口駅前文化交流施設」は、
図書館と美術館がくっついているのですが、人の流れや拠点のような広
がりと結び目を生み出すプロジェクトです。機能も重要ですけれども、
人が集まるたびにいろいろな快適要素を組み合わせ、からませていくと
いうものです。屋上に植物を植えて、木漏れ日で本を読めるようにもし
ます。全体として大きな〈流れ〉のようなものをつくります。

188　第5章　Flow_er

オープニングパーティで振る
舞われた HORO Kitchen の色
とりどりのスープ

The colorful soups from Horo
Kitchen that were served at
the opening party.

when someone she was traveling with fell ill but then recovered
completely after being given a local soup to drink. Soup is like a kind
of energy-rich medicine.

Hirata — When it comes to beautiful images of water, the poster that
Saori Matsuda of Suimok Design created for us was really something,
wasn't it?

Tsukada — That's right. She placed a mirror beneath a flowering tree
to capture the reflection of the sky and tree and flowers, dripped
water on its surface, and then post-processed the photographs
to create a graphic that seemed to reveal a whole new kind of
relationship between architecture and plants. I really liked it a lot.

Subsequent Developments

Kawamukai — It's been a few years since the Flow_er exhibition.
Could you each talk a bit about what you've been up to since then?

Hirata — The Ota Station North Entrance Center for Culture and
Exchange that I'm working on now combines a library and an art
museum. It's the kind of project that involves generating expanses
and nodes that are like flows and meeting points for people.
Functionality is important, but I also want there to be a tangled
combination of all sorts of pleasant elements whenever people
gather. There will be greenery on the roof that makes it possible to
read a book by sunlight filtering through the trees. From the whole, I
intend to create one great flow.

I've also started up the Ishii Tree-ness House project again after a
hiatus. It's a project that came about as a result of meeting Tsukada,
and is moving forward in much the same basic direction as the
Flow_er exhibition, so I hope to ask for his help again. For Flow_er we

「石井邸 Tree-ness House」
（平田晃久建築設計事務所）。
模型（左）と断面図（右）

Model (left) and section
drawing (right) of the Ishii
Tree-ness House (Akihisa
Hirata Architecture Office).

そして、中断していた「石井邸 Tree-ness House」のプロジェクトが再開しました。塚田さんと出会うことになったプロジェクトですが、基本的に同じ考え方で進めるので、また塚田さんに協働をお願いできればと考えています。

「Flow_er」展では短い展示期間で植生を考えたわけですが、「石井邸 Tree-ness House」ではメンテナンスを必要とするものの、野生に近い状態で半永久的に建築にからむ植生のプロジェクトが実現しそうです。

川向 ── 塚田さんの、その後の展開は、いかがですか。

塚田 ── 音、身体、風土が「Flow_er」展でかなり結びつきました。最近は、音楽や物語の朗読などを僕の花活けと組み合わせるコラボレーションをいくつか試みています。例えば、バンド・デシネのフランスの作家と「『かわいい闇』〜物語としての花活け〜」というイベントを行います。それから、アンソロジスト／文芸評論家の東雅夫さんに、例えばある花に関する物語を集めて、文学史的な背景を説明し、さらにその花についてシンボリックな話もしてもらう。その後、東さんに朗読してもらい、それに合わせて、僕が花を活けるというコラボレーションなどです。あるコンセプトに従って花の世界をつくり上げ、想像の世界、非日常の世界に〈遊ぶ〉試みです。

ワークショップで行った「廻り花」も日本各地で行っています。植物は土地の「声」ですし、花は「歌」ですから、まず植物から自分の暮らす風土のことを感じ直していくことを各地でやっていきたいと思っています。建築家と組むことも多く、平田さんとは特に面白い試みができそうです。どんどんからまりたいですね。植物や町の声や風や虫たちの営みをそっと引き寄せる大きな樹木のような建物が戻ってくると、自然という母胎へのかかわり方が新たに見えてくると思います。

川向 ── 結局、新しいコンセプトを立てて実践しなければ、新しいものは生まれない。おふたりの話を伺っていると、逆に、新しいものが次々に生まれそうで、それが実に愉快で、あっという間に予定の時間になりました。どうも、ありがとうございました。

only had to think about vegetation over the short term. With the Ishii Tree-ness House, though, I think we'll be able to create a vegetation project that, although it will require maintenance, should constitute a semi-permanent tangling with the architecture in a nearly wild state.

Kawamukai — And Tsukada, what have you been up to?

Tsukada — The *Flow_er* exhibition really tied together sound, the body, and *fudo*. Recently I've been involved in a number of collaborations that combine my flower arranging with music or narratives or recitations. For example, there was the event *"Kawaii yami": monogatari to shite no hanaike* [Beautiful Darkness: Flower Arranging as Narrative] that I did with a French writer of *bande dessinée.* I also work with anthologist and literary critic Masao Higashi. He gathers stories related to a certain flower, explains the literary-historical context, and relates symbolic stories about the flower. I then perform flower arranging as he does recitations. These are efforts to play at building a world of flowers around a given concept, an imaginary, out-of-the-ordinary world.

I also do *meguribana* events like the one we did for the workshop, all around the country. Plants are the voice of the earth, and flowers are its song, so I hope to continue traveling around inspiring people to re-think—or re-feel—the climate in which they live, starting with plants. I frequently collaborate with architects, and working with Hirata seems especially likely to lead in interesting directions. I look forward to getting even more tangled up. If we can see the return of buildings that are like massive trees, quietly drawing in the voices of plants and neighborhoods, the workings of insects and wind, then I think we'll be able to see our connection to Mother Nature in a new way.

Kawamukai — Ultimately, nothing new is created unless new concepts are developed and put into practice. Talking with you both, though, gives me hope of seeing new things created one after the other, and has been a lot of fun. Thank you very much.

CHAPTER —— 6

Invisible White

白
い
闇

ARCHITECT
Makoto Yokomizo

建築家
ヨコミゾマコト

OLFACTORY ARTIST
Maki Ueda

嗅覚のアーティスト
上田麻希

194　第 6 章　白い闇

CHAPTER-6　Invisible White　195

この展覧会では、私が憧憬する無限に広がる境界
のない空間をつくってみたいと考えています。そ
もそも、有限なこの地球上に無限に広がる空間を
つくり出すなど土台無理な話です。しかし、物理
的には不可能でも、人の持つ感性と想像力に頼れ
ば可能かもしれません。そこで、嗅覚のアーティ
スト上田麻希さんに参加して頂くことにしまし
た。空間と時間を、形あるものでデザインする建
築家と、形がないものでデザインする嗅覚のアー
ティストとのコラボレーションです。
　想定されるのは、白いだけのまったく何もない空

間です。しかしそこは、とても静かで豊かな空
間です。嗅覚と聴覚が研ぎすまされます。視覚
は役に立たないからです。匂いは日常に溢れて
いるものながら、未解明の部分が多いようです。
嗅覚は、視覚や聴覚に比べて初源的かつ直感的
であり、記憶に直結しているとも言われていま
す。その嗅覚に刺激を与えることで人のもつ無
限の感性と想像力を活性化させたいと考えてい
ます。　　　　　　　　　　（展示コンセプト文より）

For this exhibition I wanted to try and create the kind of boundless expanse that I long for, one that stretches out forever. Trying to create an infinitely expansive space in our finite world, of course, is impossible right from the very beginning. Still, even though physically impossible, I thought this might be achieved by relying on human sensitivity and imagination. I decided, therefore, to ask olfactory artist Maki Ueda to join me in working on the project. Our collaboration brought together an architect who designs space and time through things that have form and an olfactory artist who designs things that are formless. What I imagined was an empty space filled with nothing but whiteness, yet one that was also very quiet and abundant, a place where the senses of smell and hearing would be acutely felt since vision was of no use. Although smells are all around us in our everyday lives, much about them remains a mystery. Smell is said to be more primitive and intuitive than either sight or hearing, and more directly linked to memory. I hope that by stimulating their sense of smell this exhibition will invigorate people's boundless sensitivity and imagination.

(Exhibition concept, July 2013)

視覚と嗅覚を科学して
無限空間を楽しむ

ヨコミゾマコト
上田麻希
川向正人

建築家
ヨコミゾ マコト

1962 年 神奈川県生まれ。東京藝術大学美術
学部建築科大学院修了後、伊東豊雄建築設計
事務所を経て、2001 年 aat+ ヨコミゾマコト建
築設計事務所開設。東京藝術大学美術学部建
築科准教授 (2009-)。新発田市庁舎 (2016)、
釜石市民ホール (2017) が進行中

ARCHITECT.
Makoto Yokomizo

Born in Kanagawa prefecture in 1962, Yokomizo
completed his graduate studies at the Tokyo
University of the Arts Department of Architecture.
After working with Toyo Ito & Associates,
Architects, he established AAT + Makoto
Yokomizo, Architects Inc. in 2001. Since 2009 he
has been an Associate Professor at the Tokyo
University of the Arts Department of Architecture.

川向 ― まず、ODS-R 第 11 回の企画を引き受けるときに、どんなことを
お考えになったのか、そこからお話しいただけますか。

ヨコミゾ ― やはり、今、自分の関心のあることから離れることはできま
せん。ですから、日頃の仕事ではできないことを、この場で試してみた
いと思いました。それは 2 つあって、 1 つは現実の条件、例えば、法律
とか地球の重力とか、そういうものに妨げられてできないことです。も
う 1 つは、自分がイメージしたものがストレートに実現できない。ふさ
わしい素材が見つけられないとか、形にするためのスタディの方法が思い
つかないなどの理由からです。この 2 つのもどかしさが常にありますが、
できるだけそれらから開放されるようなものをやってみたいと考えました。

A Boundless Space
Built of the Science of Sight and Smell

MAKOTO YOKOMIZO
MAKI UEDA
MASATO KAWAMUKAI

嗅覚のアーティスト

上田麻希

1974 年 東京都生まれ。アートと嗅覚の融合を
試みる「嗅覚のアーティト」。世界的に流行の兆
しを見せている「嗅覚のアート」のリーディング・
アーティストのひとり。視覚的な要素を排除し
た、匂いだけによる嗅覚体験を提供する作品
を発表する

OLFACTORY ARTIST

Maki Ueda

Born in Tokyo in 1974, Ueda is an "olfactory
artist" who seeks to combine art and the sense of
smell. As one of the world's leading practitioners
of olfactory art, a field showing signs of growing
popularity around the world, she creates works
that eliminate visual elements to present
olfactory experiences that rely on smell alone.

Kawamukai — I'd like to begin by asking what you thought when you
first agreed to take on the 11th ODS-R.
Yokomizo — Well, it's impossible, of course, to move very far from
the things that interest me now. I did, though, want to use the
opportunity to try something I can't do in my everyday work. Such
things come in two flavors. First, there are times when real-world
conditions—like the law, or perhaps the law of gravity—get in the
way. Second, there are times when I can't carry out what I imagine
straightaway. This might be because I can't come up with the right
material or the right method for doing the studies that would give
the thing form. These two sources of irritation are constantly with

自分を包み込む、無限に広がる空間

川向 ── では、関心のある、手がけてみたいテーマとは何ですか。

ヨコミゾ ── 無限に広がり、境目がなく、どこまでも広がっていって自分自身が包み込まれるような空間でしょうか。例えば、海の中にダイブしたときとか、夜の砂漠とか。もしかしたら全宇宙に自分しかいないのではと感じるような瞬間は、感覚が高揚しているときなど日常生活の中でもあります。普段見えているものがすごく遠くに感じ、音もはるかかなたから聞こえてくるように思えて、一瞬ワクワクするような、そういう感覚を空間化できたらいいなと思ったのです。

吉本隆明の『ハイ・イメージ論』(1989) に出てくる、天井ギリギリの所から自分が寝ている姿を見下ろしている視点とか、電車の中からビルで働いている人が見えて、その向こう側のビルで働いている人も見え、さらに向こうの向こうの向こうまで見えるような瞬間とか、そういう普段われわれが意識しない視点みたいなものを、現代テクノロジーによって一瞬手に入れたりする面白さともいえますが、そんなものを試してみたい。

川向 ── 日常の向こうとか隙間に広がっている不思議な空間に、偶然に出合ったと感じることは、確かにあります。いくつもの条件の重なりで、ある一瞬に、ほとんど偶然のように出合う。それは、単純に光と闇、明るさと暗さといったものを空間的につくってみるのとは、全然違います。なるほど、「白い闇」とは、そういうものですか。

ジェームズ・タレルにも同じような試みがあります。彼も、「宇宙の広がり。通常意識しない状態の光」と言っています。モダンアートには、サイエンスあるいはテクノロジーとの協働で、日常では出合わない宇宙、世界を体験可能にする、あるいは、そういったものに対する人間の新しい感じ方を開拓することが含まれていたように思うのですが、「白い闇」も同じ系譜に立つといえますね。

さて、では「白い闇」をどう具体的につくっていくのですか。

ホワイトアウトあるいは暗闇順応

ヨコミゾ ── つくり出したかったのは、人が昼間、静かにまぶたを閉じた状態です。まぶたを閉じた状態では、何も見えていないが、実は、何か見えているんです。それは、空間において定量的に数字で書き表せるようなものではないし、物理的なものは存在しない。おそらくは、意識の中に残っている残像みたいなものの積み重ねだけで、それを色で表現しようと思えば、やっぱり、やや青みを帯びた昼間の太陽光の白でしょうか。雪山で起きるホワイトアウトという現象に似て、上下左右の方向感覚を

me, and I wanted to do something that freed me from them as much as possible.

Boundless Expanses that Swallow You Up

Kawamukai — So what topic of interest did you decide you wanted to tackle?

Yokomizo — I guess boundless spaces that stretch out forever and seem to swallow you up, like when diving in the ocean or being in the desert at night. Even in everyday life, there are moments of heightened sensitivity when it feels like you just might be the only person in the entire universe. Things you're used to seeing suddenly seem terribly far away. Sounds, too, fade as if they've traveled a great distance. There's a moment of tremendous exhilaration—a sensation that I thought I'd really like to try to recreate spatially.

I wanted to try using contemporary technology to enable people to enjoy grasping for a moment the kind of perspectives we're not usually conscious of—like the idea of looking down on your own sleeping form from a spot up against the ceiling that Takaaki Yoshimoto describes in *Hai imeji ron* [On High Images] (1989), or when you look out the window while riding the train and see people working in an office building and it feels as though you can see people working in the building beyond it, and then the one beyond that, and so on.

Kawamukai — Yes, sometimes it can feel as though you've peered through the gaps in the everyday and caught a glimpse of some mysterious space on the far side. These moments are encountered only when a number of conditions overlap, only for an instant, and almost entirely by chance. That's nothing at all like simply trying to spatially create light and dark, brightness and gloom. Now I can see what *Invisible White* was all about.

James Turrell seeks to do something similar in his work. He talks of the vastness of the universe, and about light conditions we're not normally conscious of. I think the notion of modern art encompasses working with science and technology to enable experiencing worlds and universes not encountered in everyday life, or pioneering new ways to appreciate such things, and I suppose we could say *Invisible White* stands in this same lineage.

But tell me, how did you set about actually putting *Invisible White* together?

失わせるようなものです。

川向 ── 闇の中でポワーッと明るく白く見えてくるという意味では、安藤忠雄さんとタレルのコラボレーションによる、直島の「南寺」(1999) が一番近いと思いますね。体験的にはまったく同じですが、企画としての「白い闇」展は、空間に無限の広がりを感じさせるために、われわれを包み込む空間そのものからエッジを消すなど、用意する空間の形態や色をもっと積極的に考えています。包み込まれる体験が、タレルよりもさらに一歩進んでいます。

ヨコミゾ ── 闇に目が慣れていく体験型のインスタレーションは、私自身も、過去に手がけています。「colony」(デジタル PBX / 2001　青木淳著『原っぱと遊園地──建築にとってその場の質とは何か』に掲載) では闇をつくり、闇の中で次第に見えてくる暗闇順応を体験してもらったのです。今回は、闇ではなく白くホワイトアウトした状態、上下左右の区別がない霧の中のような状態をつくりたかった。身体の中に潜在する宇宙的なものにかかわるような作品をつくることに関心がある点では、タレルに共感する部分もあります。できれば、視覚に由来する空間体験でなく、全感覚を起動させざるを得ないようなものを目指したいと思いました。

川向 ── 星空の美しさとか、太陽が昇り、沈むときの美しさ、そこで感じる宇宙の大きさやある種の憧れをただ自然現象として体験するだけではなく、建築・アートの世界で凝縮し、より強烈な印象を与えることも、人類がずっと願ってきたことですね。

闇と光～宇宙につながる内部空間

ヨコミゾ ── 建築でいえば、きちんと内部と外部を隔てる機能性や、形に意味を付与する論理性の獲得を建築家がずっとやってきたとすれば、今、それらに加えて、日常的な感覚を超えるもの、形では表すことのできないものにもう少し関心を持ってもいいのかもしれません。

川向 ── 北川原温さんの「中村キース・ヘリング美術館」(2007) や三分一博志さんの「犬島精錬所美術館」(2008) では、意図的に暗闇を導入しています。一般の鑑賞者が入るミュージアムに暗闇を導入して、ま

加藤弘行とヨコミゾマコトによるユニット「デジタル PBX」のインスタレーション「colony」(2001)。暗闇の中に発光性植物が広がる

The *Colony* (2001) installation by Digital PBX, a creative unit composed up of Hiroyuki Kato and Makoto Yokomizo, involved an expanse of luminescent plants in the darkness.

Adjusting to Darkness or a Whiteout

Yokomizo — What I wanted to create was the condition of quietly closing your eyes during the day. You can't see anything with your eyes closed, but you're actually not seeing nothing. It isn't a space you can express quantitatively using numbers, and there isn't anything physically there, but if I had to describe the layered afterimages that linger in consciousness in terms of color I suppose I'd call it the white of daylight with a slightly bluish cast. Like a whiteout on a snowy mountain, it's the sort of thing that makes you lose all sense of direction.

Kawamukai — In terms of a bright whiteness that emerges from the darkness, the closest example I can think of is Turrell's collaboration with Tadao Ando, Minamidera [Southern Temple] (1999) in Naoshima. The works are experienced in much the same way, but as a project I think *Invisible White takes* a more aggressive approach toward the shape and color of the prepared space enclosing the viewer, eliminating edges to create the impression of a boundless expanse. The experience of envelopment is a step ahead of Turrell.

Yokomizo — I've done installations myself in the past that worked with the experience of the eyes adjusting to the darkness. For *Colony* (Digital PBX / 2001, included in *Harappa to yuenchi: kenchiku ni totte sono ba no shitsu to wa nani ka* [Open Fields and Amusement Parks: What, for Architecture, is the Quality of a Place?] by Jun Aoki), I created total darkness and then had people experience things become visible as their eyes adjusted. This time I wanted to create something different, using a state of whiteout rather than darkness to put people in a kind of fog where spatial distinctions disappear. Insofar as I am interested in making works that relate to aspects of the cosmic that are latent within the body, there may be something in common with Turrell. If possible, I wanted to aim for a spatial experience that was not grounded in sight but instead was compelling to all of the senses.

Kawamukai — Humanity, I think, has always longed for a way to experience the scale of the universe—that sense of awe that we feel when looking into the night sky or when watching the rising and setting of the sun—not only through natural phenomena but also through its condensation in architecture or art to leave an even more powerful impression.

さに包み込まれる空間そのものが、鑑賞といいますか体験といいますか、その対象になっているわけです。人間の意識とか心理への働きかけが、アートの目的・手段になってきている。

建築の環境工学の領域でも、日常の生活や仕事に必要な明るさを考えたり、便利で効率的な照明方法を考えたりする次元から、人間の意識とか心理との関係で光、照明を考える次元へと関心がシフトしています。非日常とか偶然の世界がどんどん侵入してきて、結果として、光とか照明が生み出す環境が、非常に多様になっています。そういう意味で、アートとサイエンスが融合していて、美術館が環境実験室になったり、環境実験室が美術館のようになったりと、面白い時代になってきました。

今回の「白い闇」というのは、すごく洗練されたアートの世界ではありますが、どこか環境実験室の延長みたいなところがあります。展示場所がオカムラのショールームの打合せコーナーですから、まさに日常のオフィス空間で、徹夜明けの早朝に出合うかもしれない状況がつくられているようで、そこがすごく面白いと思いました。

ヨコミゾ ── 現代美術の流れの1つに、サイトスペシフィックというのがありますが、サイトとして、あの場所は創作意欲をかき立てる場所ではありません。でも、そのことが逆に着想のきっかけにもなりました。

川向 ── サイトとして無機的で、無性格な場所ですね。でも、美術館のホワイトキューブでもない。まさにオフィス空間です。どこか、都市空間そのものにも思えて、私は、けっこう面白い空間だなあと思えるようになっています（笑）。

ヨコミゾ ── 20世紀半ばから美術館の展示室はホワイトキューブが定番化していて、ホワイトキューブを前提に作品をつくるアーティストもいます。それはそれで、ある性格を持った1つの環境になっていると思うのです。ところが、オフィスの打合せコーナーは、どう考えてもアーティストを刺激する空間ではないですね。

アニッシュ・カプーアとヘルツォーク＆ド・ムーロンとのコラボレーションプロジェクト「56 Leonard」で、ニューヨークのコンドミニアムの一番下でシルバーの球体がブチュッとつぶれて地面との間に挟まったような作品があります。それに似て、宇宙のように全方向に無限に広がるものが、あのオフィス空間の低い天井高に合わせ、つぶれて挟まれている感じでしょうか。だから今回の無限に広がる空間の提案は、実在する空間の特性を逆手に取ったところがあります。

川向 ── 結果として、閉じて内部空間をつくった上で、内部に無限の広がりをつくり出す。日常の光空間ではなく「白い闇」を使う。

ヨコミゾ ── 光はあるけれども、どこからやってきているのかわからない

多木浩二氏撮影の「中野本町
の家」(伊東豊雄建築設計事
務所、1976)

Photography by Koji Taki of
the House in Nakano Hon-
cho (Toyo Ito & Associates,
Architects, 1976).

Darkness and Light: Interiors That Connect With the Cosmos

Yokomizo — If architects have always sought to secure a functionality
that separates inside and out and a rationale that gives meaning to
form, then perhaps what we need to add now is a bit more interest
in what transcends the everyday and cannot be expressed through
form.

Kawamukai — Atsushi Kitagawara's Nakamura Keith Haring
Collection (2007) and Hiroshi Sambuichi's Inujima Seirensho Art
Museum (2008) both intentionally incorporate darkness. Both of
these museums, which serve the general public, do so in a way that
their enveloping spaces themselves become objects of appreciation
to be experienced on their own terms. Appealing to human
perception and psychology has become part of the objective and
methodology of art.

In architecture's environmental engineering field, too, a dimensional
shift is underway in the way people think about lighting, moving
from an interest in the amount of light needed in daily life or work,
or in devising convenient, efficient lighting methods, to thinking

光です。「白い闇」という言葉は、多木浩二さんが伊東（豊雄）さんの「中野本町の家」（1976）で、「この住宅の内部は白い闇だ」って、夢中になってシャッターを切ったという逸話からきています。

川向 ── オープニングに、師匠の伊東さんが来てくださっていましたね。

ヨコミゾ ── 伊東さんから、「おまえがつくるものはエロい」と言われてしまいましたが……（笑）。

〈か〉と〈かたち〉

川向 ── 物質らしいものがないにもかかわらず、ヨコミゾさんのつくられた空間に入ると、何か充満するもの、何か包み込んでくるものを感じました。しかも今回は、そこに匂いが加わっています。

伊東さん、菊竹（清訓）さん、さらには菊竹さんの『代謝建築論　か・かた・かたち』（1969）に戻っていくのですが、重要なのは伊東さんが菊竹事務所の〈か〉のグループだったことです。〈かた〉はタイプで、〈かたち〉

「白い闇」展の平面図
Invisible White exhibition plan drawing.

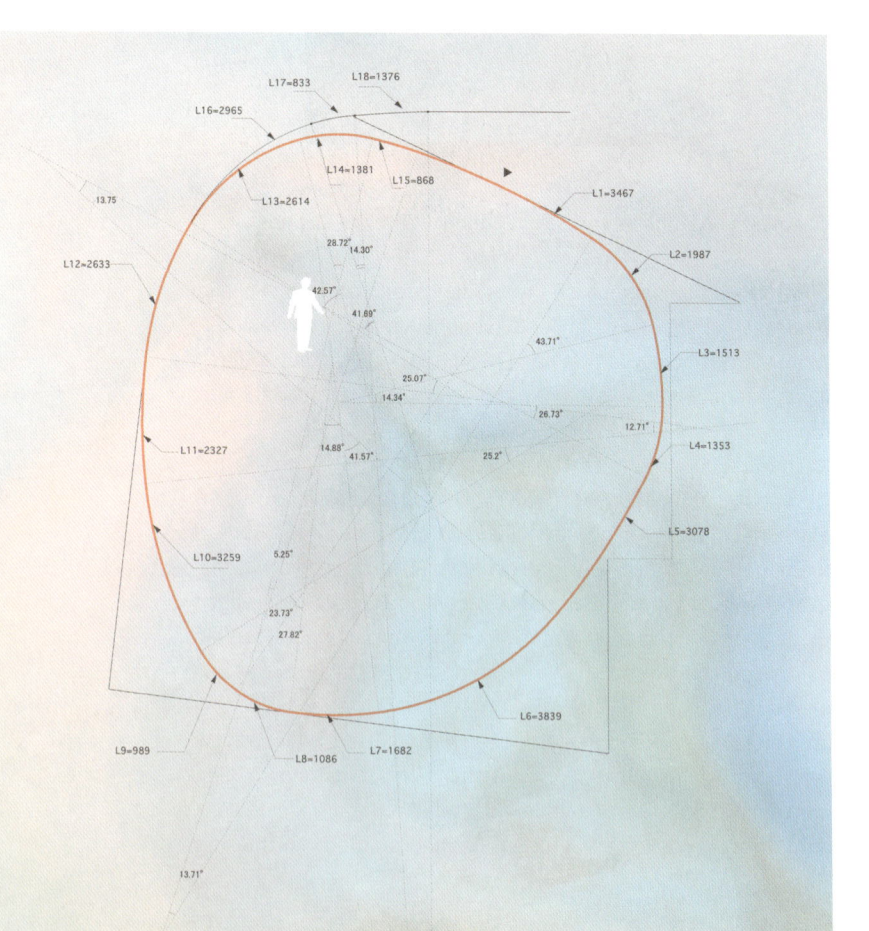

about the relationship of light and lighting to human perception and psychology. This rapid influx of the out-of-the-ordinary and the serendipitous has resulted in an extremely varied range of environments generated through light and lighting. In this sense there has been a kind of fusion between art and science; we live in an interesting time when museums are like environmental laboratories and environmental laboratories are like museums.

Invisible White was a highly refined work of art, but in some ways it also seemed like an extension of an environmental laboratory. Because it was installed in the meeting area of the Okamura showroom—in the middle of an everyday office space—I find it intriguing that it created the sort of state you might encounter early in the morning after staying up all night.

Yokomizo — Site-specific works are a trend in contemporary art these days, and in that sense the site isn't really one that stimulates the creative juices. On the other hand, that itself is something that actually helped inspire the concept.

Kawamukai — It *is* a rather inorganic, characterless space. But it isn't the white cube of a museum, either. It truly is an office space. You know, in a way it feels like the quintessential urban space. I'm starting to warm to it! (*Laughs*)

Yokomizo — White cubes became a fixture in art museum exhibition spaces starting in the middle of the twentieth century, and some artists even premise their work on them. And I do think such environments have a distinctive character. But no, by no stretch of the imagination is an office meeting space the kind of site that excites an artist.

56 Leonard (2015), the collaboration between Anish Kapoor and Herzog & De Meuron, is a silver sphere that seems to have been squashed under a New York City condominium and become trapped between it and the ground. In the same way, maybe this thing that wanted to spread out endlessly in all directions like the cosmos was squashed and trapped beneath the low ceiling of that office space. So my proposal to create a boundless expanse essentially turned the tables on the characteristics of the actual site.

Kawamukai — The result, then, was that you created a closed, interior space, built a boundless expanse within it, and used "invisible white" lighting instead of ordinary everyday lighting.

Yokomizo — There is light, but it is a light whose source is indeterminate. The term "invisible white" comes from Koji Taki's

はシェイプですが、〈か〉は、それになる前の混沌とした、実在するが説明するのが難しい無限の広がりのことです。今回、ヨコミゾさんが目指したのは、その〈か〉だったのではないか。

ヨコミゾ ── 確かに……〈かたち〉をつくる場所でも、その機会でもないと思いました。

川向 ── 先ほどの伊東さんの言葉を聞くと、伊東事務所時代、ヨコミゾさんは〈か〉を一番期待されていたのではないでしょうか。建築の〈か〉を無限の広がりのまま建築化するのが伊東流のやり方で、それが既存の建築を徹底的に破壊する力にもなっています。〈か〉をストレートに〈かたち〉にするにもかかわらず、やはり〈かた〉は使われる。では、どんな〈かた〉を使うかに、ものすごいエネルギーをかけるのが、伊東さんの建築設計ではないか。建築設計をするときに、つまり、〈か〉から〈かたち〉に行くときに、ごく限定的に〈かた〉を入れるが、既存の建築ボキャブラリーをできるだけ排除しようとする。だから、一発でスペースが立ち現れたようにも見えます。

ヨコミゾ ── なるほど。〈か〉から〈かたち〉へ直結しているかのように、つまり、いかに〈かた〉を感じさせないか、ということですね。

川向 ──「白い闇」を取り囲む外周壁のつくり方に、できるだけ〈か〉がそのまま〈かたち〉になったように感じさせようという気遣いが出ています。無限の広がりを生むためには、内部空間をつくる外周壁が必要でしたが、逆の方法で、つまり外周壁をつくらず、光の操作だけで、求めるものがつくり出せたのではないかとも、私は考えるのですが。

ヨコミゾ ── 光の操作だけですか、とても難しそうですね。しかし、今回のように、きわめてアナログな手法によらず、何種類かのセンサーに直結された環境制御装置を導入すれば、可能かもしれませんね。でも正直なところ、自分のどこかに、形態に対する圧倒的な信頼性があり、形ではないと言いながらも、やはり形でしょ⁉ というような自己矛盾があることも否定できません。一方で、そのような説明し得ない要素を持たない作品は、面白みも少ないのではないかと思います。

川向 ── それが、自然現象とは違うアートの特質ですね。固定され、反復可能でもある世界です。「白い闇」が建築・アートとして誕生する経緯がとてもよくわかったように思います。ODS-R は個展ではなく、コラボレーション展です。そこで、「どなたかと組んでください」というお願いをしましたが、コラボレーターに上田麻希さんを選ばれた理由は何ですか。

" 匂い " 〜空間をコントロールする

ヨコミゾ ── 無限に広がる空間が仮にあったとして、その空間は真空なの

description of Toyo Ito's White U, also known as the House in Nakano Honcho (1976), as "a house with an interior of invisible white" that he found completely engrossing as he composed his shots.

Kawamukai — Your old mentor Ito came to the opening, didn't he?

Yokomizo — Yes. He said, "Everything you make is so erotic." (*Laughs*)

Ka and Katachi

Kawamukai — When I step inside spaces that you've made I often feel, even though they are bare of anything material, as if they were filled with something, that I was being enveloped by something. And this time you've also added the element of scent.

Going back to Ito and Kiyonori Kikutake, and Kikutake's *Taisha kenchiku ron: ka, kata, katachi* [Metabolist Architecture: *Ka, Kata,* and *Katachi*] (1969), I think the important thing is that Ito was part of the *ka* group in Kikutake's office. Where *kata* might be described as a thing's form or type, and *katachi* the thing as a phenomenon, its specific shape, *ka* refers to something fundamental—the Platonic *idea*—a boundless expanse that pre-exists *kata* and *katachi* but is rather difficult to explain. I think perhaps you were aiming for *ka* with this project.

Yokomizo — Indeed. I felt this wasn't the time or the place for playing with shapes.

Kawamukai — Given what Ito said to you, I wonder if, when you were working at his firm, he had high hopes for what you would do with *ka*. Ito's way of doing things is to express the *ka* aspects of architecture directly as boundless expanses within his buildings, which enables him to be so thorough in demolishing existing structures. He turns *ka* directly into *katachi,* but not, of course, without using *kata*. I think Ito probably spends a tremendous amount of energy deciding what kind of *kata* to use in his designs. When designing buildings—that is, when making the move from *ka* to *katachi*—he incorporates *kata* in a very limited way, seeking to do away with received architectural vocabulary as much as possible. That's why his spaces so often seem to appear all at once out of nowhere.

Yokomizo — I see, moving directly from *ka* to *katachi*. The question, then, is how to keep *kata* from rising to the level of consciousness.

Kawamukai — The way the peripheral walls surrounding *Invisible White* are made shows your concern for leaving the impression of a direct route between *ka* and *katachi.* In order to generate a

かというと、実はそうではなく、昔の人が考えたように"エーテル"みたいなもので満ちているわけです。そういう捉え方をすると、空間に匂いのあることが、ごく自然に必要だと思えたのです。ただ、それをコントロールできるかどうかがわからなかったのです。

川向 ── 先ほど、展示とするには何をしなければならなかったかを話されましたが、意図したものにするには、いかに空間をコントロールするかが、ポイントになりますね。

ヨコミゾ ── それも、デザイン対象にしたかったのです。空間だけではなく、その内部の気、つまり空気をコントロールしたい。それを手っ取り早く、確実にできるのは、匂いではないか、と。そこで偶然、インターネットで見つけたのが上田さんでした。

川向 ── ヨコミゾさんからの連絡を受けて、どう内容を理解して、何をしようと考えたのですか。

上田 ── まず、「白い闇」のイメージとホワイトアウトの話と、「無限に広がる感じを匂いでどうやって表現するのか」という質問をいただいて、香水業界には数種類の"宇宙的な香り"があるので、それを使えば空間性を感じさせやすいことを、最初に思い浮かべました。実際に、そのうちの1つは使いましたが、それをただ使うのではなく、私もアーティストとして、エフェクトではなくて体験という方面からアプローチしたかった。企画「白い闇」の設計図を見て、そのもとになったヨコミゾさん設計の「空蓮房」（2006）にも行きました。角のない、白い闇に満たされた空間で、歩いていると突然壁があったりして、確かに遠近感のわかりづらい空間でした。そこで、自分自身が中に入って動くシミュレーションをしてみて、どんな香りをどんなふうに知覚できたらよいだろうかと考えました。

「空蓮房」（aat＋ヨコミゾマコト
建築設計事務所、2006）

Kurenboh (AAT + Makoto
Yokomizo, Architects Inc.,
2006).

boundless expanse, you needed peripheral walls that would make an interior space, but I wonder if you could also have taken the opposite approach, that is, manipulated light to create the desired effect without constructing peripheral walls at all.

Yokomizo — By manipulating light alone? I think that would have been very difficult. Actually, it might be possible by introducing environmental control equipment directly linked to a variety of sensors rather than relying on the decidedly analog methods we employed here. To tell you the truth, though, somewhere inside I have an overpowering dependence on form, and I can't deny a certain internal contradiction—saying on the one hand that it isn't all about *katachi* and then on the other that it comes down to *katachi*, after all. But any work that doesn't incorporate something inexplicable like that probably just isn't all that interesting.

Kawamukai — This is a property of art that differs from the world of natural phenomena, doesn't it, this ability to fix and to repeat? I think I have a much better understanding now of the process by which *Invisible White* was born as a work of art and architecture. ODS-R, of course, is not a solo show but a collaborative exhibition. You were asked to choose a collaborator, and I'm curious to know why you selected Maki Ueda?

Scent: Controlling Space

Yokomizo — Let's say you have a boundless space. Would it be a vacuum? Not really. It would be filled with something akin to the ether that people used to believe in. Seen in this way, it felt perfectly natural to think of the space as needing a scent. I wasn't sure, though, whether this was something I would be able to control.

Kawamukai — You were talking earlier about the things you had to do to prepare for the exhibition, but the key to creating what you intend is really how well you can control the space, isn't it?

Yokomizo — The space was something I wanted to design. And I wanted to control not just the space, but also the mood within it—its atmosphere. I thought scent would be the easiest, most reliable way to do so, and then happened to come across Ueda on the Internet.

Kawamukai — When Yokomizo contacted you, Ueda, did you understand what he was proposing and how did you decide to approach the project?

Ueda — Well, he explained his concept for *Invisible White*, the

「白い闇」展の匂いの検討図。3種類の匂いの"色"をどのように混ぜるか、また全体の匂いを嗅ぐ効果的な順番を検討

Study drawing of scents for the *Invisible White* exhibition, used when considering how to mix the "colors" of the three scents and in determining the most effective overall order for encountering the scents.

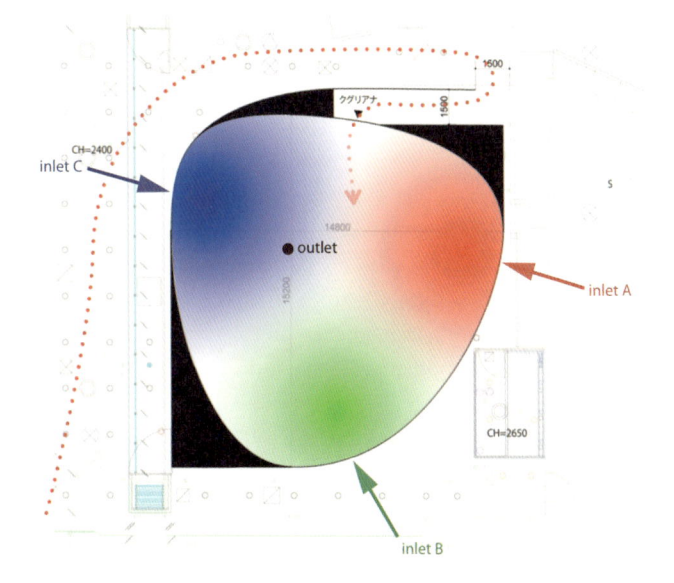

結論としては、空間の中で視覚的には無限なのですが、常に香りが刺激してくる状態をつくることにしました。ただ、香りのパーティクルはすぐに混ざって、香りが均一化してしまいます。これが常識です。そこで、次々に新しい香りが刺激してくるという常識破りに挑戦しようと思い立ったのですが、これまでの経験から多分できるだろうと。もちろん今回は、人が歩くことが前提だったので、1点に香りがとどまるのではなく、空間軸と時間軸を考える複雑な課題になりました。

あとから、「自分の記憶の奥深いところが引き出される香りだった」といったコメントも頂いたのですが、それは二次的なもので、とにかく私の考える知覚体験をしっかり実現させることに集中しました。

流動と差異

川向 ── 位置が変われば何か変わったなと意識させる方法として匂いの変化を使ったということですか。ディファレンス（差異）のアートですね。

ヨコミゾ ── 最初は、イメージに直結する宇宙の匂い、都市の匂い、森の匂い、水の匂いなどで満ちている状態しか考えていなかったのです。ですが、上田さんと話しているうちに、イメージはわれわれがデザインするのではなく、匂いを嗅いだ人の頭の中で生成されればよくて、そこまでデザインするのは too much であると考えるようになりました。

そうではなく、複数の匂いをそこに満たし、どっち向きにどういう順番で匂いを嗅ぐかで、生成するイメージが違ってくること自体に着目する。

左：匂いを嗅ぐ順番を検討。
右：東京藝術大学の校舎内
で行われた匂いの拡散実験
風景

Left: Scent diffusion experiment conducted at the
Tokyo University of the Arts.
Right: Determining the order
for encountering the scents.

idea of a whiteout, and asked how he could express a boundless expanse through the use of scent. There are a few "spatial scents" in the perfume industry and the first thing that came to mind was that using these might make it easier to foster a sense of space. I did use one of these, in fact, but as an artist I wanted to go beyond just creating an effect and instead approached the project hoping to create an experience.

After seeing the plans for *Invisible White*, I also visited the Kurenboh meditation gallery (AAT + Makoto Yokomizo Architects, 2006) on which they were based. A space without corners filled with a white dimness—one in which walls suddenly appeared as you walked around—it was certainly a place where gauging perspective was a challenge. I ran a simulation of my own, moving around in the space and thinking about what kind of scents I could use and how I would want them to be perceived.

As a result, I decided that although the interior space was visually boundless, I would create conditions in which the sense of smell was constantly stimulated. The problem, as anyone knows, is that different fragrance particles quickly dissolve and saturate a space. I decided I wanted to take on the unconventional challenge of stimulating a series of aromas one after the other. This was something that experience told me I could probably pull off. It was a given that people would walk around in the space, so the project was complicated in that it meant not just keeping the scent in one spot but also thinking about how the scent would hold up spatially and over time.

Someone later said, "It was a scent that elicited something from a place deep in memory," but this was a secondary effect; I was just concentrating on trying to bring about the sensory experience I had envisioned.

CHAPTER–6 Invisible White **215**

その多様な環境が、現実には狭いあの空間の中につくり出される。空気に色をつけるように匂いをつけて、隣の色といかに混ざるかが重要で、混ざり具合やそれを嗅いで何を想起するかは体験した人ごとに違うのですから、その状況をつくり上げるだけでいいと、途中から考えるようになりました。それが、上田さんとコラボして一番面白かった点です。

上田 — 匂いは受取り方が多様で、嗅覚は非常に曖昧な感覚器官ですから、自分が思う匂いと相手が思う匂いには、ズレが起きる可能性が高い。いろいろな道筋を考えてはいたのですが、最終的にあの空間で香りを薫き、組み合わせているうちに、香りの意味づけの部分は完全にそぎ落とされてしまったというか、一番エフェクティブなものという観点から香料を選ぶことになりました。だから、私の場合、コンセプトは一切なしです。

川向 — 差異を刻むことが重要で、前もってストーリーやイメージは想定しなかったということですか。

個人のデータベースの大切さ

上田 — ひとつ気をつけたのは、嗅覚は個人のデータベースを参照するので、まったく嗅いだことのない香りばかりだと、本当に"嗅げない"という問題が出てくるのです。そうなると、嗅いでも何も感じなくなります。今回香料を3種類選びましたが、まったく嗅いだことのない香りは1種類だけにとどめて、2種類は、わりと経験に結びつきやすいものを選びました。

川向 — 何かを嗅いだだけではいけなくて、できれば「何の匂いかな？」と思ってもらったほうがいいということですか。

上田 — はい。そのほうがより意識に上りやすいのです。実際に、匂いの分子を感知する鼻の中の嗅粘膜に分子が付いたというシグナルが脳に送られただけでは、匂いを嗅いだことにはならないのです。一生懸命、意識を集中すれば微細な匂いを嗅ぎ分けられるはずなのですが、それがシャットアウトされてしまうのは避けたい。意識的に嗅ごうとするのは1つのアクションですが、嗅いだことがある匂いが漂ってくると、自分の体験と結びつけて何かを思い出すことはありますよね。私の作品では「香りがありますよ」と伝えることが、まず重要なのです。今回は、入り口で中と外の空気をうまく仕切れたので、中に入った瞬間、香りがすぐに意識に上ったのでしょうね。

設計段階では計算できない要素がたくさんあって、その場合、勘と想像力で想像して決定しました。換気扇のスペック、香りの蒸散の方法、香りを吹き出す方法も何種類かの中から選びました。タイミングをずらして香りを出す方法を選んで発注し、その組合せを同時進行で決めなけれ

Fluidity and Difference

Kawamukai — You used changes in scent as a way to make people conscious that something was changing as they moved around. It was an artwork of difference, wasn't it?

Yokomizo — At first, all I could think of was a space filled with scents directly related to images of the cosmic, like the smell of the city, or the forest, or water, but as I spoke more with Ueda I realized that this would be too much, that we should not seek to design such impressions but rather allow them to be conjured in the minds of those who are doing the smelling.

I realized that by infusing the space with a number of scents, it would be possible to generate different impressions depending upon which direction people turned and in what order they encountered the scents. We could create a variety of environments in what was really a rather small space. When coloring the air, the way adjacent colors mix is incredibly important. At some point in the project I changed my thinking and decided that it was the same with scents, and that it was enough to create a situation in which different images were conjured by each person who experienced the work. I think this was the most interesting part about collaborating with Ueda.

Ueda — Smell is an extremely ambiguous sense, and the same aroma can be perceived in a variety of ways, so there is always a strong possibility that the way you perceive a scent is out of sync with the way someone else does. I considered a lot of different paths, but as I infused the space with various combinations of scents their semantic aspects dropped away completely and I ultimately decided to choose the scents that were the most effective. In my case, then, there really wasn't any conceptual component.

Kawamukai — So even though carving out difference was important, you had no preconceived story or image in mind, right?

The Importance of Personal Databases

Ueda — One thing I was careful about was that the sense of smell relies on referencing each individual's personal database, so using only scents that people had never smelled before could lead to the problem that they might not actually register as smells. If that happened, they wouldn't conjure any impressions at all. I ended up choosing three scents. One was a fragrance that people would be

ばなりませんでした。自分でも、いつ、どういうふうに決定したかを詳しくは思い出せないほど複雑な要素がありましたが、最終的にうまくいきました。

川向 ── 移動に伴って匂いがどう変わるように設計されたのですか。私も何度も体験しましたが、あらためてお尋ねしたくなりました。

上田 ── 歩いていて視覚に気を取られているうちに、フッと違う匂いが迷い込んでくる。そうしてまた歩いていくと、別の香りが出現する。それなら、もっと歩いてみようかと思うようになるはずです。無限だけれども時間軸がある。そういう意味では、私がやりたかったことができたといえるかなと感じています。

匂いをコントロールする

川向 ── 建築的にいえば、吹き出す香料の量を非常に繊細にコントロールしていたということでしょうか。香料を吹き出し続け、排出しないと、どのような状態になるのですか。

上田 ── 均一な香りの空間になってしまうので換気力が必要ですが、設計段階で注意するのは、香りの吹出しと排出のバランスです。あとは、香料の濃度と質とか、化学香料なのか天然香料なのか、いつ、どのくらい薫いて、蒸散の状態、分子が散らばる空気の状態を、頭の中でシミュレーションしていきます。人が内部をだいたい左回りで動くだろうと予想して設計しました。

川向 ── 同じ香りが出続けているよりは微細に変化するほうがいいわけですか。

上田 ── はい。この部屋でも、ある1つの香りを薫いていれば、最初に入

「白い闇」展の上田氏による匂いのワークショップ。目隠しをして匂いを嗅ぐ体験の様子

Scent workshop with Ueda at the *Invisible White* exhibition, with participants experiencing scents while blindfolded.

unfamiliar with, but the other two would be relatively easy to tie to personal experience.

Kawamukai — Do you mean that it's not enough for the nose to simply pick up a scent—that you'd rather cause people to question what the scent is?

Ueda — It makes it easier to rise to the level of consciousness. The fact is that just sending a signal to the brain from the nasal receptors that detect odor molecules isn't enough on its own for something to register as a smell. It ought to be possible to sniff out minute difference between scents by concentrating hard enough, but you really want to avoid having people come up blank. Consciously focusing on one's sense of smell is one action people can take, but having familiar scents waft through can also elicit memories tied to one's own experience. Still, in my work the most important thing to convey first is that there is something to smell. This time we managed to cleanly separate the inside and outside air at the entrance so scent was probably something people were conscious of as soon as they entered.

There are a lot of elements that are impossible to calculate at the planning stage, and in those cases I just had to decide based on intuition. I had to look at a lot of options when deciding on specs for the exhaust fans and how to vaporize and emit the fragrances. I had to commit to a staggered-timing emission method—and place the order— at the same time as I was deciding what combination of scents to use. There were so many things to decide that I can't really remember how I made all the decisions, but everything fell into place in the end.

Kawamukai — How did you intend for the scent to change as people moved? I experienced it myself many times but I'd like to ask you to touch on this again.

Ueda — You're walking along, absorbed in your sense of sight, when you suddenly catch a whiff of an unusual scent. You start walking again and encounter a different smell. That should be enough to create a sense of anticipation, a desire to walk further. It's boundless, but grounded in time. In that sense I feel I can probably say I accomplished what I set out to do.

Controlling Scent

Kawamukai — Surely you must have exercised very precise control, architecturally, over the amount of fragrance that was emitted. What

った瞬間だけ匂いを感じて、あとは感じなくなります。人間の鼻は匂いを一定時間嗅ぐと、匂いを感知できなくなるので、香りを排出しながら、香りを吹き出すのはタイマー仕掛けにしました。

川向 —— まさに、匂いを科学する、テクノロジーで徹底的に使いこなす感じですね。

さて、「白い闇」展から1年がたちましたが、その後の展開をお話しいただけますか。

匂いへの挑戦〜オランダ、東京、石垣島

上田 —— 私はオランダ、東京の拠点のほかに、石垣島にアトリエを構えました。アトリエの前の畑で育てたものから香りを抽出したり、香水をつくったりしています。香りのワークショップも開催しています。季節に合わせて島内を巡る匂いのツアーも企画していて、石垣島ならではのリトリート・ツアーも考えています。

東京でベリーダンスのステージ「Ruhani Belly Dance Celebration 〜 PERFUMUM」（2014）で香りづけを頼まれて、ダンスに合わせて空間に目まぐるしく香りを薫きました。

川向 —— それは新しい試みですね。

上田 —— そういうことをしている人は、ほとんどいないでしょう。単にBGM的に単一の匂いを流すのは可能ですが、空間全体を対象に複数の匂いをコントロールするのは、非常にリスキーなので、みんな避けるのです。ダンスの振りやステージが変化する瞬間に合わせて、匂いを切り替えてどんどん展開できるように、空間の3カ所にサーキュレーターを使ってやりました。

川向 —— 与えられた時間の中でどのぐらい変えるのですか。

上田 —— 1時間に30種類くらいです。ベリーダンスの方々が「白い闇」展のワークショップに参加して、「感銘を受けた。匂いで何かやろう」と言ってくださったので実現したのです。ダンスあり、音あり、匂いありで、

2点とも：上田氏の石垣島のアトリエ

Left and Right: Ueda's studio on Ishigaki Island.

would have happened if you continued to emit fragrance without discharging any of it?

Ueda — Well, the space would end up with a uniform aroma, so ventilation is absolutely essential. During the planning stage I paid a lot of attention to the balance between fragrance emission and discharge. Later I did simulations in my head to decide on the concentration and characteristics of the fragrances, whether to use natural or chemical fragrances, how much to infuse and when, the state of vaporization, and the condition of the air to ensure dispersal of the molecules. I designed things on the assumption that people would generally tend to move counterclockwise around the interior.

Kawamukai — It's better, then, to exercise such precise control rather than to just have the same scent infused continually?

Ueda — Even in this room, if you just kept pumping in the same scent you would smell it when you entered but you wouldn't notice it after that. After smelling a given scent for a certain amount of time, the human nose becomes desensitized to it, so when infusing the fragrances I decided to use a timer.

Kawamukai — I sense you've really made a science of scent, and are employing technology effectively, too. It has been about a year since the *Invisible White* exhibit. Could you share what have you been up to since then?

Testing the Limits of Scent:
The Netherlands, Tokyo, and Ishigaki Island

Ueda — In addition to bases in the Netherlands and in Tokyo, I also opened up a studio on Ishigaki Island in Okinawa. I extract fragrances and make perfume from the things I grow in the garden out in front, and I hold workshops and organize seasonal fragrance tours around the island. I'm also thinking about putting together a retreat tour that would take advantage of the unique things Ishigaki Island has to offer.

In Tokyo I was asked to compose fragrances for a belly dancing event, the Ruhani Belly Dance Celebration: Perfumum (2014), and produced a dizzying array of scents to go with the performances.

Kawamukai — That's something new, isn't it?

Ueda — Well, I suppose there aren't very many people doing that sort of thing. It's easy enough to create a constant stream of some uniform scent, almost like background music, but there's a lot of risk

会場の皆さんが泣いていらっしゃるのです。「感動した」とおっしゃって。香りをどんどん薫いているので忙しいのですが、会場の人たちが泣いているのがわかって、私も涙がツーッと。言葉にはならない、どうしようもなく突き動かされるような感情が、いろいろな感覚要素がそろうと生まれることがわかりました。

川向──強烈な体験ですね。空間の振動にシンクロする匂いの演出というのは、すごい試みです。ヨコミゾさんのその後は、どうですか。

〈境内〉～都市や農村の無限空間へ

ヨコミゾ──あの年の冬にプロポーザルコンペ「(仮称) 釜石市民ホール及び釜石情報交流センター」があって、今、830人ほど収容のホールを設計していますが、匂いとか無限の広がりが表現できる機会かというと、どうでしょうか。求められているのは、実に現実的な、まるで町中の公民館のようなホールです。しかし、震災復興という短期的な視点だけで物事を判断せず、地域の文化的醸成の舞台となるべく50年、60年先まで見据えたものにしなければ、と苦闘している最中です。「白い闇」と、現実とのギャップは大きいですね。

川向──どう広がりを持たせるか。人と人とのつながり、自然とのつながり、そういう思考の延長線上に、「白い闇」に現れたのだと、私は受け止めています。人が集まる空間も〈かたち〉の問題ではなく、〈かた〉でもなく、〈か〉の状態でどう空間化するか、いつもそのことを考えていらっしゃるのでは？

ヨコミゾ──確かに、人が集まる場所性が気になっています。今、考えているのは「ホールか、境内か？」ということです。〈ホール〉は戦後、前川 (國男) さんから始まって、ヨーロッパで熟成された文化をいかに日本に取り入れるかに躍起になってやってきて、その頂点が「新国立劇場」(1997) ですよね。でも今、それを再生産しても仕方ないと思います。原点に立ち返り、少し見方を変えると、劇場のような空間とは、人々が集まってきて、見せたいと思う人が演じ、見たいと思う人がその周りに座って、目の前で演じられるものを眺め、楽しむ場所といえるのではないか。そのような人と人の初源的な関係性を考えると、そこは、神社の〈境内〉のような場所ではないかと思うのです。普段はひっそりしていて、野良猫と鳩くらいしかいない。たまに掃除している老人がいたりして。しかしいざ縁日となれば、老若男女が集い、怪しげなテキ屋までやってきて最高に盛り上がる。終わればまた普段の状態に戻る。そのような場所でいいのではないか。ですから、これからの公共の〈ホール〉は普段は開けっ放しにしておいて、演奏会や講演会などを開催するときだけ扉を閉

involved in trying to control multiple scents across an entire space, so everyone avoids that sort of thing. I used three circulators in three locations in order to switch scents one after the other in time with shifts in the choreography or other changes taking place on stage.

Kawamukai — How frequently can you make such changes within a given time?

Ueda — About thirty scents in the course of an hour. Some of the belly dancers had taken part in the *Invisible White* workshop. It left such an impression on them that they approached me about doing something with scent for their performance. And we made it happen; the music and the scents left everyone in the audience so moved they were in tears. During the performance I was furiously busy behind the scenes infusing scents but when I saw the audience crying it bought tears to my eyes, too. I realized that several different sensory elements in combination could really be indescribably, powerfully, moving.

Kawamukai — It was an intense experience, then. Trying to synchronize fragrances with the vibrations in the air of a performance space is an amazing experiment. And Yokomizo, what have you been up to?

From "Precincts" To Boundless Urban and Agricultural Spaces

Yokomizo — That winter there was a competition for a project tentatively called the Kamaishi Municipal Hall and Information Center, and I'm now designing an 830-person capacity auditorium. It's hard to say whether or not it presents an opportunity to use scent or to express a boundless expanse. What I've been asked to do is something very practical, very much like a downtown community center. Still, right now I'm struggling with the feeling that I really have to make decisions based not only on the short-term perspective of post-earthquake reconstruction but also on how to nurture local culture for the next 50 or 60 years. It's a world away from *Invisible White*.

Kawamukai — I understood *Invisible White* to be an extension of thinking about how to convey breadth, the connections between people, or our connection to nature. I imagine that when designing spaces where people assemble you must spend a great deal of time thinking not so much about *katachi* and *kata* but rather about how to convey *ka*.

Yokomizo — Indeed, there is a particular character to places where

「(仮称)釜石市民ホール及び釜石情報交流センター」プロポーザルコンペ時の模型。広場、ホワイエ、ステージがひとつながりとなる

Model used in the competition proposal for the Kamaishi Municipal Hall and Information Center, showing its interconnected plaza, foyer, and stage.

めて特別な場所にすればいい。古谷(誠章)さんの設計した「茅野市民館」(2005)も、オープンにできるホールをやっていましたよね。

川向 — 古谷さんは〈お堂〉とか〈がらんどう〉と言っています。

ヨコミゾ — 僕の感覚では〈お堂〉じゃなく、やはり〈境内〉かな……。社殿に見立て得るステージから、平土間を抜けてホワイエへ、ロビーを抜けて都市広場へ、そして家々が建ち並ぶ街へと連続するひと続きの空間。その連続性の中に、あらためて〈ホール〉を位置づけたいと考えています。地方における集落と神社との関係など、とても参考になると思っています。

川向 — いいじゃないですか、〈境内〉みたいな劇場。ただ単に壁を取り払ったというだけではなく、無限に広がっていく感じがあります。完成が楽しみです。

people gather. The question I'm asking myself now is whether a concert hall or theater constitutes a kind of precinct. After the war, beginning with Kunio Maekawa, many such halls were built in a frantic effort to transfer to Japan aspects of a culture that had matured in Europe, with the pinnacle of this movement being the New National Theater, Tokyo (1997). But there doesn't seem to be much point in doing the same thing today. Going back to basics and shifting perspective a little bit, aren't theatrical spaces really just places where people assemble, and where those who have something to show perform while those who want to watch gather and enjoy the entertainments played out before them? Considering the primal aspects of such interpersonal relationships, I have come to think that maybe such places are really like the precincts of a shrine. Ordinarily enveloped in a quiet disturbed only by the screeching of stray cats and perhaps the occasional elderly person tidying up, on festival days they erupt in a great swell of excitement that draws young and old alike, and even a confusion of dodgy street vendors. And then, when the festival is over, everything returns to normal. Why not build such a space? Going forward, I think public halls ought to be places that are normally left wide open, with the doors only shut to enclose a special space when there are concerts or lectures being held. Nobuaki Furuya created a hall that could be opened up in this way when he designed the Chino Cultural Complex (2005).

Kawamukai — Furuya has described it as being like the main hall of a temple or shrine.

Yokomizo — To me, though, I must say it feels more like the precincts of a shrine. In one spatial continuum you move from the stage, which might be likened to the main building in a Shinto shrine, through the main floor of the theater and out into the foyer, then through the lobby to the urban plaza, and finally out into the town and its rows of houses. I really want to reposition the auditorium for the Kamaishi project within this kind of continuum, and I think the relationship between a rural village and its local shrine may be a point of reference for me.

Kawamukai — Wonderful. I love the idea of a theater as the precincts of a shrine. It not only removes the walls but also creates a sense of boundless expanse. I look forward to seeing how the project turns out.

CHAPTER —— 7

Ripple

波・紋

ARCHITECT	HANANOFU (IKEBANA MASTER)
Nobuaki Furuya	Shuho
建築家	花士
古谷誠章	珠寶

228　第7章　波・紋

CHAPTER-7　Ripple　229

230　第 7 章　波・紋

CHAPTER-7 Ripple 231

この展覧会の依頼があったとき、協働する作家と
して、私は真っ先に珠寶さんを想いました。その
「花」はただの花でなく、私たちとの間におかれた、
まさに「賜物」。たちまち空間がさざめき、そし
て静かにひとつになっていきます。
花は、摘まれてひととき生命を絶たれ、ふたたび
水面に立てられて活かされます。その指先に波立
つ波紋の広がりが、やがて私たちまでをも包み込
んでいきます。私はそんな空間をイメージして、
この会場をデザインしました。

（展覧会コンセプト文より）

When I was first approached about doing this exhibit, I thought of Shuho right away as the artist I would most like to collaborate with. Her flowers are not ordinary flowers; they are truly gifts set among us. A stir sweeps though the space, which then quietly unites as one. When picked, a flower's life is momentarily ended, and then given new life as she places it in the water's surface. The ripples that spread from her fingertips eventually envelop us all. Such is the kind of space I imagined while designing the venue.

(Exhibition concept, July 2014)

「花」の波紋が
生きた空間のかたちをつくる

古谷誠章
珠寶
川向正人

建築家
古谷誠章

1955年 東京都生まれ。早稲田大学大学院博士課程前期修了。文化庁芸術家在外研修員としてマリオ・ボッタ事務所に在籍。1994年 NASCA を八木佐千子と共同設立。1994年 早稲田大学助教授、1997年から同大学教授。主な作品に、茅野市民館（2005）ほか

ARCHITECT
Nobuaki Furuya

Born in Tokyo in 1955, Furuya received his master's degree in architecture from Waseda University. He later worked at the studio of Mario Botta through the Japanese Government Overseas Study Program for Artists. He co-founded Nasca with Sachiko Yagi in 1994. He became an Professor at Waseda University in 1997. Major works include the Chino Cultural Complex (2005).

川向 —— ODS-R の第 12 回を引き受けるにあたって、どのようなことをお考えになられましたか？

空間を使いこなしてほしい

古谷 —— オフィス家具のショールームという日常空間を劇的に変えるということは、普通のギャラリーで行うのとは違う面白みがあると思いました。ほかのアーティストとの協働が条件でしたが、建築というのは〈器＝空間の構え〉をつくって、住みこなしたり使いこなされたりすることがうまく重なり合って本当の空間が立ち上がるというのが、日頃からの自分の考えでもありましたから、何かアート作品のために容れ物をつくると

Ripples of Flowers
Shape a Living Space

NOBUAKI FURUYA
SHUHO
MASATO KAWAMUKAI

花士 (はなのふ)

珠寶

1967 年 兵庫県生まれ。2004 年 慈照寺初代花
方に就任。慈照寺「花道場」での指導や『同仁』
誌の編集などに携わる。2008 年よりフランスほ
かで慈照寺国際交流を開始。2011 年 一視同仁
の精神を基に「慈照寺研修道場」が開場。企画
運営も担当。2015 年独立。花の活動を開始

HANANOFU (IKEBANA MASTER)

Shuho

Born in Hyogo prefecture in 1967. Appointed the
first *hanakata* of Jisho-ji Temple in 2004. In 2008
she began conducing international exchange
activities for Jisho-ji Temple. In 2011 the Kenshu
Dojo (study center) at Jisho-ji Temple was
established, with Shuho responsible for planning
and operations. She became independent in
2015 and is active in flower arranging.

Kawamukai — What were your thoughts when you agreed to take on
the twelfth edition of ODS-R?

Making Full Use of a Space

Furuya — My first thought was that dramatically transforming an
everyday space like an office furniture showroom was sure to be
interesting in ways that differed from using an ordinary gallery.
One of the conditions for the project was to find another artist with
whom to collaborate, and as someone who approaches buildings
like containers that only emerge as real, living spaces through the

いうよりは、ある空間をつくり、それが、家が住みこなされるように、あるいは服が着こなされるように、何かをもたらしてくれる形で協働していただける方がいいなと思いました。

そこで、まずピンときたのが珠寶さんでした。ある機会に、珠寶さんが銀閣 慈照寺の研修道場でお花をされるのを拝見して、そのときの珠寶さんの一挙手一投足から空間に何かが生じる、それまでの普通の空間に灯がともっていくような感覚を新鮮に覚えていたからです。

川向 ── 珠寶さんは、コラボレーターとして参加してくださいませんかというお誘いを受けて、どんなことをお考えになりましたか。

珠寶 ── 古谷先生からお話を頂いたときに、直感的に楽しそうだと思いましたので、お引き受けいたしました。オフィス空間という、通常〈花立て〉をしております畳とか床の間のある空間ではないところでも、花はできます。逆に、しつらえが変わることで、非常にワクワクします。

人がつくる空間

古谷 ── 珠寶さんの〈花立て〉は、最初に花器や花材が用意されていて、そこに珠寶さんが現れて始まります。その場面をみんなが取り囲み、息をひそめている〈人がつくる空間〉が、とても鮮やかに感じられたので、それを再現したいと思いました。

さらに花器の縁すれすれまで水が注がれ、そこに一挿し、一挿し、花を立てていきますが、そのとき、水面に波紋が生じます。水面に生じた波紋が器の縁を越えて、固唾をのんで見守る人々の間まで広がっていくような、まるでそれが目に見えるような感覚があったので、大変驚きました。ピンと張り詰めていますが、ふうわりと空気の〈波紋〉が庭へと広がっ

珠寶氏の花立て。京都にて
（2014）

Shuho arranging flowers in
Kyoto (2014).

superimposition of being lived in and put to use, I was really hoping to find someone I could work with not to create a receptacle for a work of art but a space they might breathe life into in the same way a house comes alive when lived in, or clothing comes alive when worn well.

The first person to come to mind was Shuho. I had an opportunity to observe her performing ikebana flower arrangement once at the Kenshu Dojo (study center) at Ginkaku Jisho-ji Temple in Kyoto. I could still remember with absolute clarity how her every movement seemed to breathe life into the room—the way an ordinary space was suddenly suffused with light.

Kawamukai — Shuho, what were your thoughts when you were invited to collaborate?

Shuho — When Furuya approached me I intuitively knew it would be fun, and accepted immediately. I was certain I could do arrangements even in an office space that was nothing like the tatami mat rooms and *tokonoma* alcoves where ikebana is customarily done. Indeed, I found myself very excited by the idea of working in a space that was appointed in a completely different way.

Spaces Built by People

Furuya — When Shuho arranges flowers, the equipment and materials to be used are set out in advance and the performance begin when she enters. When I saw her at the temple, the way everyone gathered around with bated breath left a real impression. It was a space formed by people, and this was something I wanted to recreate for the ODS-R.

She used a flower vessel filled to the brim with water, and as each flower was added, one at a time, it generated ripples in the surface. What was astonishing is that I could almost see the ripples extend beyond the edge of the vessel and spread among the breathless observers gathered round. There was an acute tension in the air and yet the ripples seemed to spread out gently, extending even to the garden. It left a powerful impression.

I thought the project would be a huge success if we could create the same sort of thing in an everyday space like a showroom bustling with a bigger group of people, an environment so unlike the Kenshu Dojo at Ginkaku Jisho-ji Temple.

Kawamukai — The notion of a space made by people is really

ていくような感じが、とても印象的だったのです。

これを、銀閣 慈照寺の研修道場とは違う、もう少し大勢の人でガヤガヤする日常空間のショールームの中で生じさせることができたら大成功なのではないかなと思いました。

川向 ──〈人がつくる空間〉というのは魅力的な言葉ですね。人が自らの身体でつくる空間、まさに始原の空間です。人々が眺めながら、同時に空間づくりに参加するという、空間生成の始まりの姿がそこにあります。

古谷 ──もともと建築は立体的なもので、こちら側から見る視点があれば、向こう側から見返す視点もある。そのように人が介在することで建築が成立します。

よく私がお話しする〈がらんどう〉という概念の場合も、「がらんどう」だけでは意味がなくて、「がらんどう」に人が入って初めて意味が出てきます。人の入り方には、1点を見つめて固唾をのんで集合する場合もあれば、三々五々、バラバラの場合もあるでしょうし、ワァッと一斉に外を向いて眺めたりと、いろいろな立ち位置で出現する空間が、〈がらんどう〉に現れる空間の醍醐味ですよね。それをやってみたいと思いました。

求心的な空間がいくつも生成する

川向 ──〈がらんどう〉の中に成立する空間は、それを生み出す人々の意識とか身体のありようによって、大きく変化するのですか。何となく求心的なものかなという印象を持っておりました。

古谷 ──〈がらんどう〉の中に成立する空間には自由度がありますが、珠寶さんのお花は〈波紋〉と〈向き〉を感じる、非常に求心的なものです。取り囲んでいるわれわれのほうに向かって、珠寶さんが1輪お花を挿し

〈がらんどう〉の一例。「小布施町立図書館まちとしょテラソ」（NASCA、2009）

Obuse Town Library Machi Tosho Terrasow (NASCA, 2009), an example of a *garando* empty space.

appealing. A space that people create through the use of their own bodies is a primordial space, one that begins to take shape when people watch together, taking part in something simultaneously.

Furuya — Architecture exists in three-dimensions; you can look at it from one side, and someone else will be looking back from the other. In this way, architecture is realized through the intervention of people.

I often talk about the concept of *garando* (empty spaces), but *garando* are meaningless on their own; meaning only emerges when someone enters. People may enter looking intently at one spot—holding their breath, lost in concentration—or enter separately in groups of threes or fives. They may all turn at once to look outside, and it's the way different spaces emerge from different perspectives that makes *garando* so appealing. This is the sort of thing I was hoping to accomplish.

Generating a Number of Spaces With Centripetal Pull

Kawamukai — Do the types of spaces that can be realized within *garando* vary widely with the consciousness or physicality of the people who create them? I had the impression you meant something with centripetal pull.

Furuya — There's a degree of freedom in the kinds of spaces that form within *garando*, but Shuho's ikebana is extremely centripetal, with a sense of rippling and directionality. She added a single flower facing those of us who were gathered around. At first this was surprising—*Huh? She's directing the flower toward us?*—but then she added one facing the far side, and then one facing herself, and the notion of displaying flowers in an alcove to be viewed from a single direction fell away.

Kawamukai — What you've just said really puts the exhibition layout sketch that you shared at our first ODS-R meeting into perspective. It was centripetal, but rather than ending with one circle you drew a number of circles.

Furuya — That's right. You're familiar, of course, with the phrase from the opening lines of the classic text *Hojoki* [The Ten Foot Square Hut]: "Foam floats upon the pools, scattering, re-forming, never lingering long." * Right from the start I was imagining something similar, with something small and centered that flowed out by degrees, so I wanted to use the corridor as part of the venue, too, and make the

* Kamo no Chomei. *Hojoki: Visions of a Torn World.* Translated by Yasuhiko Moriguchi and David Jenkins. Berkeley, Calif.: Stone Bridge Press, 1996.

てくださる。「あれ？ こっち向きの花なのかな？」と最初驚きますが、続けて向こうに1輪、ご自分のほうに向かって1輪と挿していきます。床の間に花を飾り正対して拝見する、という概念がにわかに崩れるわけです。

川向 ── 今のお話で、ODS-R の最初の打合せのときに示された展示構想のスケッチの意図がよくわかりました。求心的であるけれども、1つの円で終わらず、いくつかの円が描かれていました。

古谷 ── そうですね。「淀みに浮かぶうたかたは、かつ消え、かつ結びて、久しくとどまりたる例^{ためし}なし」（方丈記）ではないけれども、小さな求心性はあるのですが、だんだん流れていくイメージは最初からありましたので、会場は廊下も使い、広く、どんどん伸びていきました。

何かを見ようと思って、身を乗り出したり、取り囲んだり、あるいは、反対側に回って見たり、意志を持って動く〈人がつくる空間〉です。珠寶さんの花にはそれができる求心力があると思いました。

次々に小さな世界が立ち上がる

川向 ── 珠寶さんの花は、完結したスタイルを持って展示された花ではなくて、1つの世界が立ち上がるプロセスそのものを人々が囲んで拝見するという花です。この10年、20年、テレビや雑誌などに取り上げられてきた、パフォーマンスが過剰で、絢爛豪華に見せ、ワッと驚かせる花とは対照的で、珠寶さんの花は、1輪の花、1本の草がまっすぐに立ち上がってきます。つまり、1つの世界が静かに立ち上がること自体を拝見し、また、立ち上がった花と対話する花です。静かに花と向き合い、対話しつつ、その姿に触発されて自分の記憶をたどるような花だと思いました。

プロセスそのものを見せ、なおかつ場所を変えて、複数のしつらえを試みるところに、要所要所を押さえる確かさがあって、きわめて建築的だとも感じました。互いに異なる多様なものが、ある距離をもって、緊張

古谷氏による「波・紋」展のイメージスケッチ

Furuya's sketch of the *Ripple* exhibition.

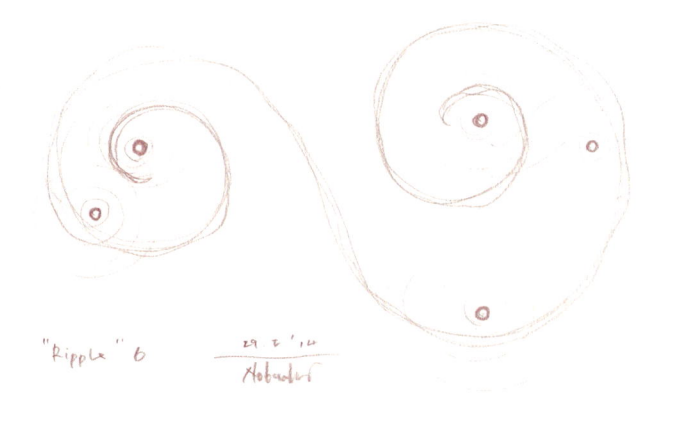

"Ripple" 6

space as broad and expansive as possible. I wanted it to be a space where you could lean forward or move closer to try to get a better look at something, or move around to the other side—a space created by people who moved willfully. I knew Shuho's ikebana had the centripetal pull to make that happen.

Small Worlds That Emerge One After the Other

Kawamukai — Shuho, your ikebana is not exhibited as an example of a perfected style, but rather shown as a process, witnessed by a gathering of people, through which a unique world emerges. Unlike the kinds of ikebana that have drawn attention on television and in magazines over the last decade or two—over-the-top performances designed to overwhelm and surprise through lavish pageantry— your ikebana involves single flowers, single blades of grass, standing straight and tall. It offers the opportunity to witness a unique world emerging quietly, and then to engage in a dialogue with the arrangement that results. You face the flowers quietly, and engaging with them seems to trigger a retracing of memory.

In showing the process itself, in changing locations and experimenting with various kinds of environments, you seem to have an almost architectural attentiveness to nailing down the key points. Various things that are unalike maintain a certain distance as they form relationships of tension. Is this typical of your normal style?

Shuho — My daily duties start with cleaning, picking flowers in the garden, and arranging flowers for each location. The sketch that Furuya showed me included a number of circles and I was easily able to imagine arranging flowers at each in turn.

Furuya — I first saw Shuho doing ikebana in the Japanese-style room at the Kenshu Dojo. When I heard that she ordinarily did ikebana for various locations throughout the temple, I must have been left with a powerful image of her walking around the grounds arranging flowers. I suppose this is why, instead of crowding things together into one area for the *Ripple* exhibition, I must have subconsciously wanted to recreate the feeling of swift transitions to new locations. And indeed, she did move very fast....

Kawamukai — Shuho, does that you mean that when arranging the flowers it was more like an extension of the way you live your life than something you consciously thought about as being exhibited?

Shuho — I wasn't thinking at all about creating a work of art or about

感のある関係をつくり出しています。珠寶さんが普段なさっているスタイルに近いのですか？

珠寶 ── 毎日の作務は、掃除をして、畑で花を摘んで、各所に花を生けることから始まります。古谷先生のスケッチに円が何カ所かありましたので、これは順番に花を生けていけるのかなと、スッとイメージできました。

古谷 ── 珠寶さんのお花を拝見したのは研修道場の和室でしたが、「普段は、花を生けて回るのですよ」と伺ったので、珠寶さんが毎朝、銀閣 慈照寺の中で花を生けながら歩き回る様子が頭にすり込まれていたのでしょう。だから、「波・紋」展では、1カ所でにぎにぎしくやるのではなくて、サッと移っていく感じを再現したいと、無意識に思ったのでしょうね。実際には本当に速かったのですが……。

川向 ── ことさらに展示を意識することなく、あくまでも日常の生、生きることの延長で花をされたということでしょうか。

珠寶 ── 作品をつくるとか、展示をしているという感覚はありませんでした。常に動いている日常の延長線上です。

銀閣 慈照寺の花〜〈むこう〉とのつながり

川向 ── 先ほども申しましたが、珠寶さんの花には、現代の華道家といわれる方々とは異なる、つまり作家の個性の現れとは違う、何か深い日本の伝統文化とのつながりが感じられます。ここが決定的に新しい（笑）。ここで少し、花を生けることがどのような意味を持つ生活をされているのかをお話しいただけますか。

珠寶 ── 花方というお花の専門職として銀閣 慈照寺でお仕事させていただいています。（足利）義政公の時代から室町時代の末くらいに〈いけ花〉という、立てるお花や、なげ入れるお花ができてきました。その時代から学んでいきますと、人のほうからの視点ではなくて、まずは、〈むこう〉〈あちら〉ありきだったようです。左右を逆に描く『相阿弥花伝書』の図絵を拝見したときに、私自身が〈むこう〉に行くべきことに気づきました。そこからですね。ほろほろと、ほどけるようにわかるようになったのは。いけ花が室内を飾る美しい装飾、芸術になったところから、もう一度、原点に戻って、命を生かすとか、自分自身が自然の中に入っていって草木や虫や鳥などと同列に並んで、もう一度目の前の花を眺めてみることを考えるようになりました。お寺でする仕事も、お花だけをしているわけではなくて、掃除も畑仕事も事務仕事もしていますし、何をしてもいけ花につながっていくという意識を持つようになりました。

川向 ── 〈むこう〉の花ですか。そのいけ花は、どなたのための花なのでしょう？

exhibiting. It was just an extension of a daily life in which I am in constant motion.

The Flowers of Ginkaku Jisho-ji Temple:
A Connection to the Other Side

Kawamukai — As I mentioned earlier, Shuho, your arrangements are different than those of others who are known as contemporary masters of ikebana—rather than expressing an artist's personality they connect in some profound way to Japanese traditional culture. Indeed, this seems decidedly new! (*Laughs*) Could you talk a little bit about the significance of flower arranging in your life?

Shuho — I work at Ginkaku Jisho-ji temple as its *hanakata,* the "flower person" responsible for all matters concerning ikebana. Between the time of Shogun Ashikaga Yoshimasa (the mid-15th century) and the end of the Muromachi period (1573), ikebana developed as a practice encompassing both the *rikka* "standing flowers" and *nageire* "thrown-in" styles. In studying that period, I could see that what was most important was not the viewer's perspective but the view from the other side, from "over there." When I saw the paintings in Soami's *Kadensho* [Book of Flowers], which are reversed left-to-right, I realized that I needed to go to the "other side" myself. That was when things started to come untangled and make sense.

I needed to shift from this position where ikebana had become beautiful displays for adorning interiors, a kind of decorative art, and return to fundamentals, to the notion of keeping something alive— to go out myself into nature and stand at the level of the flowers and grasses, the insects and birds—and I began thinking about really looking at the flowers in front of me. My work at the temple is not limited only to flowers. I clean, and tend the gardens, and do administrative work, too, but no matter what I'm doing, now I'm better able to see it within an ikebana context.

Kawamukai — Flowers on the "other side"? Who is such ikebana done for?

Shuho — The first thing is to be clearly conscious of things that you cannot see, like Yoshimasa, for example. It's only because he existed that I'm now able to do to the work I do, and for this I feel grateful. I think many people become conscious through ikebana of their ties to their ancestors, or to the gods of nature, or to other things that go unseen, and I believe that in this lies the meaning of practicing

珠寶 ── まずは、目に見えないものを、はっきりと意識しているように感じます。例えば義政公。公がおられたから、今、私がこういう仕事ができていることに感謝する気持ちがあります。あるいは、皆様も、ご先祖や大自然の神々など、目に見えないものとのつながりを、いけ花を通して意識なさることがあると思いますが、それが花を生ける意味だと思います。来られた人とも、お花があることで、人と人のつながりをはっきり意識できます。

川向 ── すごく建築に通じるお話です。地霊に対し、そして地霊から、建築は立ち上がってきます。むろん個人の施主を強く意識することもあります。さて、そうして立ち上がってくる花の姿は、どのように決まるのですか。

珠寶 ── 一般論としては、目的によって決まるといえます。どなたに対してということも含めて。今日は何のためにお花をするのか。お客様をお迎えするためか、あるいは、仏様に向かっての花なのか。フォーマルなものからカジュアルなものまで何通りもあります。実際に花をする場所、空間もその姿を決める大きな要因です。そして、それに合った道具の見立て、最後に、季節です。

〈始まり〉と〈終わり〉

珠寶 ── お花に関しては、季節の新鮮なものを、お寺の畑で、自分の手で摘みます。「お客様をお迎えする日に、咲いてくれるかな」と思いながら畑を見て回ります。そこから「いけ花」が始まっています。頂戴したお花をどうやって生かそうかと考える場合もありますので、どうしても自分で摘まなければいけないというわけではありません。ただ、この順序、プロセスだけは変わりません。

川向 ── 今、どういけ花が始まるかをお話しくださいましたが、珠寶さんの花を実際に拝見して強く私の印象に残ったのは、もう１つ、〈どう終わるか〉ということでした。どこで終わるのか。どの状態で、もう十分とお考えになるのか。

珠寶 ── 私は、お花１輪の存在はすごいと思います。お花がたくさんあるからといって、あるだけ使おうとは思わないのです。つまり、お花の数量は重要ですが、それだけで決定要因にはなりません。やはり重要なのは、始まりについて申し上げた、目的であり、花をする場所です。何もないところに１輪でも花が出現すると空間が変わります。

その日の主となる花を１本立てたときに、私のイメージの中で、天井も床も壁もボワーッとなくなる感覚が広がるかどうか、なのです。それができると、〈あちら〉へどうぞと、次の手に動いていきます。

珠寶氏の花立て。フランス・ドルドーニュにある Dhagpo Kagyu Ling チベット仏教センターにて（2013）

Shuho arranging flowers at the Dhagpo Kagyu Ling Center for Tibetan Buddhism in Dordogne, France (2013).

ikebana. The presence of flowers brings to visitors, too, a clear awareness of the connections between people.

Kawamukai — What you say is true of architecture, too. Buildings face, and arise from, spirits living in the ground. And architects, of course, are also very conscious of their clients. But tell me, how do you decide what form to give the flowers you arrange?

Shuho — Generally speaking, you could say it depends on the objective, including for whom the flowers are being prepared. Why am I arranging flowers today? Is it to welcome a guest, or am I preparing flowers for the Buddha? There are all sorts of ways to do things along a range from formal to casual. And, of course, the space where the flowers will actually be placed is an important factor. I select appropriate equipment and finally, of course, there is the season to consider.

Beginnings and Endings

Shuho — I use fresh, seasonal flowers that I pick myself from my

CHAPTER-7   Ripple   **245**

〈波紋〉の広がり

川向 ── このようなコラボレーターをお迎えして、花をする瞬間を想定しつつ、建築家として展示空間の設計をなさいました。珠寶さんの花のお考えを伺うと、今回、古谷さんが、ODS-Rでこれまで使ってきたショールームの一角の「打合せコーナー」から、広いショールーム空間そのものに展示スペースを移された理由も、何となくわかるような気がしてきます。この展示スペースの選び方についてご説明いただけますでしょうか。

古谷 ── 珠寶さんが花をなさる場所をいくつかつくり、その場所の間に距離感が欲しかったのです。ある距離と広さが必要でした。それに何よりも、日常的な空間であるショールームが変貌する幅を大きくすることにチャレンジしたかったので、ややニュートラルな打合せコーナーよりも、いかにもショールーム然とした空間に踏み込みたいと思いました。その中で、珠寶さんが緊張感をつなぎつつ次に移っていくための距離をとることを考えました。

ショールームのあの位置だと、外に広がるニューオータニの庭が見えて、珠寶さんが花立てをする空間から外の庭まで〈波紋〉が広がっていくような感じを生み出すことができます。私がいつも求めている、建築の境界を越えて外にまで延び広がる空間性も意識しました。

「波・紋」展の平面図。ショールームを歩き回りながら見ることができる

Plan drawing of the *Ripple* exhibition. The exhibit could be seen while walking about the showroom.

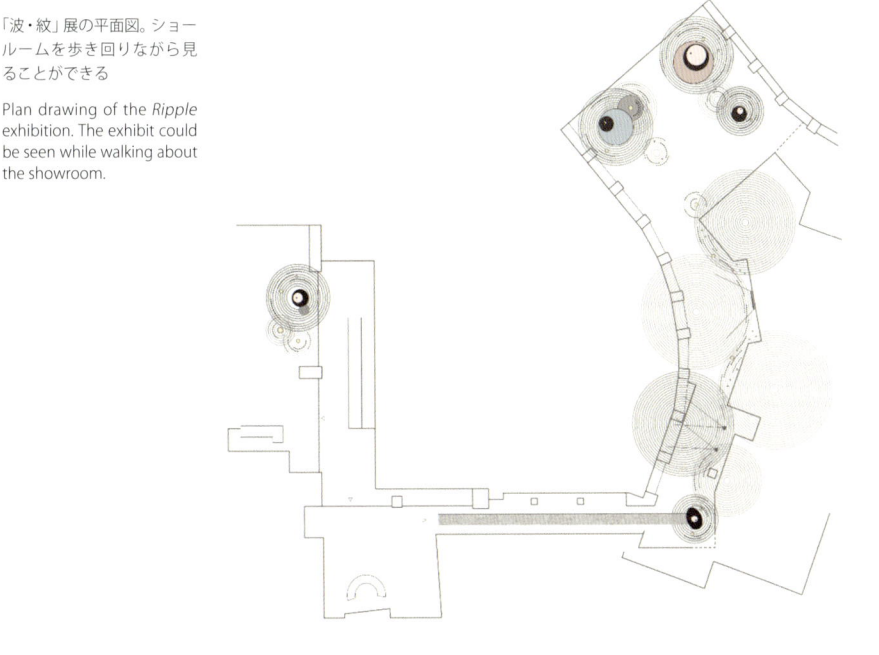

246　第7章　波・紋

private garden at the temple. I walk around the garden wondering what will blossom on the day a guest is expected. At that point, the ikebana has already begun. Sometimes I have the opportunity to think about how to give life to flowers I have received, too, so it's not as if I absolutely have to pick them myself, but the order of things, the process, is the same either way.

Kawamukai — You spoke just now about the point at which ikebana begins, but another thing I was very interested in when I saw you arrange flowers in person was how you know when to stop? What tells you that you've done enough?

Shuho — I believe even a single flower is an incredible thing. Just because there are a lot of flowers available doesn't make me feel compelled to use them all. The quantity of flowers is important, but it's never a deciding factor on its own. What is important, as I mentioned when talking about beginnings, is the purpose and location. Even a single flower in an otherwise empty space changes the space completely.

The question is whether, when I have placed the primary flower for the day, I am able to imagine the ceiling and the floor and the walls all fading away. If I can do this, then I can show the way "over there" and move on to the next step.

The Spreading of Ripples

Kawamukai — As an architect, Furuya, even as you were imagining the moment when your collaborator would arrange flowers, you were also designing the exhibition space. Having just heard Shuho's approach to ikebana, I feel like I have a better understanding of why you decided to extend the exhibition beyond the meeting space in the corner of the showroom—the location used for previous editions of the ODS-R—to the broader showroom itself. Could you explain a bit about why you chose the exhibition space you did?

Furuya — I wanted to create a number of areas for Shuho to arrange flowers, and to maintain a sense of distance between them. I needed a measure of distance and breadth. Most of all I wanted to try to transform the everyday space of the showroom as extensively as possible; rather than staying within the somewhat neutral meeting area, I really wanted to push deep into the showroomiest parts of the space. There, I hoped to tie things together with the sense of tension I knew Shuho would create, while leaving enough distance for her to

珠寶さんの「花を一回殺し、そして、もう一度それを生かす」という言葉が印象的で、僕がつくる空間的しつらえを、珠寶さんの流儀で殺し、そして再び生かしてもらいたいと思いました。建築は、実は本質的にそういうプロセスをたどるもので、建築家がつくった空間に住み手が入り、そこに自由に家具を持ち込んで、いろんな切り崩し方をされます。今回はそれを、美的な感覚でやっていただけた。花と一緒に建築的しつらえをも変え、花と建築空間との間の境界線を消し去る。そんなコラボレーションを想定しました。

珠寶 ── 古谷先生から、布で囲われたいくつかの展示スペースについて、「ひとつひとつが花だと思ってください」という説明がありましたので、建築的しつらえを、お花と同じように足したり引いたり、好きにさせていただきました。

川向 ── 建築空間と花を立てる行為をつなぐ道具として、いくつかスケールの違うものを介在させ、その結果、複数の場が生まれていました。大きい水盤、大きな藁を束ねたもの、台の上に置かれた花器などです。

花を生けない〈いけ花〉

珠寶 ── 大きな藁の束は、古谷先生がつくってくださいました。若杉聖子さんの花器の独特な白がよく合うだろうなとひらめきましたので、制作をお願いしました。若杉さんがたくさん送ってくださった花器から実際に花瓶として使ったのは 2 つだけですが、あとは、床に寝転がらせたりして遊ばせていただきました。

ライブでお花を始めると、私の場合、もう花瓶だけが花入れではなくなります。大きな水盤もその外側の床も、あらゆるところが、お花と組み合わせられます。逆に、大きな水盤に花瓶を置いても、花を生けないことがあります。

川向 ── 空間の波紋の広がりがあれば、そこにあえて花を加えなくてもいいと。

珠寶 ── はい。古谷先生が先に波紋をつくってくださっていますし、それ

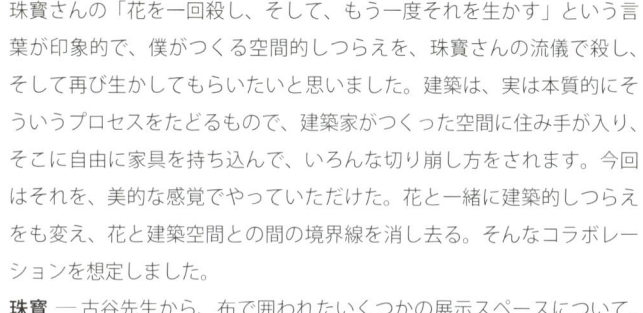

「波・紋」展の花のプレゼンテーション。花から花へ、来場者を引き連れて長い通路を移動し、その先でプレゼンテーションする珠寶氏

Flower presentation at the *Ripple* exhibition. From flower to flower, Shuho led attendees down a long corridor and then gave her presentation where it led.

move from one area to the next.

The expansive gardens of the New Otani are visible from the showroom so I knew it would be possible create the sensation that the ripples from where she was arranging flowers were spreading out into the garden. I was very conscious, as I always try to be, of creating a spatiality that stretches beyond the boundaries of the building to the outside.

I remember Shuho talking about "killing a flower and then bringing it back to life," words that left a deep impression on me. I hoped that by doing things her way, Shuho would kill the space I had prepared and then bring it back to life. Architecture actually follows much the same process insofar as when residents move into a home built by an architect they bring with them whatever furnishings they please and undercut things in all sorts of ways. For the exhibition, Shuho did so with an aesthetic sensibility. I imagined a collaboration in which, through flowers, we would change the architectural layout in a way that erased the boundaries between the flowers and architectural space.

Shuho — When he explained that there would be various exhibition spaces enclosed by fabric, Furuya asked me to think of each one as a flower, so I added and subtracted from the architectural layout just as I would with flowers, and did as I pleased.

Kawamukai — You connected the architectural space with the act of arranging flowers through the intervention of equipment that varied in scale—a large shallow water basin, a great bundle of straw, a vase set on a table—resulting in the creation of multiple spaces.

Ikebana Without Flowers

Shuho — Furuya made the big bundle of straw for me. I asked him to do so as I had the feeling it would go very well with the distinctive white of ceramic artist Seiko Wakasugi's flower vessels. Of the many that she sent, I only ended up using two to actually hold flowers; the rest I had fun with, doing things like laying them out on the floor.

When I begin arranging flowers for a live performance, I don't limit myself only to placing flowers in vases. I might combine the flowers with any location, whether a large water basin or the floor just beyond its edge. On the other hand, even after positioning a vase in a large water basin, there are times when I won't place any flowers in it at all.

までに、お花を置いた時間の流れがあるので、お花を置かずに通り過ぎても、私としてはよいかなと思いました。会期中のパフォーマンスでも、いろいろな方とコラボレーションをしましたが、ライブで神郡宇敬先生が書かれた書を水に浮かべたら、紙から墨がパーッと離れていったのは、私にとっては、まさに〈いけ花〉でした。

川向 ── 私たちには、〈花を生ける〉とはこういうことだという、ある種の先入観があります。ですから、花を生けると言いつつ〈花を生けない〉のは、なかなか勇気のいることですね。ただ、期待があるから、花を生けないという動きに、かえって何らかの意図を感じます。

珠寶 ── あの場にいる人々が何か感じることが〈いけ花〉なので、そこが大事です。できあがった花ではなく、花がつなぐ役割をし、何か次につながることが最も大切なのです。「お花を床の間に飾ることだけがいけ花ではない」ということをライブでお伝えできる、すごくいい機会を頂いたように思います。

川向 ──「波・紋」展では、集まっている人々の様子を見たり、外からの光を感じたり、大きな水盤に墨が広がる様子を見たりと、状況の変化を一瞬に把握しては、花を生ける、生けないの判断が下されました。静謐な時間のもとでの、その種の瞬間のつながりが目指す展示スタイルだったとすれば、かなり革命的な試みでしたね。

古谷 ── すべては珠寶さんの花をする行為が、その生き生きした時間の継続を生み出しています。もともと、会期中に何回かリピートする時間軸の構想がありましたが、ひとつ前の花の〈波紋〉が残っていて、そこに新たに〈波紋〉が生じるというのは、珠寶さんの花の最大の特徴ですから。

「波・紋」展より。書家・神郡宇敬氏と珠寶氏とのコラボレーションのパフォーマンス。水盤に浮かべた書に花びらを散らした

At the Ripple exhibition. Performance collaboration between Shuho and calligrapher Ukyo Kamigori, in which flower petals were scattered on calligraphy placed in the water basin.

Kawamukai — Is that because there's no need to do so if the ripples are already spreading?

Shuho — Exactly. For this exhibition, Furuya had already created ripples in advance, and there was a temporal flow in the placing of flowers up to that point, so I felt it would be all right to pass on by without placing any more. During the period of the exhibition I took part in collaborative performances with a number of people. When the calligraphy that Ukyo Kamigori made was floated on the water and the ink suddenly dropped away from the page, that—to me—was ikebana.

Kawamukai — We make certain assumptions about what it means to do ikebana, so it seems to require a measure of courage to "arrange flowers" without actually arranging flowers. At the same time, given these expectations, the decision not to do so seems like it must be purposeful.

Shuho — The important thing in ikebana is that people in a given place feel something. The critical thing is not the resulting arrangement but that the flowers tie something together and lead to something else. I think this exhibition was a tremendous opportunity to convey to people that ikebana is about more than just arranging flowers for a *tokonoma* alcove.

Kawamukai — At the *Ripple* exhibition, you watched the people who had gathered in attendance, and felt the light coming in from outside, and saw the ink spreading out in the pool of water, and made snap decisions about whether or not to place a flower based on your grasp of such changing conditions. If you were aiming for an exhibition style that was a series of such moments enclosed in a period of peace and calm, then it was a really revolutionary effort.

Furuya — It was entirely Shuho's acts of ikebana that generated this succession of vivid moments. We started out working with the idea of a temporal cycle that repeated a few times during the period of the exhibition, but the most distinctive part of Shuho's ikebana is the way the ripples of a new flower are generated while the ripples of the previous flower still linger.

Minimalism: Theatrical Connections

Kawamukai — What you say reminds me a lot of the world of theater.

Furuya — Yes, there is a connection. I'm a huge fan of the play *Water Station* (1981) by Shogo Ota's Tenkei Gekijo (Transformation Theater).

ミニマリズム～演劇とのつながり

川向 ── お話を伺っていると、演劇の世界とのつながりを感じます。

古谷 ── ええ、つながっています。僕は、太田省吾さんの劇団「転形劇場」の代表作で『水の駅』(1981) という芝居が好きなのですが、その舞台にあるのは、蛇口から一条の水がチーッと音をたてて流れている水道だけです。少女が 2 m を 5 分かけて舞台上を歩くのですが、時々動くのではなく、本当に少しずつ動いていて、いつの間にか水道の脇に着いたところで、バスケットから赤いコップを取り出して、その一条の水にツッとコップを差し出すのです。それまで、ずっと会場に音をたてていた水の音がフッと消えた瞬間に、サティの音楽が流れて芝居が始まります。そしてまたボジョボジョボジョと音がたって。

舞台上のほとんど何もないミニマルな空間に、何かちょっとしたものが一瞬にして空気を止め人を引き寄せる力がある。それが予想通りだったり、新鮮に裏切ったりする。それに近いものが、珠寶さんの花にはありますよね。

川向 ── ごく限定されたものと人の動きが、観衆の目や耳を完全に捉えています。

古谷 ── そうですね。今の劇場は座席に番号が振ってあり、整列されて固定されていますが、それがどうも不自然だなと思っていまして、もっと自由に人垣の間から覗き込むようにして興味の対象に見入る。その〈人がつくる空間〉そのものが劇場だと僕は思うのですが。

「波・紋」展では、できあがった花の形だけではなくて、花をしていただいている間、人が何重にも取り囲んでいる感じをつくりたかったのです。

川向 ── 複雑につくり込まないで、むしろ「これが展示空間なの？」というような場で、自由に演じ、自由に見てください、というやり方でしょうか。

とはいえ、やはりミニマルに何かを用意する必要があったわけですね。

〈まとう〉と〈脱ぐ〉

古谷 ── ショールーム空間を最小限の操作で非日常に変えようとしたのですが、会場の相談をしていたときに、珠寶さんがオカムラのチェアのメッシュの張り地に非常に興味を持たれて「メッシュを着られないかしら」とおっしゃった。それを聞いた瞬間に「これなら大丈夫。シンクロしていける」と思いました。

珠寶 ── 今回、オカムラさんに、メッシュ・チェアに張る生地を少し分けていただけないかと無理を申しまして、何色か使わせていただきました。

The only thing on stage is a tap with a stream of water trickling from the faucet. A girl walks across the stage, taking about five minutes to cover just two meters. Rather than moving only now and then, she's constantly moving, but just a little bit at a time. Suddenly she arrives by the water tap, pulls a red cup from a basket, and thrusts it beneath the stream of water. At the moment the trickling of the water, which has carried through the venue throughout, disappears, the music of Eric Satie kicks in and the play begins. And then the trickling returns. In the nearly bare space of a minimalist stage, even something very minor can have the power to bring everything to a halt, to pull people in. This can happen in ways that are utterly predictable, or that are fresh and defy expectations. I think there is something similar to this in Shuho's ikebana.

Kawamukai — By stringently limiting the people and things that appear, you can seize the audience's eyes and ears completely.

Furuya — That's right. Theaters today have numbered seats that are fixed in place in orderly rows. I can't shake the feeling that there's something unnatural about this, and that a real theater is a kind of space made by people, one where there is greater freedom of movement and you look at the objet of interest as if peering through a crowd.

For the *Ripple* exhibition, I really wanted not only to show the form that the completed flowers took but also to create a sense of layers of people crowded around during the process of arranging them.

Kawamukai — So perhaps by keeping things from getting too complicated—choosing instead to make people wonder if that was all there was to the exhibition space—you encouraged freer performance and freer observations. Even in a minimalist space, though, you still had to prepare something.

Putting On and Taking Off

Furuya — I tried to transform the showroom space into something extraordinary with the least possible manipulation. When we were discussing the venue, Shuho expressed an interest in the mesh fabric used to cover Okamura's chairs, saying she wondered if it could be worn. As soon as I heard that, I knew we were all right, that we were in sync.

Shuho — I asked Okamura to provide some of the fabric used in its mesh chairs and they kindly made a number of colors available. I then

京都の長艸縫巧房さんにお願いして、生地の特性に合い、花の所作がしやすく、巫女の装束のようなイメージでつくっていただいたのが、今回の衣装でした。

川向 ── 空間を徹底してミニマルに構成するとか、布を使うにしても、チェアのメッシュ地がそうであるように硬い布を使うこともできたはずですが、薄く半透明のオーガンジーで場を包んでいったのも、この衣装と関係があるのですか。

古谷 ── メッシュを服に仕立てる話がありましたので、建築のしつらえも衣服のように〈まとう〉ものがいいなと思いました。夏には脱いで、冬には厚着をして襟を立てるような〈重ね着する家〉ができないかと僕はよく言っているものですから、今回の展示も〈脱いだり・着たり〉できるしつらえにしようと思いました。ある程度は用意しておいて、「あとはご自由に〈脱いだり・着たり〉してください」という発想につながりました。珠寶さんの「メッシュを着たい」というお話から、インスピレーションを得たものです。

川向 ── そして実際、ワークショップを重ねるたびに、花立ての場の周りのオーガンジーの〈囲い〉が取り払われて、次第に元のショールーム空間に戻っていきました。

古谷 ── 人工的なオーガンジーの花のような〈囲い〉の部分を、珠寶さんが花のようにスパッとあしらって、どんどん〈脱いでいく〉ことで、最後はほとんどショールーム空間に戻っていました。その変化を、僕も設計者として本当に楽しませていただきました。

ショールームにもともとあった椅子が前面に出てきたのは、見事でしたよ。僕が思っていたのより何倍も見事にやってくださったと感謝しています。

次第に会場のオーガンジーが取られていき、ショールームの元の姿が現れてきた。
左：2回目のプレゼンテーション後。右：4回目のプレゼンテーション後

As the organdy in the venue was gradually removed, the showroom returned to its original state. Left: After the second presentation. Right: After the fourth presentation.

asked the Nagakusa Embroidery Atelier in Kyoto to create clothing that would take advantage of the characteristics of the fabric, be easy to arrange flowers in, and leave an impression reminiscent of the robes worn by maidens at Shinto shrines. For the exhibition, I wore the clothing that they produced.

Kawamukai — Was the decision to create a thoroughly minimal space—and to wrap it in thin, translucent organdy rather than the stiffer mesh chair fabric that you might also have elected to use—related to this clothing in some way?

Furuya — Shuho talked about turning the mesh into clothing, but I wanted the architectural appointments to feel like they were "put on" in the same way that clothes are worn. I often talk of my interest in creating a house that can be "dressed in layers"—stripping down in summer but bundling up and turning up its collar in winter—and I wanted the appointments for the exhibition to be the sorts of things that could be put on and taken off. This ties into the idea of preparing things up to a point and then saying, "Put things on and take them off as you like." I was really inspired by Shuho's comment about wanting to wear the mesh.

Kawamukai — In fact, more and more of the organdy "enclosures" surrounding the flower arranging spaces were removed with each workshop, gradually revealing the original showroom space.

Furuya — Shuho cut away the flower-shaped, man-made organdy enclosures as if she were snipping stray blossoms, "taking them off" in such a way that by the end the showroom was almost back to its original state. As the designer of the space, this was a transformation I really enjoyed. The way the chairs that had been in the showroom from the start gradually came to the fore was just brilliant. I am grateful for the way she made things turn out so much better than I had imagined.

The Spirit of Ikebana: In the Everyday

Kawamukai — The common theme of all ODS-R exhibitions is collaboration: they're not solo shows. I always look forward to seeing how the cross-stimulation will draw out things that are different from the kind of work participants usually do. Shuho, did taking part in the *Ripple* exhibition bring any new realizations?

Shuho — A lot of people assume a certain stance as soon as they hear words like "ikebana" or "the way of flowers" or "this-or-that school,"

花の精神〜日常の中で

川向 ── ODS-R の共通テーマは「コラボレーション」であって、個展ではありません。互いに刺激し合うことで普段なさっていることとは違う何かが引き出されるのではないかと、毎回、期待しているわけですが、珠寶さんは「波・紋」展に参加して何か気づかれたことはありましたか。

珠寶 ──「華道」とか「いけ花」とか「何々流」とか、言葉のイメージだけで身構えられる方もいらっしゃいます。けれども伝統と現代は同じ延長線上です。今の連続が過去になり、未来になります。現代の作家さんとお仕事をご一緒すると、そのことがよくわかります。今回の企画はまさにそれをいろいろな視点から見つめることができました。

私の花の持ち味を引き出してくださったことに感謝申し上げます。自分のお花のいろいろな可能性とか役割、そして、まだまだ皆さんにお伝えしなければいけないことがあると確認できる非常にいい機会でした。

川向 ── 建築設計の場合、施主という使い手がいて、その人たちの生活行為をいろいろと思いながら案を練られると思うのですが、今回は、応答し合う醍醐味のようなものが、うまく表現されたのではないですか。

古谷 ── 振り返ると、そうですね。普通の家の場合は、ここまで見事にならなくて、もう少しごちゃごちゃして終わります。これほど見事にできたのは、やはり花の精神があったからではないでしょうか。増えるのではなく、むしろ減っていき、最後は本当にスッキリとした姿に収斂する。現実の建築でもこのようにできたら、本当に素晴らしいですね。

川向 ── ミニマルに、本当に必要なものだけで世界を構築する思想や精神が確立されれば、物質的なものは減らすことができるのかもしれません。十分に楽しみ、たくさんの何かを得て、すべてが終わったときには元の姿に戻っているというのは、素晴らしいことですね。何か晴れ晴れした爽やかな気分です。

古谷 ── 最近、僕が考えているのは〈着られる家〉というもので、その住宅「N-House」(2014) が竣工しました。服を〈着たり・脱いだり〉するように、家族みんなが〈脱いで〉出ていき、帰ってきて〈着る〉という概念に逢着したのです。

「波・紋」展の場合も同じで、会場に集まった皆さんは〈着て〉、会が終わったときには〈脱いで〉、出ていかれたのではないかと思います。

川向 ── 共に着ることで共通体験をし、内面的に豊かになり、そして脱いで、爽やかな心持ちでお帰りになったのでしょうね。

(この鼎談は 2014 年 9 月に行われた)

but tradition and the contemporary are part of the same continuum. Both past and future are made up of a succession of nows. You can seen this quite clearly when working with contemporary artists. This exhibition enabled me to examine this issue from a variety of perspectives.

I'm thankful that the exhibition drew out the distinctive qualities of what I do with flowers. It was a terrific opportunity to be reminded of the many possibilities and roles my ikebana can play, and to reconfirm how much there is that I still need to convey to everyone.

Kawamukai — When you design a work of architecture, I imagine you have client-users whose life activities and ideas serve to guide you as you develop your proposal. For this exhibition, too, it seems like you were able to really enjoy that kind of interactivity and feedback.

Furuya — Looking back on it, yes, I think you're right. With an ordinary home, though, things don't usually fall into place so nicely. They end up a bit messier. I'm sure the reason things turned out so well this time is due to the spirit of ikebana. Rather than adding, we removed, and by the end there was a convergence on something really clean. It would be wonderful to be able to do the same thing with a real work of architecture.

Kawamukai — Having the idea or mentality of building a minimal world containing only what's really necessary might enable us to reduce our reliance on the material. It's fantastic when you can enjoy yourself thoroughly, gaining so much, and then at the end return everything to the way it was before—really refreshing.

Furuya — Lately I've been thinking a lot about "houses that can be worn." My recently completed N-House (2014), for example, is based on the concept of family members shedding the house when they leave and putting it back on when they return, much as they might put on and take off clothing. I suspect it was the same for the Ripple exhibition, with those who gathered at the venue "putting on" when they arrived and then "taking off" as they left.

Kawamukai — I suppose people had the shared experience of wearing something together, becoming inwardly enriched, then removing it and returning home feeling refreshed.

(This roundtable discussion was held in September 2014)

オカムラデザインスペースRの記録
A Record of Okamura Design Space R

Vol. 1　THEORIA
企画建築家：北川原温
コラボレーター：高木由利子
開催期間：2003年7月3日（木）―7月18日（金）
Vol. 1 Theoria
Architect: Atsushi Kitagawara
Collaborator: Yuriko Takagi
Dates: Thursday, July 3 to Friday, July 18, 2003

Vol. 2　粒子がレスポンスする場＝ニワ
企画建築家：隈研吾
コラボレーター：廣瀬通孝
開催期間：2004年7月12日（月）―7月23日（金）
Vol. 2 Niwa: Where the Particle Responds
Architect: Kengo Kuma
Collaborator: Michitaka Hirose
Dates: Monday, July 12 to Friday, July 23, 2004

Vol. 3　AWARENESS　今日の結界
企画建築家：芦原太郎
コラボレーター：山田宗徧
開催期間：2005年7月14日（木）―7月29日（金）
Vol. 3 Awareness: Divided Spaces of Today
Architect: Taro Ashihara
Collaborator: Sohen Yamada
Dates: Thursday, July 14 to Friday, July 29, 2005

Vol. 4　TIME SCAPE　時間に触れる
企画建築家：内藤廣
コラボレーター：アルバロ・カシネリ、石川正俊
開催期間：2006年7月13日（木）―7月28日（金）
Vol. 4 Timescape
Architect: Hiroshi Naito
Collaborators: Alvaro Cassinelli, Masatoshi Ishikawa
Dates: Thursday, July 13 to Friday, July 28, 2006

Vol. 5　都市を歩く表象
企画建築家：江頭慎
コラボレーター：岡村製作所技術開発チーム
開催期間：2007年7月12日（木）―7月27日（金）
Vol. 5 Flat Elephant Walks
Architect: Shin Egashira
Collaborator: Okamura Corporation Advanced Engineering Team
Dates: Thursday, July 13 to Friday, July 27, 2007

Vol. 6　風鈴 ─────────

企画建築家：伊東豊雄（建築家）

コラボレーター：takram design engineering（デザインエンジニアリングファーム）

開催期間：2008 年 7月28日（月）─ 8月22日（金）

シンポジウム：「風鈴から都市まで」 2008 年7月30日（水）

　　パネラー：伊東豊雄、高橋麻実、アンドレ・ギモンド（以上、伊東豊雄建築設計事務所）、

　　田川欣哉、渡邉康太郎（以上、takram design engineering）、畑中元秀（ex-takram）、瀧口範子、川向正人（アンカーマン）

ギャラリートーク：「伊東豊雄× takram design engineering 」 2008年8月7日（木）・20日（水）

DM・ポスター制作：佐藤卓デザイン事務所

Vol. 6　Furin

Architect: Toyo Ito (Architect)

Collaborator: Takram Design Engineering (Design Engineering Firm)

Dates: Monday, July 28 to Friday, August 22, 2008

Symposium: "From Wind Chimes to the City," Wednesday, July 30, 2008

　　Panelists: Toyo Ito & Associates, Architects (Toyo Ito, Asami Takahashi, Andre Guimond);

　　Takram Design Engineering (Kinya Tagawa, Kotaro Watanabe), Ex-Takram (Motohide Hatanaka);

　　Noriko Takiguchi; Masato Kawamukai (Moderator)

Gallery Talks: Toyo Ito and Takram Design Engineering; Thursday, August 7 and Wednesday, August 20, 2008

DM & Poster: Taku Satoh Design Office Inc.

Vol. 7　透明なかたち ─────────────────────────
企画建築家：妹島和世（建築家）
コラボレーター：荒神明香（アーティスト）、佐々木睦朗（構造家）
開催期間：2009年7月21日（火）─ 8月7日（金）
シンポジウム：「透明なかたち」 2009年7月25日（土）
　パネラー：妹島和世、荒神明香、佐々木睦朗、周防貴之（妹島和世建築設計事務所）、川向正人（アンカーマン）
ギャラリートーク：「荒神明香 × 周防貴之（妹島和世建築設計事務所）」 2009年7月30日（木）
協力：大光電機株式会社
DM・ポスター制作：GRAPH（制作）、新津保建秀（写真）

Vol. 7 Transparent Form
Architect: Kazuyo Sejima (Architect)
Collaborators: Haruka Kojin (Artist), Mutsuro Sasaki (Structural Engineer)
Dates: Tuesday, July 21 to Friday, August 7, 2009
Symposium: "Transparent Form," Saturday, July 25, 2009
　Panelists: Kazuyo Sejima, Haruka Kojin, Mutsuro Sasaki, Takashi Suo, Masato Kawamukai (Moderator)
Gallery Talk: Haruka Kojin and Takashi Suo; Thursday, July 30, 2009
Support: Daiko Electric Co., Ltd.
DM & Poster: Graph (Production), Kenshu Shintsubo (Photography)

Vol. 8　PARTY PARTY

企画建築家：小嶋一浩＋赤松佳珠子（建築家）

コラボレーター：諏訪綾子（フードアーティスト）

テクニカルアドバイザー：岡安 泉（照明デザイナー）

開催期間：2010年7月21日（水）― 8月6日（金）

シンポジウム：「出来事のデザインと建築」 2010年7月23日（金）

　パネラー：小嶋一浩、赤松佳珠子、諏訪綾子、岡安泉、川向正人（アンカーマン）

協力：三菱電機オスラム株式会社、株式会社空間コム、株式会社木村硝子店

DM・ポスター制作：アキタ・デザイン・カン

Vol. 8 Party Party

Architects: Kazuhiro Kojima (Architect), Kazuko Akamatsu (Architect)

Collaborator: Ayako Suwa (Food Artist)

Technical Advisor: Izumi Okayasu (Lighting Designer)

Dates: Wednesday, July 21 to Friday, August 6, 2010

Symposium: "The Design and Construction of Happenings," Friday, July 23, 2010

　Panelists: Kazuhiro Kojima, Kazuko Akamatsu, Ayako Suwa, Izumi Okayasu, Masato Kawamukai (Moderator)

Support: Mitsubishi Electric Osram Ltd., Kuu-Kan.Com Inc., Kimura Glass Co., Ltd.

DM & Poster: Akita Design Kan

ぼよよん

青木淳 + MONGOOSE STUDIO

2011.7/26 (tue) — 8/12 (fri)
オカムラデザインスペース R

EXHIBITION 9: "BOYOYONG" JUN AOKI + MONGOOSE STUDIO

OKAMURA
Design Space R

Vol. 9　ぼよよん ──────────
企画建築家：青木淳（建築家）
コラボレーター：MONGOOSE STUDIO（クリエイティブ 集団）
開催期間：2011年7月26日（火）― 8月12日（金）
シンポジウム：「ぼよよんのこと」 2011年7月30日（土）
　パネラー：青木淳、MONGOOSE STUDIO、川向正人（アンカーマン）
ワークショップ：「アンニンドウフは、ぼよよん！？」2011年7月27日（水）、「ぼよよん狩り」2011年8月12日（金）
制作：青木淳建築計画事務所（青木淳、園田慎二）、MONGOOSE STUDIO（大橋卓也、猪口健司、
鍋島久和、平原真、松山真也、八木澤優記）、神山友輔、松村充、イエムラ・タマヨ・オフィス
協力：カラーキネティクス・ジャパン株式会社
オープニングパーティフード：ホテルニューオータニ
DM・ポスター制作：MONGOOSE STUDIO

Vol. 9 Boyoyong
Architect: Jun Aoki (Architect)
Collaborator: Mongoose Studio (Creative Team)
Dates: Tuesday, July 26 to Friday, August 12, 2011
Symposium: "About Boyoyong," Saturday, July 30, 2011
　Panelists: Jun Aoki, Mongoose Studio, Masato Kawamukai (Moderator)
Workshops: "Does Almond Jelly Boyoyong?," Wednesday, July 27, 2011 and "Boyoyong Hunting," Friday, August 12, 2011
Production: Jun Aoki & Associates (Jun Aoki, Shinji Sonoda); Mongoose Studio (Takuya Ohashi, Kenji Inoguchi,
Hisakazu Nabeshima, Makoto Hirahara, Shinya Matsuyama, Yuki Yagisawa)
with Yusuke Kamiyama and Mitsuru Matsumura; Iemura Tamayo Office
Support: Color Kinetics Japan
Opening Party Food: Hotel New Otani
DM & Poster: Mongoose Studio

Vol. 10　Flow_er

企画建築家：平田晃久（建築家）

コラボレーター：塚田有一（ガーデンプランナー／フラワーアーティスト）

開催期間：2012年7月24日（火）―8月10日（金）

シンポジウム：「Flow_erの風景」　2012年7月28日（土）

　パネラー：平田晃久、塚田有一、川向正人（アンカーマン）

ワークショップ：「廻り花」2012年8月2日（木）

公演：「水の音」　2012年8月3日（金）

　出演：安田登（能楽師／ワキ方）、槻宅聡（能楽師／笛方）

協力：岡安泉照明設計事務所、株式会社富士清水

オープニングパーティフード：HORO Kitchen

DM・ポスター制作：SUIMOK DESIGN

Vol. 10　Flow_er

Architect: Akihisa Hirata (Architect)

Collaborator: Yuichi Tsukada (Garden Planner, Flower Artist)

Dates: Tuesday, July 24 to Friday, August 10, 2012

Symposium: "The Flow_er Landscape," Saturday, July 28, 2012

　Panelists: Akihisa Hirata, Yuichi Tsukada , Masato Kawamukai (Moderator)

Workshop: "Meguribana," Thursday, August 2, 2012

Public Performance: *The Sound of Water*, Friday, August 3, 2012

　Performers: Noboru Yasuda (Noh Supporting Actor), Satoshi Tsukitaku (Noh Flutist)

Support: Izumi Okayasu Lighting Design, Fujiseisui

Opening Party Food: Horo Kitchen

DM & Poster: Suimok Design

Vol. 11　白い闇 ———

企画建築家：ヨコミゾ マコト（建築家）

コラボレーター：上田麻希（嗅覚のアーティスト）

開催期間：2013年7月23日（火）— 8月9日（金）

シンポジウム：「知覚と空間」　2013年7月27日（土）

　　パネラー：ヨコミゾマコト、上田麻希、川向正人（アンカーマン）

ワークショップ：「嗅覚と空間認識〜犬のように空間を探る〜」　2013年7月27日（土）

ギャラリートーク：「アーティスト達と匂いや建築、空間や知覚について語らう場」

2013年7月24日（水）、8月2日（金）、5日（月）、8日（木）

協力：山本香料株式会社

DM・ポスター制作：Soonhwa Kang

Vol. 11　Invisible White

Architect: Makoto Yokomizo (Architect)

Collaborator: Maki Ueda (Olfactory Artist)

Dates: Tuesday, July 23 to Friday, August 9, 2013

Symposium: "Perception and Space," Saturday, July 27, 2013

　　Panelists: Makoto Yokomizo, Maki Ueda, Masato Kawamukai (Moderator)

Workshop: "Smell and Spatial Recognition: Investigate Space Like a Dog," Saturday, July 27, 2013

Gallery Talks: "A Forum for Talking With the Artists About Odor, Architecture, Space, and Perception",

July 24, August 2, 5, and 8, 2013

Support: Yamamoto Perfumery Co., Ltd.

DM & Poster: Soonhwa Kang

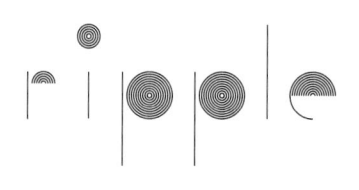

Vol. 12　波・紋 ────

企画建築家：古谷誠章（建築家）

コラボレーター：珠寳（花士）　※ポスターの名前・肩書は開催当時のもの

開催期間：2014年7月8日(火)ー7月25日(金)

シンポジウム：「波・紋をめぐって」　2014年7月11日(金)

　パネラー：古谷誠章、珠寳、川向正人（アンカーマン）

プレゼンテーション：「珠寳氏による会場での花立て」　2014年7月7日(月)、11日(金)、15日(火)、22日(火)

協力：長艸縫巧房（衣装制作）、若杉聖子（花器制作）、大光電機株式会社（照明提供）

施工：株式会社Celia、株式会社スペース

オープニングパーティフード：野村友里（フードプロデューサー）

DM・ポスター制作：菊地敦己

Vol. 12　Ripple

Architect: Nobuaki Furuya (Architect)

Collaborator: Shuho (*Hananofu* [Ikebana Master])　Note: Name and title on poster were current at the time of the exhibition.

Dates: Tuesday, July 8 to Friday, July 25, 2014

Symposium: "About Ripple," Friday, July 11, 2014

　Panelists: Nobuaki Furuya, Shuho, Masato Kawamukai (Moderator)

Presentation: "Ikebana by Shuho at the Venue," July 7, 11, 15, and 22, 2014

Support:　Nagakusa Embroidery Atelier (Costume Production), Seiko Wakasugi (Flower Vessel Production),

Daiko Electric Co., Ltd. (Lighting Provision)

Construction: Celia; Space Co., Ltd.

Opening Party Food: Yuri Nomura (Food Producer)

DM & Poster: Atsuki Kikuchi

コラボレーションという変曲点

北川原温　建築家・東京藝術大学教授・ODS-R企画委員

21 世紀の特徴のひとつは、コラボレーション。ただひたすら、がむしゃらにやっていればよかった 20 世紀が終わって、協働の関係を構築しなければ何もできない時代になって、人々の頭が切り替わったように思います。そして 20 世紀は大きな理念を掲げてそれを共有する時代でしたが、今は、もっと身近なところに大事なことを発見して多様に共有するようになってきました。

今、僕が日本館の建築プロデュースを担当している 2015 年ミラノ万博のテーマは「Feeding the Planet, Energy for Life（地球に食料を、生命にエネルギーを）」です。各国で何を食べているのかをお互いに知って理解するという身近なテーマですが、地球全体で見れば、大量に余った食料を捨てている国もあれば、食べ物がなくて困っている国もあるという社会問題、さらに食の問題を通して科学や環境などを問い直していくことにも言及しています。20 世紀の万博は技術や自然といった大きな理念を掲げたわけですが、21 世紀の万博は日常生活の中の身近なテーマを掲げながら、その背後に大きな課題を浮かび上がらせます。

コラボレーションというと、ジョン・ケージの「チャンス・オペレーション」という言葉を磯崎新さんが使っていたのを思い出します。都市計画で何か物事を進めるときにタイミングを見ながら、条件がうまくそろって「ここだ」というところで、そのチャンスを生かして都市をオペレーションしていくという考え方です。つまり、都市のマスタープランを描くのではなく、プロセスをデザインしていけばよいというわけです。

僕が参加した第 1 回「THEORIA」展（2003）では、写真家の高木由利子さんとご一緒させていただきました。彼女と話しているなかで一致するところが何カ所か出てきて、それが共有され、だんだんと情景が描かれていきます。ジャズの世界のインプロビゼーションのように、楽譜はなくても互いの何かを共有して音楽が生まれるような即興のものづくりをしました。

若い人も年をとった人も男も女もフラットに、違う者同士が何か一緒にやろうと、お互いに努力してコミュニケーションする言語を見つけ出しては議論し、他分野の人とコラボレーションすることで、さまざまな突破すべき問題／解が自然に共有できます。

ODS-R の12組の建築家もアーティストも、コラボレーションして多くの問題、矛盾、課題を発見したのではないかと思います。それは、コラボレーションを試みないとわからない類いのものです。ODS-R の試みが新しい問題／解を生み出す突破口となり、次の仕事に必ず影響する変曲点になっているのではないでしょうか。

Collaboration as Inflection Point

Atsushi Kitagawara

Architect, Tokyo University of the Arts Professor
ODS-R Planning Member

One of the characteristics of the twenty-first century is collaboration. With the end of the twentieth century—when it was enough simply to work like mad—I think people have switched mindsets for an age in which it is impossible to do anything without building collaborative relationships. And while the twentieth century was an age for raising and sharing great principles, now people discover important things near at hand and share them in diverse ways.

The theme of Expo Milano 2015, where I am producing the architecture for the Japan pavilion, is "Feeding the Planet, Energy for Life." It is a theme that hits close to home, on developing a better mutual understanding of what people eat in countries around the world, but also touches on the social issue of some countries having so much extra food that it goes to waste while others struggle with not having enough, and reexamines issues of science and the environment through the lens of food. The expos of the twentieth century held up big ideas about technology and nature, but those of the twenty-first century are raising more familiar topics at the heart of everyday life to bring into relief the big issues beneath them.

When I hear the word "collaboration" I am reminded of when Arata Isozaki used it to describe John Cage's "chance operations." The idea is that when trying to move anything forward in urban planning, you keep an eye on timing and act when the conditions are right, leveraging opportunities to operate the city. In other words, rather than drawing up a master plan for the city, all you need to do is design the process.

I participated in the first ODS-R exhibition, *Theoria* (2003), working together with photographer Yuriko Takagi. In talking with her I found that we agreed on a number of things, and by sharing these we gradually drew up the scene. We worked much as in the manner of jazz improvisation, where sharing something together generates music even in the absence of a score.

When different people—young and old, men and women—come together at the same level and decide to do something together, each making the effort to discover a common language for communication and discussion, collaboration with people from different fields enables a natural sharing of all sorts of problem to be overcome, and solutions, too.

I suspect the collaborations between architects and artists in the twelve ODS-R editions have discovered all sorts of problems, contradictions, and issues. These are the kind of thing you cannot understand without giving collaboration a try. I am sure the experiments of the ODS-R have led to breakthroughs that create new problems and solutions, serving as inflection points that influenced subsequent work.

時間に触れる異空間

内藤 廣　建築家・ODS-R企画委員

　企画委員を務めさせていただいています。この企画では、建築家が普段考えたことのない回路で
向き合わねばなりません。日常の仕事に追われる建築家としては、新たな挑戦を試みる貴重な機会
です。建築家を選定し、提案される企画を吟味していくのは、大変な作業だったと推察します。
この企画がここまで続いてきたのは、川向先生の指導あってのことです。深甚の敬意を表したいと
思います。

　第4回に、私自身もプレーヤーとして展示をするように言われました。実際に展示する側になって
みると、その困難さがよくわかります。まず、アイデアがなかなか思い浮かばない。クリエーター
と組むという以外、具体的な条件はないのですから、それこそ雲をつかむようなものです。

　ちょうどそのころ、NHKでデジタル時代の新しい映像をプレゼンテーションするデジスタという
番組があって、その中でとても面白い試みをしている若者がいました。格段に発想がユニークで、
なおかつ先端的だったのです。それがアルバロ・カシネリ君でした。どうやら彼は、私の勤めてい
た大学の情報理工学科に留学生として所属しているらしく、私の研究室から50mほどの距離にいる
ことがわかりました。情報理工学科の石川正俊先生の研究室に所属していると知って、石川先生に
相談したところ、カシネリ君を紹介してくださり、彼と共同で提案することになりました。

　彼は映写されている画像の背後にある時間をコントロールしようとしていました。柔らかい映写
幕に映されている画像に手をふれて押し込むと、押し込む深さをセンサーがオンタイムで感知して、
その深さが深いほど映されている画像が過去に戻っていくシステムをつくり出していました。風景
でも植物写真でも、対象は何でもいいのです。例えば、渋谷の交差点を渡っている人たちの動画を
押し込むと、押し込むほどに人々が後ろ向きに戻っていきます。押されていない所は何も変化しな
いのですが、それが押された曲面に従って連続的に過去に向かっていくのです。不思議な風景が映
し出されます。まさに「時間に触っている」感覚です。あまりに面白いので、即座に彼に展示の協
力をお願いしました。

　せっかくの機会ですから、できるだけ多くの人に、この工学的に生み出された最先端の技術を
使って、その面白さと可能性を見てもらいたいと思いました。あとは会場を幕でどのように構成す
るかです。押し込むのに適切な幕の素材を手に入れ、それで会場構成をし、そこにカシネリ君のつ
くった映像を映し出しました。時間にふれることのできる見たことのない異空間ができあがりました。

　建築家の能力にはさまざまな可能性があります。その1つが、最先端の技術や知見を誰もが感じ
取れるように翻訳することです。ここでは、その機会をいただいて表現ができたのではないかと思っ
ています。

Another Dimension for Touching Time

Hiroshi Naito

Architect, ODS-R Planning Member

I serve as an ODS-R planning member. The ODS-R project is one that an architect must approach with a different way of thinking. For an architect swamped with everyday work, it is a precious opportunity to take on a new challenge. I can only imagine how difficult it must have been to select the architects and to carefully weigh their proposals. That the project has continued for so long is undoubtedly due to the leadership of Dr. Kawamukai, for whom I wish to express my deep respect.

For the 4th edition I was asked to take part as the exhibiting architect. Being a principal to the exhibit gave me a chance to see just how difficult it is. First of all, I struggled to come up with an idea. With no specific criteria other than to pair with another creator, it felt much like grasping at clouds.

Right around that time, NHK was broadcasting a program called *Digital Stadium* (also called *Digista*) that presented new kinds of moving images for the digital age. In one episode the show introduced a young man who was doing really interesting things. His remarkable ideas were unique and also very cutting edge. His name was Alvaro Cassinelli and it turned out he was studying in Japan in the department of information physics and computing at the very university where I was teaching at the time—in fact, only about 50m away from my office. Learning that Cassinelli was based in the research lab headed by my colleague Masatoshi Ishikawa, I discussed the matter with Ishikawa, was introduced to Cassinelli, and we ended up working together.

Trying to control aspects of time behind projected images, Cassinelli had created a system in which applying hand pressure to images projected on a soft screen caused them to move back in time according to the depth of the depression as picked up by sensors in real time. The subject of the image could be a landscape or a photograph of a plant or anything. If, for example, one were to press an image of the scramble intersection in Shibuya, the people would walk further backward the deeper one pushed. Areas not pushed would not change, but the rest would move backward along a continuity following the curvature of the depression made. This created truly fantastic landscapes. It felt like touching time. It was so fascinating that I immediately asked him to collaborate with me on the exhibition.

The exhibition seemed like a tremendous opportunity to show a great many people just how fascinating this carefully engineered, cutting-edge technology really was and what it was capable of doing. The question for me was how to structure the screens at the venue. I was able to obtain material that seemed just right for use as screens that could be pressed in, laid out the venue, and then projected the images Cassinelli had made onto the screens. This created a never-before-seen, other-dimensional space in which it was possible to touch time.

The abilities of an architect can be put to all sorts of potential uses. One of these is translating cutting-edge technology or knowledge into a form that anyone can grasp. I think I was given an opportunity to do so here, and succeeded in doing so.

気づくことの大切さ

芦原太郎　建築家・ODS-R企画委員

　ODS-Rが12回も継続できたことに驚くとともに、オカムラ中村会長や委員長の川向先生など、この企画にご尽力いただいた関係者の皆様に敬意を表したいと思います。

　毎回、参加した建築家たちの思考を建築作品とは違った形で知ることは貴重な機会でした。本書には第6回以降が収録されていますが、最初のころは、北川原温さん、内藤廣さん、そして私という企画委員が自ら企画建築家となって1つの回を担当するという、振り返ってみれば、この場所で、コラボレーションで、この準備期間で、この予算で、毎回オリジナルなものが提案できるのかと、多少手探りをしていた時期だったのかな、という感じもしています。

　私が企画建築家となった回では、茶道宗徧流の家元とコラボレーションを行って、オフィスワーカーたちが感性をリセットできるような、オフィス空間に置かれたコンテナ型の非日常空間を提案させていただきました。伝統と革新、制度と精神の自由、感性への働きかけと美意識。建築と茶道の違いはあっても、家元と問題意識を共有することができました。そして、今日の結界として伝統的な茶室空間、バール形式の場、建築家が提案する新しい空間の3つを実際につくり、その場を使って気づきの環境実験を行いました。家元は、茶道の心得のない学生を使ってバール形式での新しい御点前づくりを工夫されていましたし、私は、伝統的な茶室空間で本物の御点前に果敢に挑戦することができました。

　建築家として空間をつくるだけでなく、その空間を実際に使って茶道の家元と＜おもてなし＞をあれこれ工夫できたことは貴重な経験でした。どんな場所にも、上質の＜おもてなし＞の場が用意され、しかも、その場その場で一工夫されているのは日本文化の誇るべきところで、これからオフィスの中にも都市の中にもさらに積極的に出てくるとよいと思います。

　あの場に参加して＜おもてなし＞を受けた方々にもさまざまな気づきの体験があったのではないでしょうか。茶道は空間や道具そして作法が一体化した総合芸術であり、そこには人が豊かに生きていくためのさまざまなヒントがちりばめられています。

　こうした機会をいただき、環境をつくるさまざまな分野の人間が問題意識を共有してコラボレーションすることの大切さをあらためて確認することができたことを、ODS-Rに感謝したいと思います。

The Importance of Noticing

Taro Ashihara
Architect, ODS-R Planning Member

While a bit surprised that the ODS-R exhibitions have managed to continue through twelve editions, I wish also to convey my respect to Okamura's Chairman Nakamura, ODS-R Planning and Executive Committee Chairman Kawamukai, and everyone else who has worked so hard on behalf of this project.

Each edition has been a valuable opportunity to learn about the participating architect's thinking through a form other than a work of architecture. This volume compiles exhibitions beginning with the sixth edition but the early days—when planning members Atsushi Kitagawara, Hiroshi Naito, and I each took turns doing one edition as the exhibiting architect—now seem to have been something of a grasping phase when we wondered whether it was really possible to create something original each time in such a place, while collaborating, with such limited preparation time, and within the given budget.

In the edition for which I served as exhibiting architect I collaborated with the head of the Sohen school of tea in proposing an out-of-the-everyday space in the shape of a shipping container where office workers could reset their sensibilities. Tradition and innovation, institutions and spiritual freedom, the sensory and the aesthetic—despite the differences between architecture and tea, I was able to find in the tea master a shared awareness of the issues. We created three spaces— a traditional tea ceremony room as a space apart from today's world, a bar-like space, and a new space proposed by the architect—and applied them to a field test of noticing. The tea master used students with no training in the ways of tea to devise a new, bar-like ritualized form for preparing and serving tea, while I was able to boldly try my hand at serving tea in the traditional manner in the tea-ceremony room space.

To not only create the space as an architect but also to actually use the space together with a tea master to devise different forms of *omotenashi* hospitality was a valuable experience. All of the spaces provided forums for fine quality *omotenashi*, with each offering a twist on an aspect of Japanese culture of which Japan can be proud and which really should be actively promoted both within the office and out in the city.

I imagine that those who attended and received our *omotenashi* probably found themselves noticing all sorts of things. The tea ceremony is a comprehensive art unifying space and tools and etiquette, and is scattered with a variety of hints for more bountiful living.

I am grateful to the ODS-R for the opportunity to participate and for the chance to reconfirm the importance of collaborating and sharing an awareness of issues with people from different fields who are involved in the creation of environments.

ショールームを展示空間に使うこと

中村留理 株式会社岡村製作所 オフィス研究所

　ODS-R を開催するショールームは、ホテルニューオータニ・ガーデンコート内にありますので、設営に関しては通常のギャラリーとは異なり、ホテルや消防署との調整が必要です。ライティングも、残念ながら可変可能な状態になっていません。防火対象物内に展示するということで素材を防炎仕様にしたり、ショールームの運用が最低限できるように調整するなど、いろいろな制約がかかってきます。

　例えば、「風鈴」展は、ショールームの打合せスペースを使う展示でしたが、あのころは下がり天井の部分がありました。吊り下げられた数百の風鈴で大きな波を生み出すにあたって、天井はフラットな面にしたいということで、天井の改修を行いました。その際、風鈴を設置するピッチに合わせて下地材を入れ、会期終了後にダウンライトを設置して、打合せスペースとして通常使用するようにしました。そのほか、予期せぬ出来事に驚くこともありました。展示にあたって、会場のライティングパターンを制御するセンサーを天井面に設置したのですが、翌朝、会場に来てみるとライティングの調子がおかしい。原因はビルの空調のインバータがセンサーに影響していたのです。オープニングまでに takram さんが原因を突き止めて無事に調整を終えられました。こういうこともあるのだと勉強になった出来事です。

　「透明なかたち」展では、外光を取り入れた明るい展示にしたいということで、既存の壁の一部が青だったものを白に塗装し直しました。また、アクリルを搬入する際、通常使用しているエレベータでは入らず、夜間に搬入していただきました。最終段階で妹島先生が確認にいらした際、アクリルにダウンライトの映り込みがかなり出ることを気にされ、妹島事務所のスタッフの方が最後まで照明関係の調整を行っていたことが印象に残っています。アクリル面の透過とか反射に関係する問題だったのですね。

　「PARTY PARTY」展では、しつらえるテーブルをオカムラと一緒に制作できないかと小嶋先生、赤松先生からご相談がありました。テーブル支柱部分の直径が 18mm で、しかも管の中に配線したいというご要望だったので、弊社スタッフとともに造作家具として制作から設置まで担当させていただきました。テーブルが一般のものよりも高かったので、転倒しないように、急遽、床に固定しました。また、会場全体を暗くしたいということで、天井面にも黒いオーガンジーのクロスを設置することになりました。シーラカンスのスタッフの方に防炎スプレーで防炎処理していただき、それを使って、暗さを演出しました。この回もセンサリングによるライティングが演出に盛り込まれ、7種のライティングパターンが用意されていましたが、パーティションのしつらえなどで会場全体が

Using a Showroom as an Exhibition Space

Ruri Nakamura
Okamura Corporation Office Research Center

Because the showroom where the ODS-R is held is located within the Hotel New Otani Garden Court, arrangements for the exhibits require, unlike at an ordinary gallery, coordination with the hotel and the fire department. Regrettably, too, the lighting is not adjustable. The space is subject to all manner of constraints, such as the need to use fire-retardant materials and to ensure that the showroom itself remains at least minimally operational

---

The *Furin* exhibition made use of the showroom's meeting space, which at the time still had a ceiling that was lower in some places than in others. Given the collaborators' desire for a flat ceiling that would create the sense of great waves made from hundreds of wind chimes suspended in midair, we redid the ceiling. In doing so we added furrings at a pitch to match that of the wind chimes, and these then facilitated the installation of downlights when the space was returned to its normal use as a meeting space after the exhibition. There were also other surprising and unexpected happenings, too. Sensors were installed on the ceiling of the exhibition space to control the lighting pattern, but the morning after they were put in we arrived at the venue to find that the lighting was acting up. Apparently, the inverter for the building's ventilation system was affecting the sensors. Takram was able to identify the cause and make the necessary adjustments by the time the exhibition opened, so things turned out all right in the end, but it was an education to see the kind of things that can happen.

For *Transparent Form*, we repainted part of an existing blue wall white to facilitate the collaborators' desire to brighten the exhibition space with as much natural light as possible. Also, when the acrylic sheets were delivered they couldn't fit in the normal elevators so we had to have them brought in at night. When Sejima was making a late-stage inspection of the site, she grew concerned that the reflections from the downlights were too visible in the acrylic, and I can remember her staff working hard right up until the end to adjust the lighting and the relationship between the reflected light and the apparent permeability of the acrylic.

For *Party Party*, Kojima and Akamatsu asked if Okamura would work with them in manufacturing the tables for the exhibition. They wanted table pillars that were only 18mm in diameter and that would also serve as conduits for electrical wiring, so I helped coordinate with our staff on this custom-made furniture from manufacture through installation. The tables were taller than ordinary tables so at the last minute we fixed them to the floor to ensure they would not tip over. Wanting to dim the entire venue, they decided to install black organdy cloth on the ceiling. Staff from Coelacanth used fire-retardant spray to make the cloth fire-resistant and this did result in a darkened venue. This exhibition incorporated sensor-dependent lighting, too. There were seven different lighting patterns prepared but the positioning of the partitions made it difficult to visually take in the entire venue at once, so final adjustments took an entire day.

見通せず、調整に丸 1 日かかっていました。

　「ぼよよん」展では、リングの制作に青木先生とオカムラがコラボレーションしました。素材や
ロゴの入れ方など、何度も検討して、青木先生のイメージされるリングをつくり上げます。会場に
納品されたリングを、スタッフの方々がある程度のユニットに組み上げ、それを会場に設置してい
きます。白い雲のようなものが次第に広がっていくのが面白いのですが、この工程を動画で撮影して、
インターネット配信をされていました。リングの設営終了後に、光や音の演出をめぐる調整があり
ました。ずいぶん試行錯誤を重ねられて、オープニングを迎えました。

　「Flow_er」展では、巨大水盤を実現するために、まず防水工事が必要でした。防水シートを張り合
わせると強いにおいが発生するおそれがあり、ほかのテナントと機械空調を共有していることから、
ダクトで強制排気をしていただきながらの工事となりました。その後、アクリル板を組み立て、水際
の石などを設置して、いよいよ水を張ります。ポンプで循環させるときには水漏れが出ないかとドキ
ドキしましたが、無事に設営が完了して、ホッとしました。会期中、水の入替え時に水をこぼしてし
まいましたが大事に至らず、ショールーム運営に特に影響もなく展示を終えることができました。

　「白い闇」展では、床・壁・天井をふさいだ巨大な空間を構築したいという要望を実現すべく、相談
のために消防署に出向いたところ、「そもそも建築物なのか？」という問いかけがありました。そこ
で、区役所の建築指導課に相談したところ、「アートであって建築物ではない」というご判断でした。
再度、消防署を訪れてアートだとご理解いただき、最低限の消火対策を施すようにとの指導を受けて、
ようやく詳細の設計に入れるようになりました。完成時の消防検査に来られた消防署の担当者が
実際に体感して帰られ、一段落という感じでした。

　「波・紋」展では、巨大な水盤を分割で納品して施工するとのご説明でしたので、水が漏れないか
と心配でした。設営は 3 日間とかなり短い工期で進めていただきましたが、図面ではよく把握でき
なかったことが工事として行われたために、ショールームにご来場のお客様と設営がバッティング
することが若干あったものの、設営はすべて無事に終わりました。ワークショップは毎回異なる
演出を珠寶さんのほうで企画されていましたので、当日まで何が起こるか把握できずにハラハラ、
ドキドキすることもありました。

　あらためて振り返りますと、さまざまな制約があるなかで、建築家の先生や協働者の方々とご一緒
に工夫をして乗り越えることができたように感じます。毎回、素晴らしい展示がショールームに
生まれたことをうれしく思っております。

Production of the rings used for *Boyoyong* was a collaborative effort between Aoki and Okamura. There were many discussions to talk about materials and about inclusion of the logo, but ultimately I think we did manage to create the rings that Aoki had imagined. When they arrived on site, staff assembled them into units of a certain size and then installed them in the exhibition space. It was fascinating to see the "white cloud" gradually take shape and expand, a process captured on video and distributed over the Internet. After the rings were installed, there was a great deal of coordination still to be done concerning lights, sound, and stage direction, which led to a lot of trial-and-error adjustments right up to the opening.

Before the giant water basin for the *Flow_er* exhibition could be installed, we first needed to do some waterproofing. Fusing together waterproof sheeting can create a strong smell, and since we share the mechanical air-conditioning with other tenants we had to run forced ventilation ducts while the work was underway. The acrylic sheets were then assembled and stones placed at the water's edge, and finally the exhibit was ready to fill with water. I was nervous that the circulating pump might leak, and was very relieved when its installation went smoothly. There was some spillage when changing the water during the event, but it was not anything serious and we were able to bring the exhibition to a close without any adverse affect on showroom operations.

For *Invisible White,* the collaborators wanted to build a huge space that was closed off at its floor, walls, and ceiling. When I went to the fire department to discuss the matter, they asked if what was being built was even a "building" at all. I then went to the Building Guidance Division at the city office and they determined that it was not a building but a work of art. I went back to the fire department, convinced them that what we were building was art, was advised to implement the minimum necessary fire-prevention measures, and finally we were able to move on to the detailed design phase. The responsible party from the fire department came to inspect the site once everything was done and it felt like we had passed a milestone when he departed after experiencing the piece for himself.

For the *Ripple* exhibition, we had heard that the great water basin would be delivered in three pieces and assembled on site, so we were concerned it might leak. The construction moved forward on a fairly tight three-day schedule. There were some elements we had not fully grasped based on the plans, and these created some minor inconvenience for showroom visitors, but the construction itself all went well. Shuho planned something different for each of the workshops and it was always a thrill not to know what would happen until the day of the event.

Looking back, I feel we were able to find ways to help the architects and their collaborators overcome the many limitations of the site, and I am very pleased that they produced such wonderful exhibitions in the showroom every time.

謝辞

　18 世紀の哲学者イマヌエル・カントは、「啓蒙とは何か」という有名な論考に、次のように書いています。「この世の中には、人間に自然から与えられた能力を発揮させようと種々の決まりごとが設けられているが、それが現実には、さまざまな足枷になっている。それをはずして自由になる勇気をもてば、人間は誰もが、みずから考え、実践できるようになる」。

　この「自由」の考えは、建築界でも G. ゼムパー、O. ヴァーグナー、A. ロース、F.L. ライトなどを経て、連綿と今日まで受け継がれてきました。

　ODS-R の基本理念のひとつに、この「自由」がありました。どの回も建築家とアーティストが力を合わせ、いわば「自由の王国」をつくり上げることに心を砕いてくださいました。対等で自由な協働関係の構築です。それによって、ODS-R は毎回、刺激的に、創造的に展開することができました。まず、各回の建築家とアーティストの皆様に御礼を申し上げます。

　オカムラの中村喜久男会長は、ODS-R を 12 年にわたって開催し、足枷となるものをすべて取り除き、徹底してサポートする社内態勢をつくり上げてくださいました。会長が出席される月 1 回のミーティングは、どんなに厳しい局面でも、和やかなものでした。岩下博樹専務は事務局の核となって、もうひとつ大きな協働の輪をつくってくださいました。紙幅の関係で個別にお名前を挙げることができませんが、代々のショールーム所長をはじめとして大勢のオカムラ（岡村製作所）社員、そして多くの専門家と企業が、ODS-R の開催にご協力くださいました。ここに、あらためて感謝申し上げます。

　本書の制作にあたっては、彰国社編集部の前田智成氏、編集のいしまるあきこ氏、デザインの佐村憲一氏にお骨折りいただきました。各事務所のスタッフの皆様には、写真と情報の提供にご協力いただきました。ありがとうございました。

　最後になりましたが、ODS-R 企画委員を務める芦原太郎氏、内藤廣氏、北川原温氏の変わらぬ友情に、衷心より謝意を表します。

2015 年 3 月 10 日

オカムラデザインスペース R 委員長　川向正人

Acknowledgements

In his famous essay "What is Enlightenment?," eighteenth-century philosopher Immanuel Kant wrote how the various rules that people establish in this world to facilitate the exercise of their naturally given abilities in fact become shackles, and how anyone with the courage to cast them aside and be free can become able to think and act for himself. In the world of architecture, this notion of freedom has been continually passed down through such figures as Gottfried Semper, Otto Wagner, Adolf Loos, and Frank Lloyd Wright.

This freedom is one of the basic principles of the ODS-R. In every edition, the architect and the artist have combined their strengths and taken great pains to create a "kingdom of freedom," to build an equal, free, collaborative relationship. As a result, every edition of the ODS-R has developed in a stimulating and creative way. I would like first, therefore, to express my thanks to all of the architects and artists who have taken part.

Okamura Chairman Kikuo Nakamura has held the ODS-R for twelve years, sweeping away every obstacle and putting together an in-house team that has provided conscientious support. The monthly meetings he attends have always been conducted harmoniously no matter how difficult the situation. Senior Managing Director Hiroki Iwashita served as the core of the secretariat, building a second great circle of collaboration. Space limitations make it impossible to name every individual, but the ODS-R would not have been possible without the cooperation over the years of showroom directors and many other Okamura employees as well as numerous outside experts and companies. I wish to take this opportunity again to express my thanks.

Tomonari Maeta of the Shokokusha editorial department, editor Akiko Ishimaru, and designer Ken'ichi Samura all went to great lengths in producing this volume. The staff of each architect and artist's offices cooperated by providing photographs and other information. Thank you very much.

Finally, I wish to express my deepest gratitude to ODS-R planning members Taro Ashihara, Hiroshi Naito, and Atsushi Kitagawara for their steadfast friendship.

Masato Kawamukai
Chairman, Okamura Design Space R Planning and Executive Committee
10 March 2015

写真・図版クレジット
Credits

●風鈴　Furin

p19, 20-21, 24, 25, 30　河野政人（ナカサアンドパートナーズ）／ Masato Kawano (Nacása & Partners Inc.)

p22-23, 39, 44　川向正人／ Masato Kawamukai

p26, 27　オフィース YUKIMATSU ／ Office Yukimatsu

p34　望月孝／ Takashi Mochizuki

p38, 42　takram design engineering ／ Takram Design Engineering

p45　宮城県観光課／ Miyagi Prefecture Sightseeing Section

p46, 48　伊東豊雄建築設計事務所／ Toyo Ito & Associates, Architects

p50　阿野太一／ Daici Ano

p51　石黒写真研究所／ Ishiguro Photographic Institute

p52　NHK

p53　Iwan Baan

●透明なかたち　Transparent Form

p55, 56-57, 58-59, 61, 75　新津保建秀／ Kenshu Shintsubo

p62, 63　オフィース YUKIMATSU ／ Office Yukimatsu

p66, 70, 74　妹島和世建築設計事務所／ Kazuyo Sejima & Associates

p72, 74　荒神明香／ Haruka Kojin

p78　畠山直哉／ Naoya Hatakeyama

p81　川向正人／ Masato Kawamukai

p82, 84　目【め】／ Mé

● PARTY PARTY　Party Party

p87, 88-89, 90, 91, 92, 93, 96, 112, 113, 115　堀田貞雄／ Sadao Hotta

p94, 95　オフィース YUKIMATSU ／ Office Yukimatsu

p100　池田ひらく／ Hiraku Ikeda

p104-105, 110, 114　CAt

p107　岩崎寛／ Hiroshi Iwasaki

p108　宮原夢画／ Muga Miyahara

p116　アキタ・デザイン・カン／ Akita Design Kan

p118　西川公朗／ Masao Nishikawa

p120, 121　井田宗秀／ Munehide Ida

●ぼよよん　Boyoyong

p123, 124-125, 126, 127, 128, 129, 152　阿野太一／ Daici Ano

p130, 131　オフィース YUKIMATSU ／ Office Yukimatsu

p132, 134, 142, 144　彰国社写真部／ Shokokusha Publishing Co., Ltd.

p138, 148, 150　MONGOOSE STUDIO ／ Mongoose Studio

p147　松岡誠太朗／ Seitaro Matsuoka

p151　ODS-R 事務局／ ODS-R Staff

p154　KAPPES ／ Kappes

p155　松山真也／ Shinya Matsuyama

● Flow_er

p157, 158-159, 160-161, 162, 163, 180, 182, 186 (right)　ナカサアンドパートナーズ／Nacása & Partners Inc.

p164, 165　オフィース YUKIMATSU ／ Office Yukimatsu

p166, 170, 174, 190　平田晃久建築設計事務所／Akihisa Hirata Architecture Office

p176　塚田有一／Yuichi Tsukada

p186 (left), 189　ODS-R 事務局／ODS-R Staff

● 白い闇　Invisible White

p193　皆川聡／Satoshi Minakawa

p196-197　新建築社写真部／Shinkenchiku-sha

p198, 199　Edwin van der Heide

p200, 201　オフィース YUKIMATSU ／ Office Yukimatsu

p204, 212　ヨコミゾマコト／Makoto Yokomizo

p207　多木浩二／Koji Taki

p208, 224　aat+ ヨコミゾマコト建築設計事務所／AAT + Makoto Yokomizo Architects, Inc.

p214, 215, 220　上田麻希／Maki Ueda

p218　ODS-R 事務局／ODS-R Staff

● 波・紋　Ripple

p227, 228-229, 230-231, 232, 233, 236, 248, 250, 254 (right)　いしまるあきこ／Akiko Ishimaru

p234, 235　オフィース YUKIMATSU ／ Office Yukimatsu

p238, 254 (left)　淺川敏／Satoshi Asakawa

p240, 246　NASCA 一級建築士事務所／Studio Nasca

p245　宮本敏明／Toshiaki Miyamoto

● オカムラデザインスペース R の記録／編著者紹介　A Record of Okamura Design Space R / About the Editors

p258, 280　オフィース YUKIMATSU ／ Office Yukimatsu

編著者紹介
About the Editors

川向正人（かわむかいまさと）　建築史家・建築評論家、工学博士

1950年香川県生まれ。1974年東京大学建築学科卒業、同大学大学院進学。1977-79年政府給費生としてウィーン大学美術史研究所・ウィーン工科大学に留学。明治大学助手、東北工業大学助教授を経て、1993年東京理科大学助教授。2002年より同教授。2005年より東京理科大学・小布施町まちづくり研究所長も務める。

ODS-Rでは、2003年より委員長として毎回、企画建築家の選定、月例会議の議長、シンポジウムの司会進行役などを務め、全体を監修する。建築家との交流は広く、シンポジウムやワークショップ等のさまざまな場で、建築家たちとの協働を実践している。

主な著書に『境界線上の現代建築』（彰国社）、『現代建築の軌跡』（鹿島出版会）、『小布施 まちづくりの奇跡』（新潮社）など。共著に『まちに大学が、まちを大学に』（彰国社）、『"Portfolio" Atsushi Kitagawara Architects』（Jovis）など。訳書も『現代建築の潮流』（鹿島出版会）など多数。

Masato Kawamukai (Architectural Historian and Critic, D.Eng)

Born in Kagawa prefecture in 1950, Kawamukai graduated from the University of Tokyo's department of architecture in 1974 and continued his studies at its graduate school. From 1977 to 1979, he studied at the Vienna University Institute for Art History and the Vienna University of Technology on a government scholarship. After working as an assistant at Meiji University and an associate professor at the Tohoku Institute of Technology, in 1993 he became an associate professor in the Department of Architecture at the Tokyo University of Science's Faculty of Science and Technology, where he was appointed professor in 2002. Since 2005 he has also served as director of the Obuse Machizukuri Institute, a joint undertaking by the Tokyo University of Science and the town of Obuse.

As chairman of the planning and executive committee, Kawamukai has exercised overall supervision of the ODS-R since 2003, including selecting architects, chairing monthly meetings, and moderating symposiums. With broad connections among architects, he frequently collaborates with them in forums such as symposiums and workshops.

Major publications include *Kyokaisenjo no gendai kenchiku* [Contemporary Architecture on the Borderline], (Shokokusha), *Gendai kenchiku no kiseki* [The Arc of Contemporary Architecture] (Kajima Institute), and *Obuse: machizukuri no kiseki* [Obuse: A Machizukuri Miracle] (Shinchosha). Co-authored publications include *Machi ni daigaku ga, machi wo daigaku ni* [A University in the Town, the Town as a University] (Shokokusha) and *Atsushi Kitagawara Architects* (Jovis). Translations include *Gendai kenchiku no choryu* [from *Architektur und Staedtebau des 20. Jahrhunderts* by Vittorio M. Lampugnani] (Kajima Institute).

OKAMURA Design Space **R**

オカムラデザインスペース R

オフィス家具のリーディングカンパニーとして国内外に広く知られる株式会社岡村製作所がスポンサーとなり、東京都千代田区紀尾井町にあるオカムラ ガーデンコートショールームの一角を会場として、2003 年から毎年 7〜8 月に、「建築家と建築以外の領域の表現者との協働」を基本コンセプトとして創出される展示とトークの空間。全体の企画運営は、川向正人（委員長）、芦原太郎、内藤廣、北川原温、中村喜久男（岡村製作所）などで構成される企画実行委員会によって進められる。毎回、旧来の枠組みを超える実験的で挑戦的なコラボレーションを展開し、新たな知と美の形式の提案を目指している。提案内容をより正確にわかりやすく伝えるために、会期中には展示のほかにシンポジウム、ワークショップ、ギャラリートークが開催され、広報のためのポスターと DM のデザインにも力が注がれている。

Okamura Design Space R

Sponsored by Okamura Corporation—known both at home and abroad as Japan's leading office furniture company—and held every year from July to August in a corner of the Okamura Garden Court showroom in the Kioi-cho neighborhood in Chiyoda, Tokyo since 2003, ODS-R is a space for exhibitions and talk events grounded in the core concept of collaboration between architects and creators from outside the field of architecture. Overall planning and operations are driven by a planning and executive committee composed of chairman Masato Kawamukai and members including Taro Ashihara, Hiroshi Naito, Atsushi Kitagawara, and Okamura Chairman Kikuo Nakamura. Each edition seeks to propose new forms of knowledge and beauty through challenging, experimental collaboration that transcends conventional frameworks. In order to properly convey these proposals, symposiums, workshops, and gallery talks are also held during the exhibitions, and great care is taken in the design of the posters and direct mailings used to publicize these events.

ODS-R 企画実行委員会 / ODS-R Planning and Executive Committee

委員長 / Chairman
川向正人 / Masato Kawamukai (Vols. 1-12)

企画委員 / Planning Members
芦原太郎 / Taro Ashihara (Vols. 1-12)、北川原温 / Atsushi Kitagawara (Vols. 1-12)、内藤廣 / Hiroshi Naito (Vols. 1-12)、赤松邦彦 / Kunihiko Akamatsu (Vols. 1-7)、中村喜久男 / Kikuo Nakamura (Vols. 1-12)、各企画建築家・アーティスト / Exhibiting architects and artists

実行委員 / Executive Members
各企画建築家・アーティスト側責任者 / Representatives of exhibiting architects and artist、牧野広司 / Hiroshi Makino (Vols. 1-4)、岩下博樹 / Hiroki Iwashita (Vols. 5-12)、向後大三郎 / Daisaburo Kogo (Vols. 2-6)、岡村経夫 / Tsuneo Okamura (Vols. 6-10)、萩原圭一 / Keiichi Hagiwara (Vols. 11-12)、甲斐慶一 / Keiichi Kai (Vols. 2-6)、大田友祐 / Tomosuke Ota (Vols. 7-10)、鈴木勇二 / Yuji Suzuki (Vols. 11-12)、山本兼司 / Kenji Yamamoto (Vols. 1-6)、花田正彦 / Masahiko Hanada (Vols. 7-8)、竹森邦彦 / Kunihiko Takemori (Vols. 9-11)、松田敏彦 / Toshihiko Matsuda (Vol. 12)、井上宏一 / Koichi Inoue (Vols. 5-12)、中村留理 / Ruri Nakamura (Vols. 1-12)

事務局 / Staff
大野隆司 / Takashi Ohno (Vols. 1-7)、佐々真康 / Masayasu Sasa (Vols. 8-9)、西山直勝 / Naokatsu Nishiyama (Vols. 10-11)、中山由稀 / Yuki Nakayama (Vol. 12)

企画	株式会社 岡村製作所
編集	いしまるあきこ
本文デザイン	佐村憲一 (Number One Design Office)
装丁・デザイン協力	いしまるあきこ
翻訳	ハート・ララビー

Planning	Okamura Corporation
Editing	Akiko Ishimaru
Text Design	Kenichi Samura (Number One Design Office)
Cover Design, Design Cooperation	Akiko Ishimaru
English Translation	Hart Larrabee

collaboration　アート / 建築 / デザインのコラボレーションの場

2015 年 5 月10日　第 1 版発行

編著者	川向正人＋オカムラデザインスペース R
発行者	下出雅徳
発行所	株式会社 彰国社
	162-0067 東京都新宿区富久町 8-21
	電話 03-3359-3231（大代表）
	振替口座 00160-2-173401
	http://www.shokokusha.co.jp
印刷・製本	三美印刷株式会社

© Masato Kawamukai + OKAMURA CORPORATION　2015
ISBN 978-4-395-32038-7 C3052

本書の内容の一部あるいは全部を、無断で複写（コピー）、複製、および磁気または
光記録媒体等への入力を禁止します。許諾については小社あてにご照会ください。